S0-ARN-825

Playing by the Rules

Georgetown University Press gratefully acknowledges the support provided by The Japan Foundation toward publication of this volume.

Playing by the Rules:
American Trade Power and Diplomacy in the Pacific

MICHAEL P. RYAN

GEORGETOWN UNIVERSITY PRESS, WASHINGTON, D.C.

To
my parents
and
grandparents

Georgetown University Press, Washington, D.C.
© 1995 by Georgetown University Press. All rights reserved.
Printed in the United States of America
10   9   8   7   6   5   4   3   2   1   1995
THIS VOLUME IS PRINTED ON ACID-FREE OFFSET BOOK PAPER.

Library of Congress Cataloging-in-Publication Data

Ryan, Michael P. (Michael Patrick), 1960–
    Playing by the rules : American trade power and diplomacy in the
Pacific / Michael P. Ryan.
        p.   cm.
    Includes bibliographical references.
    1. United States—Foreign economic relations—Pacific Area.
2. Pacific Area—Foreign economic relations—United States.
3. United States—Commercial policy.   4. Foreign trade regulation—
United States.   5. General Agreement on Tariffs and Trade
(Organization)   6. Arbitration and award, International. I. Title.
HF1456.5.P3R92   1995
337.7309—dc20
ISBN 0-87840-579-8
                                                    94-32278

Contents

Preface

With *Playing by the Rules* I have aimed to apply international relations theory and systematic evidence gathering to a vital problem of American and international public policy—the settlement of trade disputes in the Pacific. My purpose was to build policy-relevant theory regarding international trade relations and to offer policymakers, practitioners, students, and scholars theoretically derived and empirically tested generalizations about 301 trade diplomacy in the Pacific. The remarks of two of my first governmental interviewees motivated the research and writing of this book. One policymaker remarked, "No outsider ever gets what's going on here right." Another opined, "There are no generalizations to be made in this process; every case is different." Sobered by the statements of such experts, I wanted to be the outsider who got it right by producing an analytically and descriptively accurate account of 301 trade diplomacy. I also wanted to demonstrate that there were generalizations about 301 trade diplomacy that could be learned and, in turn, taught. Thus, I wanted to present at once rigorous social science and rich narrative. My hope is that the reader of this book will come to both know the generalizations about trade dispute settlement under the 301 policy and possess a "feel" for 301 trade diplomacy in the Pacific.

Playing by the Rules is deliberately not a comprehensive analysis of American trade policy. The reader interested in this policy or in the making of 301 policy by Congress should read I. M. Destler's *American Trade Politics*, Judith Goldstein's *Ideas, Interests, and American Trade Policy*, David Lake's *Power, Protectionism, and Free Trade*, and Stefanie Lenway's *Politics of US International Trade*. This book, instead, analyzes the international-trade diplomacy of 301 in the Pacific, with emphasis upon the institutions of Pacific-trade diplomacy—GATT, the Office of the United States Trade Representative, and the participating executive branch agencies of the East Asian governments. GATT establishes the rules of the game in trade diplomacy, and the executive-branch agencies play the game (if not always according to the rules).

Though my primary intellectual allegiance is to neofunctional and regime theories of international politics and to political organizational theories of comparative politics, the analytic framework employed in this study draws from structural theories in international politics and from comparative political economy. Theoretical pluralism is justified here by the goal of building policy-relevant theory: social science can be advanced by pushing a single theoretical perspective to its limits, but policy-relevant social science made with a slavish commitment to a single theoretical perspective tries to do too much with too little. A complete understanding of 301 trade diplomacy comes from recognition of the asymmetrical structure of power in the Pacific, the interests of the governments of the Pacific as a matter of political economy, the mediation effects of the rules, norms, and dispute settlement procedures of GATT, and, concomitant to all this, the behavior patterns of the national executive-branch agencies. Government decision makers employ analytic frameworks appropriate to the type of policy problem at hand; hence, so must their teachers.

In writing this book I have incurred many debts. I owe much to the many trade policymakers in Beijing, Seoul, Taipei, Tokyo, and Washington who, though I do not cite them by name, gave generously of their time to talk to me about Pacific-trade dispute settlement. They made this a much better study than it otherwise would have been. The Office of Public Affairs at the Office of the United States Trade Representative, Washington, D.C., was extraordinarily helpful.

I owe special thanks to my teachers at the University of Michigan: From Harold Jacobson I learned about international organizations and relations, from Michel Oksenberg East Asia and policy implementation, and from John H. Jackson international law and trade policy. The approach taken in this book—theory building, policy relevance, empiricism, policy implementation, international and national governmental institutions—is credited to their teachings.

Several colleagues contributed to this project by commenting on my ideas, suggesting sources, or providing help of other kinds. Without holding them responsible for the arguments presented here, I thank Kirti Celly, Ross Denton, I. M. Destler, Shawn Fagan, Gunter Dufey, Bradley Farnsworth, Gary Hawes, Heng Chiang Huang, John Kline, Stefanie Lenway, Edward Lincoln, Mitsuo Matsushita, Theodore Moran, Thomas Murtha, Henry Nau, Brian Pollins, Thomas Roehl, Mary Shimizu, Robert Snyder, Detlef Sprinz,

Marc Wall, Jimmy Wheeler, Perry Wood, and some anonymous reviewers. Special thanks to W. Christopher Lenhardt, who cheerfully read and commented on draft after draft and who taught me how to play squash. Rena Gersh offered excellent research assistance. Myrna Young provided expert secretarial help.

The Institute for the Study of World Politics, Washington, D.C., provided me with the financial resources to travel for interviews and to devote all of the 1989–90 academic year to this study without distraction. The University of Michigan School of Business Administration, Center for International Business Education, and Rackham Graduate School also provided me with financial support for travel. Between 1990 and 1993, the Michigan Business School afforded me the wonderful opportunity to teach international trade and political economy and learn from students and colleagues about international business and corporate strategy. Since fall 1993, the Landegger Program in International Business Diplomacy at Georgetown University's School of Foreign Service has offered me an extraordinary chance to teach and learn about international business diplomacy.

Sections of this book have been published in several journals. Chapter 2 appeared in the June 1995 issue of *International Studies Quarterly* under the title "USTR's Implementation of 301 Trade Policy in the Pacific." Chapter 7 appeared in the June 1994 issue of *Asian Survey* under the title "East Asian Political Economies and the GATT Regime." Chapter 9 appeared in the spring 1994 issue of *Georgetown Compass* under the title "Making Regionalism Work in the Pacific Economy." The book had its origins in my political science Ph.D. dissertation, "Leveling the Playing Field: Settling Pacific Basin Disputes Regarding Unfair East Asian Trade Policies," which was submitted to the University of Michigan in December 1990. A summary of the thesis appeared in the summer 1991 issue of *Michigan Journal of International Law* under the title "Strategy and Compliance with Bilateral Trade Dispute Settlement Agreements: USTR's Section 301 Experience in the Pacific."

Finally, I acknowledge the unwavering support and care of my parents and my grandparents: Cynthia and Jerry Ryan, Pauline and Dwight Cowan, and Dorothy and the late David Ryan. They represent the most important institutions of all, and it is to them that this book is dedicated with gratitude and love.

MICHAEL P. RYAN
Washington, D.C.

List of Acronyms

AD	antidumping
APEC	Asia Pacific Economic Conference
BoP	balance of payments
CVD	countervailing duty
DoC	Department of Commerce
FCN	Treaty of Friendship, Commerce, Navigation
GATS	General Agreement on Trade in Services
GATT	General Agreement on Tariffs and Trade
GSP	Generalized System of Preferences
IGO	international governmental organization
IPR	intellectual-property rights
ITC	International Trade Commission
LTFV	less than fair value
MFA	Multifiber Arrangement
MFN	most favored nation
MITI	Ministry of International Trade and Industry (Japan)
MOFERT	Ministry of Foreign Economic Relations and Trade (China)
MOFTEC	Ministry of Foreign Trade and Economic Cooperation (China)
MOSS	Market-Oriented, Sector-Specific
MTI	Ministry of Trade and Industry (Republic of Korea)
MTN	multilateral trade negotiations
OECD	Organization of Economic Cooperation and Development
OMA	Orderly Marketing Agreement
SII	Structural Impediments Initiative
STR	US Special Trade Representative
TRIPs	Trade-Related Intellectual Property negotiations
UNCTAD	United Nations Conference on Trade and Development
USTR	Office of the United States Trade Representative
WTO	World Trade Organization

CHAPTER 1

Introduction

This book is about the rule-oriented and power-oriented trade diplomacy practiced by USTR with Japan, Korea, and Taiwan in the settlement of trade disputes under the US Section 301 policy in the Pacific during the 1970s and 1980s. It discusses the rules and procedures of the GATT regime and American trade power in the Pacific, and looks at playing by the rules in the Pacific economy: rules about what state trade policies should and should not be; rules about how states ought and ought not to settle their trade disputes; rules that are definitive, rules that are ambiguous, and rules that do not yet exist. The analysis studies the structure of state power; global competition, market sector by market sector; the international and regional institutions of trade diplomacy; and the national governmental institutions of trade diplomacy in the Pacific. The framework for analysis helps explain the USTR 301 initiation decision; the East Asian response strategies; the dispute settlement processes and agreement outcomes; the agreement compliance records; the fit of the Japanese, Korean, and Taiwanese political economies with the rules and principles of the GATT regime; trade dispute diplomacy with China; and the capabilities of the multilateral and minilateral/regional institutions of trade dispute diplomacy in the Pacific. The conclusions of the study are based upon analysis of the largest, most systematic market-sector-specific data set presented so far on US export trade dispute settlement in the Pacific. Thus, the book brings international-relations theory and social-science analysis to vital issues of US and international public policy and aims to build policy-relevant theory on international-trade diplomacy.

The thesis of the book is that the process and outcome of 301 trade diplomacy in the Pacific are explained by the political economies of the countries in the region—a United States that is pluralist, liberal regulatory, industrialized and highly economically diversified, and hegemonic in the region; a Japan that is corporatist, capitalist developmental, lately industrialized, and free riding on the open-market regime; a statist-turning-corporatist, capitalist developmental, late industrializing, and free riding Korea; a statist-turning-pluralist, capitalist developmental, late industrializing, and free riding Taiwan; and a statist, socialist developmental, late industrializing, post isolationist China. American trade power in the region explains how the US generally negotiates a settlement agreement much closer to its preferences than to the East Asian state's preferences; American commitment to GATT multilateralism explains why it usually implements 301 policy with attention to GATT rules and rule-creation activities.

CONTEXT FOR 301 TRADE DIPLOMACY IN THE PACIFIC

No region in the world can claim to have experienced faster economic development and greater trade expansion during the 1970s and 1980s than the Pacific. No region in the world can claim to have experienced more or, for the international trading system, more interesting problems during the 1970s and 1980s than the Pacific. Transpacific trade problems are of a different character from transatlantic trade problems. Transatlantic trade problems are bound up primarily in agriculture-market-distorting subsidies, European integration and cooperation, and the entry of Russia and eastern Europe into the world economy. The trade problems of the Pacific are primarily about export-led national industrial-policy strategies and about market access. For these reasons the Pacific region's trade relations merit and receive in this study special scrutiny.

The great trade expansion and its corollary trade problems in the Pacific were caused by a variety of factors, including, importantly, the adoption of export-led development strategies by one after another of the governments of the region and, to a lesser extent, by the opening of China toward the West. Led by Japan, the governments of Korea and Taiwan, by Hong Kong and Singapore, Malaysia and Indonesia determined that the best economic strategy for greater national prosperity was to produce large quantities of manufactured goods—larger quantities than could be used in the home markets—and to export them to the large markets in the United States. The strategy worked well and produced many winners: East Asian government bureaucrats, whose policy prescriptions succeeded; East Asian industrialists, whose sales and profits rose; East Asian bankers, whose money was invested and whose capital accumulated; East Asian workers, whose salaries and standards of living rose; American industrialists and bankers, who owned investments in East Asia and whose profits increased; American consumers, who were able to purchase better-quality consumer goods at cheaper prices.

The strategy, however, also produced losers. These government development strategies encouraged new commercial competition in the Pacific economy. For American business, the new competition proved to be stiff. Many American businesses found that their capacities to compete had eroded in the 1960s and 1970s. Saddled with problems of their own making (finance-driven, short-time-horizon corporate strategies, overbureaucratized management structures, waning productivity gains) and of their government's making (high capital costs, an overvalued dollar, shortages of well-trained labor) American businesses were losing in the marketplace.[1] American industrialists struggled, often unsuccessfully, in their home markets against new, often cheaper, and sometimes better-quality competing products. For some, sales and profits dropped. Production declined; layoffs increased. Many American workers were losers: more and more spent ever-lengthening periods of time laid off, eventually losing their jobs altogether. The once-great American manufacturing cities between Boston and Chicago—from Lowell to Pittsburgh to Massillon to Warren—came to be called the Rust Belt. Like undertakers during a plague, the scrap metal dealers busily kept to their work.

Industry after industry—textiles, steel, automobiles—pressed Congress and the President to grant them relief from import competition. Protection was granted, sometimes through the GATT-compliant "escape clause" procedure, sometimes through the "negotiated protectionism" of orderly marketing agreements (OMAs) and voluntary export restraints (VERs). But, the East Asian manufacturers and their government representatives learned to adjust to US import quotas by bargaining effectively but prudently with US trade negotiators and by selling in other national markets (especially Europe) to reduce dependence on the US market.[2] East Asian business strategists also changed their product mixes toward higher-value-added, larger-profit items (as when textile manufacturers moved from yard goods to high-fashion garments or when Honda, Toyota, and Nissan moved from economy to midsize to luxury cars) and diversified into other industries to reduce dependence on a single type of product.

In American politics, trade went from being business section news and "low politics" to front-page news and top-of-the-agenda politics. The US economy had been in deep recession since the late 1970s, each quarterly report issued by the Department of Commerce noted larger trade deficits with Japan, and by 1982 the US trade deficit with the world reached astonishing proportions. Although recession and imports were only indirectly linked in the minds of economists, Japanese imports became a handy scapegoat in the minds of average citizens and the politicians who represented their interests. Thus, inside the Beltway, Congress and the President struggled over the content of trade policy and over the authority to make and implement trade policy in a crisis atmosphere.

Throughout the 1980s, students of American foreign policy-making analyzed the structure and process of trade policy formulation by Congress and the President within this protectionist milieu. These scholars tracked the genesis and gyrations of trade legislation and regulation.[3] Political scientists and economists specified the sources of, and the institutional susceptibility of the American government to, protectionist pressures.[4] They told an alarming story of a political economy unable to live up to its free-trader ideals. Indeed, an award-winning book described the situation as a "system under stress."[5] Yet even as these studies came into print, two studies noted that liberal, anti-protectionist countertendencies were visible in American trade politics. First, many American firms had by the 1980s become much more international in research, production, and marketing and were thus encouraged to oppose protectionist trade policies.[6] Second, structural characteristics of the US government and of international trade relations that insulated American trade politics from protectionism were specifiable.[7] The 1970s Pacific trade milieu—rife with demands by US manufacturers for import protection— gradually changed in the 1980s. Many American businesses in the 1980s began thinking about global competition and what that meant. It meant competing in many national markets. Thus, it meant that many American businesses confronted barriers to doing international business. Some of these barriers were problems of multinational enterprise: strategy, organization, finance, production, distribution, and marketing across geographic expanse and national boundaries. American business leaders had to solve these problems on their own. Some of the barriers, however, were national policies that discouraged or even prohibited imports, discouraged or even prohibited investment. Thus, if the proximate cause of Pacific Basin trade dispute settlement has been new competition in East Asian and American markets, the remote, deeper causes lie in differences in the political economies of the Pacific Basin. All these states are today contracting parties to the GATT regime, but all did not carry out with equal rigor the commitments they made to compliance with the rules of the regime at their times of accessions.

American business leaders stumped Capitol Hill and the US Trade Representative's office looking for help; Congress and USTR responded. Congress rewrote US trade laws in 1984 with the Trade and Tariff Act and again in 1988 with the Omnibus Trade and Competitiveness Act, each time strengthening the Section 301 trade policy—the tool of American unilateralism. The US Trade Representative's office aggressively implemented Section 301. Section 301 of the 1974 Trade Act authorizes the Office of the United States Trade Representative (USTR) to investigate allegations of "unfair" trade barriers that impede the ability to compete in foreign markets, and to impose economic sanctions on the offending country if bilateral negotiations prove fruitless. Section 301 is thus the means through which US business seeks US government help and through which the US government requests bilateral negotiations over alleged trade barriers.

USTR carried 301 policy to completion (i.e., settlement agreement) at least forty times with Japan, Korea, and Taiwan during the period 1974–1989. Many American industries have gained much from American 301 unilateralism in the Pacific. For example, the tobacco dispute with Japan resulted in the US tobacco industry increasing its exports from $100 million to $600 million in only three years. The insurance dispute with Korea resulted by 1989 (three years after dispute initiation) in ten foreign companies doing business in the $200 billion Korean insurance services markets. The International Intellectual Property Alliance reduced pirating of books, music, and videos, and the Pharmaceutical Manufacturers Association reduced unlicensed production of its patented drugs. The Rice Millers Association managed to have allegedly subsidized Taiwanese rice removed from major country markets, and the beef industry got a leg up on the growing Korean market. American 301 trade policy thus can be a useful means through which multinational-corporation managers can make the US government help them change competitive opportunities in foreign markets.

The gains, however, have come with considerable bilateral acrimony. The East Asian governments resent being bullied by the US government into changing trade policies. One critic of USTR's implementation of 301 policy declared: "The US trade policy is not consistent. USTR responds too quickly to domestic pressure. Then it uses the negotiating style of a superpower: It uses its power when it is not reasonable. It creates bitterness and weakens the hands of those in [East Asian countries] who favor market opening. The US should take a long-term view."[8] Another said: "The US is self-righteous about trade. US development has slowed and other countries have caught up. The US has many internal problems so it bashes Japan. The US used to be a great country, but can't offer much anymore. The world needs a more unbiased judge in disputes. The US cannot be both judge and jury. The US is

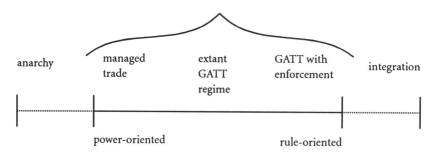

Figure 1.1:   Trade Diplomacy and World Political Economy

strong, but not fair."[9] Said another, "USTR is prosecutor, plea bargainer, judge, and executioner."[10] These views were reinforced by another critic: "The US is unilateral in interpretation of the rules, like it forgets its old waiver in agriculture. Its unilateral action is not justified."[11] For these reasons, the 301 trade policy must be used judiciously; in the words of one participant, "It must be used with finesse."[12]

RULE-ORIENTED AND POWER-ORIENTED TRADE DIPLOMACY

This study shows that Section 301 trade dispute settlement in the Pacific is rule-oriented and power-oriented trade diplomacy. GATT rules and other international trade laws help explain the processes and outcomes of Section 301 trade dispute settlement. John Jackson suggests that

> the various techniques for the peaceful settlement of international disputes can be divided into two types: (1) settlement by negotiation and agreement with reference (explicitly or implicitly) to the relative power statuses of the parties; (2) settlement by negotiation and agreement with reference to the norms and rules upon which both parties previously have agreed.[13]

Jackson calls the former power-oriented diplomacy; he calls the latter rule-oriented diplomacy. The "settlement by negotiation and agreement" of which Jackson speaks, however, cannot be carried out without regard to state power—at least in the present world political economy. Rule-oriented trade diplomacy is not power*less* trade diplomacy. Hence, it is better to think of power-oriented and rule-oriented trade diplomacy as two ends of a continuum. See Figure 1.1.

Trade diplomacy ranges from purely power-oriented in a completely anarchic world political economy to purely rule-oriented in a completely integrated world political economy. Neither anarchy nor integration is the empirical reality of late-twentieth-century world political economy. The empirical reality of our time is somewhere in the middle: a GATT-regime-ordered world political economy with some characteristics of rule-oriented diplomacy but some characteristics of power-oriented diplomacy. Thus, in Pacific trade relations some trade disputes have been settled by the two states through negotiation and agreement with the help of GATT panels of experts who apply previously agreed upon rules to particular facts and circumstances. Disputes between the United States and Japan over footwear and tobacco and between the United States and Korea over beef are examples of rule-oriented trade diplomacy. On the other hand, some trade disputes have been settled by the two states through negotiation and agreement with reference to the asymmetry in the bilateral power relationship. Disputes between the United States and Japan over automobiles and color televisions and between the United States and Taiwan over machine tools are examples of power-oriented trade diplomacy. Yet neither set of cases is pure: In the rule-oriented cases, the United States employed state power against Japan and Korea to achieve settlement. In the power-oriented cases, the United States attempted to negotiate agreements that were in technical compliance with GATT rules (albeit in violation of the spirit of the GATT). Furthermore, trade dispute settlement at times falls somewhere in the middle: for example, in disputes when rule noncompliance is articulated but not demonstrated through a GATT panel process, when appropriate rules are nascent but not extant, or when appropriate rules are nothing more than the mere declaration that "there oughta be a rule."

The present world political economy tends away from power orientation as a result of the creation of the GATT regime. This regime is based upon the 1947 General Agreement on Tariffs and Trade,[14] an agreement that was intended by the twenty-three original contracting parties to be a provisional step toward the creation of the International Trade Organization (ITO).[15] Though the ITO never came into being, the contracting parties nevertheless developed the GATT into an international regime aimed at regulating state trade policies concerning trade in goods. Jock Finlayson and Mark Zacher pointed out that the GATT is at the center of a particular international trade regime, which has for the most part been concerned with one international trade issue area, namely, trade barriers, which are *state* policies or practices that impede the access countries enjoy to each other's markets for their exports. Other trade matters, such as prices and earnings deriving from the export of primary commodities or the effect of private business practices on trade—which were both brought within the ambit of the ITO—were not addressed by the 1947 General Agreement. They have not since been brought within the GATT's regulatory-consultative framework to any significant extent.[16]

They were right, but GATT rule creation on service trade, intellectual property rights, standards harmonization, and investment carried out in the Uruguay Round Multilateral Trade Negotiation as well as on antitrust and competition policy under discussion in GATT fora indicate that the GATT has become the General Agreements on Everything regarding Commercial Policy. The creation of the World Trade Organization institutionalizes the ambitions of the GATT membership. UNCTAD and the commodity regimes have not ceased to exist, but they contradict the principles of the GATT regime and have ceased to matter much.

The GATT regime includes an international governmental organization whose activities an executive head and a secretariat staff (albeit technically leased from the United Nations) administer. In addition, rules on contracting party trade behavior have been codified into the original GATT treaty and into many subsequent agreements. The regime includes a forum—the multilateral trade negotiations—for additional rule creation, and procedures for the settlement of disputes between and among the contracting parties about their GATT rights and obligations.

The history of early negotiations for the General Agreement and failed ITO charter as well as the evolution of the regime show that the GATT regime is guided by six principles: (1) multilateralism, (2) reduction of trade barriers, (3) nondiscrimination, (4) reciprocity, (5) fair trade, and (6) economic development. These principles are the GATT regime's "meta-regime."[17] The rules and activities of the GATT regime are manifestations of the various underlying principles. The very existence of the GATT regime testifies to the multilateral expectations of the participants: greater economic and political gains from free trade are achieved in a world economy approaching universal regime membership. The tariff reductions carried out under Article II in the MTNs, the prohibition against quantitative restraints contained in Article XI, and the obligation to make trade regulations transparent in Article X implement the principle of reduction of trade barriers. The Article I most-favored-nation provision (with some exceptions, any trade benefit conferred on one member must be conferred on all) and the Article III national-treatment provision (treat foreign firms no less favorably than domestic firms) are representative of the nondiscrimination principle.

The reciprocity principle meant in the 1940s that substantially equivalent contributions to trade barrier reductions were to be offered by the members, but it seems to mean in the 1990s that substantially equivalent competitive opportunities are conferred by member states.[18] The reciprocity principle influences GATT practice and rule making. The fair-trade principle—always an ambiguous notion—resulted in rules on dumping, subsidy, and countervailing duty. In order to implement the principle of economic development, new rules (Part IV of the GATT treaty) were written in the 1960s to allow developing countries to justify legally, under certain circumstances, the protection of infant domestic industries and to receive special non-MFN tariff rates from the industrialized countries, the Generalized System of Preferences (GSP).

Disputes between and among the contracting parties about their rights and obligations within the regime occasionally occur. When they do, the regime specifies procedures for settlement. The basic dispute settlement procedure provided in the GATT treaty is "consultation," i.e., bilateral negotiation. GATT Article XXII provides that "each contracting party shall accord sympathetic consideration to, and shall afford adequate opportunity for consultation regarding, such representations as may be made by another contracting party with respect to any matter affecting the operation of this Agreement."

GATT Article XXIII explicitly obligates the contracting party states to consult when noncompliance is charged:

> If any contracting party should consider that any benefit accruing to it directly or indirectly under this Agreement is being nullified or impaired or that the attainment of any objective of the Agreement is being impeded as the result of (a) the failure of another contracting party to carry out its obligations under this Agreement, or (b) the application by another contracting party of any measure whether or not it conflicts with the provisions of the Agreement, or (c) the existence of any other situation, the contracting party may, with a view to the satisfactory adjustment of the matter, make written representations or

proposals to the other contracting party or parties which it considers to be concerned. Any contracting party thus approached shall give sympathetic consideration to the representations or proposals made to it.

Article XXIII specifies a role in bilateral-trade dispute settlement for the GATT qua institution:

> If no satisfactory adjustment is effected between the contracting parties concerned within a reasonable time, or if the difficulty is of the type described in paragraph 1 (c) of this Article, the matter may be referred to the contracting parties. The contracting parties shall promptly investigate any matter so referred to them and shall make appropriate recommendations to the contracting parties which they consider to be concerned, or give a ruling on the matter as appropriate.

Article XXIII does not, however, obligate disputants to take their problem to the GATT institution for settlement: the disputants may resolve their problem bilaterally. The practice at GATT nevertheless developed for the contracting parties, upon request of the disputants, to assist in the resolution of bilateral disputes through the formation of "working parties" (by 1948) and "panels of experts" (by 1952).[19] The panels of three to five impartial experts listen to the arguments of the disputing states, investigate the dispute with the help of the GATT secretariat, apply GATT rules to the conflict, and issue a ruling. The ruling, which culminates a yearlong process, may favor the initiator, may favor the respondent, or may encourage a negotiated settlement.[20] GATT panels have offered opinions to contracting parties in more than eighty cases. The United States initiated panel investigations against Japan in cases involving leather/footwear (three times), tobacco, wine, and agricultural products and against Korea about its beef policies. The United States won in each case. Taiwan is not a signatory to the GATT and hence cannot participate in GATT activities. (Taiwan, however, agreed with the United States that their bilateral trade relationship would be ordered by the GATT.)

Article XXIII further provides that GATT contracting parties may sanction retaliation against the noncompliant state. If the contracting parties consider that the circumstances are serious enough to justify such action, they may authorize a contracting party or parties to suspend the application to any other obligations under this agreement as they determine to be appropriate in the circumstances. The sanction of suspension of benefits is thereby explicit in the GATT regime, though granted but once in the history of

GATT, and the United States has pressed on, threatening sanctions despite the lack of authority to do so. In addition to the sanction, the policy option under Article XXIII includes termination of participation in the whole GATT regime. According to GATT law scholar Robert Hudec, to the GATT authors "[c]onsultations could not guarantee a satisfactory remedy. The only complete protection against nonreciprocity was a termination clause that would allow the disappointed party to get out of the agreement altogether, on short notice."[21] After forty-five years of regime development, however, this is no longer a viable policy option for most GATT members.

In addition to bilateral consultation aided by panels of experts under Article XXIII, the GATT regime provides other special dispute settlement procedures through its treaties. Indeed, over thirty distinct procedures can be identified in the original GATT treaty and in the additional multilateral codes of conduct negotiated in the Tokyo Round MTN.[22] Separate procedures exist under the GATT on, for example, antidumping, countervailing duty, safeguard (escape clause), and customs procedures.

Uruguay Round negotiators reached an agreement in December 1993 to improve GATT dispute settlement procedures, the "Dispute Settlement Understanding." The agreement guarantees the establishment of a panel by taking away the right of a member to block panel creation, imposes strict time limits internally on the panel investigation and decision-making process, establishes that panel reports must be adopted by the Council unless there is a consensus to reject it, and establishes an appeals process for cases in which a state believes that the panel misapplied GATT law.[23] On compliance and enforcement, the agreement sets time limits for state compliance and authorizes retaliation in the event of noncompliance with the panel report. The agreement substantially improves the working of the GATT dispute settlement procedures.

At least as important to GATT dispute settlement capabilities as the Uruguay Round agreement to improve procedures is the growth in GATT rules that the other Uruguay Round agreements offer. GATT dispute settlement has been weakened by regime rules which have been ambiguous or nonexistent in many areas of international trade. GATT dispute settlement has been empirically shown to be more effective in cases when the rules are definitive and applicable than in cases when rules are inadequate.[24] The Uruguay Round agreements that extend new rules to services (the GATS), intellectual property, and trade-related investment measures and refine rules for agricultural subsidies, import licensing, customs valuation, rules of origin, aircraft, and government procurement will likely lead to substantial improvements in

GATT dispute settlement. The growth in GATT rules will afford the multilaterally sanctioned settlement of many Pacific disputes that in the past would have been settled bilaterally. Thus, many more 301 trade disputes will be taken before GATT panels than in the 1970s and 1980s.

Despite the GATT regime and the tendency toward rule-oriented diplomacy in the world political economy, empirical reality in contemporary Pacific trade relations is considerable: regime rule noncompliance, especially among the East Asian states, and American-initiated power-oriented diplomacy in sectors such as textiles and apparel, steel, machine tools, semiconductors, and (nominally) automobiles. East Asian noncompliance with GATT rules has often been motivated by state policy to foster infant industries. American power-oriented diplomacy has been motivated by state policy to protect big and/or strategically important industries that have lost international competitiveness. The range of contemporary choice in the world political economy extends from a more-power orientation to a more-rule orientation. More-power orientation in trade diplomacy will mean more managed trade; more-rule orientation will mean a GATT regime with enhanced surveillance, dispute settlement, and enforcement capabilities. The choices made about the direction of trade diplomacy in the world political economy will matter to both world economy and world polity.

FRAMEWORK FOR ANALYSIS

This study shows empirically that 301 trade dispute settlement in the Pacific is both rule-oriented and power-oriented trade diplomacy. In order to explain the patterns of behavior, I look to international-relations theory. Realism and liberalism are the dominant research traditions in contemporary international-relations theory. By "research tradition" I mean a "set of general assumptions about entities and processes in a domain of study and about the appropriate methods to be used for investigating the problems and constructing the theories in the domain."[25] A research tradition provides "a set of guidelines for the development of specific theories"; it is a "set of ontological 'do's' and 'don'ts'." How ought research traditions be evaluated? How should realism and liberalism be compared? Synchronically, political scientists assess a research tradition's relative effectiveness at solving problems. Diachronically, political scientists evaluate its progressiveness in solving problems. "The choice of one tradition over its rivals," explains philosopher of science Larry Laudan, "is a progressive (and thus rational) choice precisely to the extent that the chosen tradition is a better problem solver than its rivals."[26] Realism and liberalism each aim to explain international relations, and the question is, Which research tradition better explains the process and outcome of 301 trade dispute settlement in the Pacific?

Classical realism in international-relations theory assumes that (1) states are the only meaningful actors in international relations, (2) military security is the dominant goal of actors, (3) military force is the most effective instrument of policy, (4) shifts in international military power set the agenda, and (5) issue linkage reinforces the international hierarchy of security, military power, and strong states.[27] In contemporary American foreign-policy thought and practice, Henry Kissinger has been the most prominent exponent of realism. Classical realism does not admit bilateral dispute settlement over trade as an interesting empirical problem and, indeed, has little to say about it. The realist research tradition has, however, come to theorize about international political economy, for, as Laudan would say, it had to change in order to continue to be a progressive research tradition capable of solving new, interesting problems. Realist political economy assumes that (1) states are the only meaningful actors in the world political economy, (2) relative gains in wealth and power are the goals of actors, (3) economic sanction is the instrument of policy, and (4) shifts in the structure of international economic wealth and power set the agenda. Realist political economy assumes that international structure determines state policy choices and international outcomes and that cooperation is exceptional.[28]

Liberalism in contemporary international-relations theory, on the other hand, assumes that (1) nonstate entities such as international governmental and nongovernmental organizations, multinational corporations, and subnational groups are meaningful actors in international relations, (2) goals of states vary by issue area, (3) instruments of policy vary according to issue area, (4) shifts in international power within issue areas, mediated by international regimes, set agendas, and (5) absence of issue linkage diminishes the hierarchy of security, military power, and strong states.[29] In contemporary American foreign-policy thought and practice, no liberal proponent has yet emerged to match Kissinger's realism, though the post–Cold War era in which we live may spawn such a leader. Liberal political economy asserts that (1) international economic organizations and regimes, multinational corporations, and labor groups are meaningful actors in the world political economy, (2) absolute gains in wealth are the goals of actors, (3) norms are an instrument of policy, and (4) shifts in international economic power, mediated by international economic regimes, set agendas. Liberal political economy concludes that international economic regimes[30] and domestic political economic factors influence state policy choices.[31] It insists that trade policy explanation cannot be reduced to international structures.[32] Thus, liberal political economy, in studying US trade policy, has pointed to its pluralist political economy and examined both the domestic interest groups that pressure for state trade policy positions[33] and the interbranch relationship between the President and Congress under the US Constitution. [34]

Yet a subtradition of liberal political-economy studies has argued that US trade policy behavior is not reducible to interest groups and that government institutions mediate interest group demands and explain why the US is less protectionist than the interest group approach would predict.[35] John Ikenberry, David Lake, and Michael Mastanduno, in a special issue of *International Organization*,[36] intended to redirect the field of US trade policy studies, recommended that "system-centered" explanations were inadequate, that "society-centered" explanations were inadequate, and that government institutions ought to be studied more. Adherents to the institutional approach draw from the "bureaucratic politics"/organization theory scholarship explanation of how organizational missions and processes influence institutional behavior.[37] Each government institution has a mission. The mission is defined by the goals of the organization and by the tasks that it is charged with carrying out. The organization socializes those who work for it, shaping their views and behavior. The mission delineates a policy area that the agency wants to control. An agency will struggle to maintain the autonomy and capabilities to carry out its mission and will resist any efforts to strip it of either its capabilities or its control.

RESEARCH DESIGN

Through US government documents, press and other secondary sources, and policymaker interviews in Washington, Tokyo, Seoul, and Taipei, I compiled the (approximate) universe of American-initiated 301 trade disputes with Japan, Korea, and Taiwan settled in the 1974–1989 period. I limited the study to 301 policy in the Pacific in order to hold the power asymmetry constant and the diplomatic and foreign-policy milieus relatively constant and to make the data collection manageable. The trade disputes arose under the US Section 301 trade law, though some were pursued informally by USTR under Section 302. Since the research aims to study the initiation of the disputes, the negotiation processes, and the outcomes of the disputes, the data set includes only settled disputes and does not include unsettled cases. There is no methodological reason to separate the 301 cases (which overtly threaten

TABLE 1.1   301 Trade Disputes in the Pacific, 1974–1989

	Manufacturing	*Services*	*Agriculture*
Japan	steel (1976)	telecom (1979)	beef (1978)
	silk (1977)	telecom (1985)	citrus (1978)
	leather (1977)	law (1986)	cigar (1979)
	baseball bats (1980)	construction (1988)	pipe (1978)
	footwear (1982)		tobacco (1985)
	wood (1985)		agriculture 12 (1986)
	pharmaceuticals (1985)		beef (1988)
	electronics (1985)		citrus (1988)
	semiconducter (1985)		
	satellite (1989)		
	supercomputer (1989)		
	wood (1989)		
Korea	footwear (1982)	insurance (1979)	beef (1988)
	steel wire rope (1983)	insurance (1985)	cigarette (1988)
	intellectual property (1985)		wine (1988)
Taiwan	home appliances (1976)	film (1983)	rice (1983)
	footwear (1982)	insurance (1986)	beer, wine, tobacco (1986)
	automobile (a) (1986)		
	automobile (b) (1986)		

sanctions) and the 302 cases (which covertly threaten sanctions), since states realize that if USTR does not achieve its goals under 302, it will formalize the dispute into a 301 case and threaten sanctions, and since the power variable is not being tested here. Thus, the compilation includes the Japan legal-services case (which was not formally initiated) but not the Japan rice case (which has never been settled). Though a few disputes undoubtedly escaped my net, my compilation of forty cases in Table 1.1 probably represents a substantial proportion of the true universe.

Aggregate analysis of the universe of forty disputes was supplemented with process-tracing case studies of nine of the disputes and with detailed analysis of the Structural Impediments Initiative and the 1989 Super 301 cases. The case study research was designed according to the method of structured, focused comparison.[38] The cases were selected in order to vary the state (Japan, Korea, Taiwan) and market (manufacturing, service, agriculture) in order to select nine cases from which to build theory. Variation by state and

Table 1.2   301 Trade Disputes in the Pacific, 1974–1989

Date	State	Dispute	Rule Violation	Settlement
1976	Taiwan	106% tariff on home appliances	none	lower tariff
1976	Japan	EC OMA diverts steel to US	none	no action
1977	Japan	thrown-silk import ban	GATT Art. XI	end quota
1977	Japan	leather import quotas	GATT Art. XI	end quota
1978	Japan	citrus import quotas	GATT Art. XI	expand quotas
1978	Japan	beef import quotas	GATT Art. XI	expand quota
1979	Japan	NTT telecom procurement	TR code	open bidding
1979	Japan	cigar distribution limits	GATT Art. III	change practices
1979	Japan	pipe tobacco distribution limits	GATT Art. III	change practices
1979	Korea	insurance-selling ban	FCN	grant licenses
1980	Japan	baseball bat regulations	GATT Art. III	change regulations
1982	Japan	footwear import quota	GATT Art. XI	end quota
1982	Korea	footwear customs procedures	TR code	change procedures
1982	Taiwan	footwear customs procedures	none	no action
1983	Korea	steel-wire rope subsidies	TR code	DoC action
1983	Taiwan	rice export subsidies	TR code	export restrictions
1983	Taiwan	film import quota	FCN	expand quota
1985	Korea	insurance-selling ban	FCN/code?	grant licences
1985	Japan	wood-products standards	none	change standards
1985	Korea	intellectual property rights	treaties/code?	write IPR laws

market introduces a variety of national environments, government agencies, and political economic interests. It also introduces a variety of dispute activities (quota, customs procedures, subsidy, etc.). I selected the footwear dispute because it was the only case that involved all three states, thus allowing me to hold the particular market constant. The nine cases are: Japan footwear, Japan tobacco, Japan semiconductor, Korea insurance, Korea intellectual property, Korea footwear, Korea beef, Taiwan footwear, and Taiwan rice.

Table 1.2, continued

Date	State	Dispute	Rule Violation	Settlement
1985	Japan	pharmaceutical standards	none	accept foreign test
1985	Japan	electronics intellectual property	emerging code?	improve patent law
1985	Japan	telecom standards	emerging code?	make transparent
1985	Japan	semiconductor imports	none	20% market goal
1985	Japan	tobacco distribution	GATT Art. III	change practices
1986	Taiwan	automobile FDI exp performance	emerging code?	end practice
1986	Taiwan	insurance-selling ban	FCN/code?	grant licenses
1986	Taiwan	automobile customs procedures	TR code	change procedures
1986	Taiwan	beer, wine, tobacco quotas	GATT Art. XI	end quotas
1986	Japan	legal services	emerging code	grant licenses
1986	Japan	12 agriculture quotas	GATT Art. XI	end quotas
1988	Japan	beef import quotas	GATT Art. XI	end quotas
1988	Japan	citrus import quotas	GATT Art. XI	end quotas
1988	Korea	beef import ban	GATT Art. XI	end quotas
1988	Korea	cigarette distribution	GATT Art. III	change practices
1988	Korea	wine import quota	GATT Art. XI	end quotas
1988	Japan	construction procurement	emerging code?	increase licenses
1989	Japan	satellite procurement	TR code	make transparent
1989	Japan	supercomputer procurement	none	throw out low bids
1989	Japan	wood-products standards	none	change standards

Each case study investigates the business reasons for bringing the case before the US government, the filing of the legal petitions that formally brought the case before the US government, the US government decision to initiate the case, the US government investigation, the US intrabureaucracy bargaining, the interstate negotiations, the dispute-resolving agreement, and the compliance record. Evidence for the case studies was marshaled through (1) interviews in Washington, Tokyo, Seoul, and Taipei with many of the

Table 1.3   301 Case Studies

State	Market	Disputed Activity	Outcome	Initiation & Resolution Dates
Japan	footwear	quota	end quota	10-25-82 12-1-85
Japan	tobacco	distribution	change practices	9-16-85 10-3-86
Japan	semiconductors	access	import quota	6-14-85 7-31-86
Korea	insurance	selling ban	grant licenses	9-16-85 7-21-86
Korea	intellectual property	protection	write IPR laws	11-4-85 7-21-86
Korea	footwear	customs	change practices	10-25-82 3-31-84
Korea	beef	quota	end quota	3-18-88 11-13-89
Taiwan	footwear	customs	no action	10-25-82 3-31-84
Taiwan	rice	subsidy	export restrictions	7-13-83 3-22-84

participants in the disputes, (2) US government documents from the Departments of Commerce and State, USTR, the International Trade Commission, and Congress, (3) GATT documents, (4) legal briefs and documents filed with the US government by trade lawyers for the disputants, (5) correspondence among US government officials, East Asian government officials, and private trade lawyers, available in public files of the US Department of Commerce and USTR, and (6) press accounts in the *International Trade Reporter*, the *Journal of Commerce*, the *New York Times*, the *Wall Street Journal*, the *Far Eastern Economic Review*, and other Pacific Basin periodicals.

The nine cases are summarized here:

Japan, Korea, Taiwan footwear (three cases):   Lawyers for the Footwear Industries of America, Inc., the Amalgamated Clothing and Textile Workers International Union, and the United Food and Commercial Workers International Union filed a massive Section 301 petition with USTR in October 1982.[39] The petition, the text of which alone ran to nearly 175 pages, complained of unfair trade policies toward nonrubber footwear by the governments of Brazil, Taiwan, Korea, Japan, the European Community as a whole, as well as France, Italy, Spain, and the United Kingdom separately. Footwear Industries charged that these governments engaged in policies of excessive tariffs, quotas, restrictive licensing practices, and subsidies.

Japan tobacco: USTR initiated a Section 301 action against Japan for its import policies on tobacco in September 1985.[40] Ambassador Clayton Yeutter announced at the time of the initiation that despite some Japanese policy steps to liberalize their tobacco market, Japan persistently maintained high tariffs, imposed discriminatory rules on marketing, advertising, and distribution, and held a monopoly on the importation and sale of tobacco products.[41] The dispute centered on the activities of the state-owned tobacco company, Japan Tobacco Inc., and five partially state-owned tobacco distribution companies, the Tobacco Haiso companies. Japan Tobacco possessed a monopoly on the import, distribution, and sale of all tobacco products in the country.

Japan semiconductor: The (American) Semiconductor Industry Association (SIA) filed a Section 301 petition with USTR in June 1985.[42] SIA charged the Japanese government with a wide range of unfair practices, from overt barriers, such as quotas and tariffs, to more subtle nontariff barriers. SIA contended that the Japanese government had identified semiconductors as an industry essential to its national economic development and security and had targeted it as an industry to be promoted. The Japanese government, said SIA, had encouraged a small number of large, integrated electronics firms, such as Hitachi, NEC, Matsushita, Fujitsu, and Toshiba, to interlink their research, development, production, and sales of semiconductors so that US firms could sell in Japan only certain types of semiconductors not produced by Japanese firms and only when there were spot market shortages. SIA claimed that despite aggressive marketing efforts by US firms and despite its dominance of American, European, and all other semiconductor markets, the US market presence in Japan in 1985 remained what it had been in 1975—about 10%.

Korea insurance: USTR initiated a Section 301 investigation against South Korean insurance trade policies and practices in September 1985.[43] Several American insurance companies charged that Korean government licensing restrictions prohibited them from competing in the Korean life insurance and compulsory insurance markets. Compulsory insurance is required by the Korean government of all citizens as a matter of national public policy.[44] The American companies charged that the 1981 agreement between the United States and the Republic of Korea to open the Korean fire insurance market had been thwarted by Korean government tolerance of the close business relationships among Korean insurance companies and banks. Korean banks, according to American firms, "directed" their customers to purchase fire insurance from Korean companies.

Korea intellectual property: USTR initiated a Section 301 investigation against South Korea's policies and practices regarding the protection of intellectual-property rights.[45] First, USTR investigated Korean patent laws, especially for chemicals and pharmaceuticals, which protected only the specific process for making the product, not the product itself. Second, USTR investigated Korean trademark protection, which allegedly offered foreign firms little redress for trademark infringements, because Korean courts employed a "famous in Korea" test for trademarks. The courts had held that a trademark merited protection only if it were well known to Korean consumers. Hence, products new to the Korean market, even if already well known in other parts of the world, were denied trademark protection. Third, USTR investigated allegations by the American publishing, music, motion picture, and software industries that Korean piracy of their books, records and cassettes, films and video cassettes, and computer software was widespread and that Korean copyright law offered little protection for foreign copyright-holders.

Korea beef: The American Meat Institute in February 1988 charged in a Section 301 petition that since May 1985 the Korean Ministry of Agriculture, Forestry, and Fisheries had banned the importation of American beef.[46]

Taiwan rice: The (American) Rice Millers Association filed with USTR in July 1983 a Section 301 complaint against the Republic of China (Taiwan) that charged the Taiwanese government with purchasing rice from its farmers at prices significantly higher than world market price and then dumping the rice to selected countries at below world market price.[47] The Rice Millers alleged that the Taiwanese government's price support system encouraged overproduction in Taiwan, which depressed American rice exports.

For the chapter on China, I carried out an intensive case study of the only major trade dispute between the United States and China during the 1980s, the dispute over textiles and apparel. Analysis is based on documentary evidence and interviews conducted in Washington and in Beijing. In the dispute, the American Textile Manufacturers Institute and the unions charged that the Chinese government was subsidizing the export of textiles and apparel. The dispute was really about US apparel makers feeling the pressure from imports from an entirely new market source—China in the era of Deng Xiaoping.

Thus, the conclusions of this study are based upon the largest, most systematic market-sector-specific data set on US export policy in the Pacific yet presented: a "universe" of forty 301/302 disputes between 1974 and 1989, nine process-tracing case studies, detailed examination of the Structural Impediments negotiations and the Super 301 cases, and a process-tracing case study of the only major trade dispute of the 1980s between the United States and China.

SUMMARY OF THE ARGUMENTS

An important finding of this study is that there are decision rules to the implementation of 301 policy by USTR, that 301 implementation is not a random exercise in American trade power, and that two explanatory variables— the commercial competitiveness of the complaining industry and the GATT regime utility of the case—explain the implementation of 301 in the Pacific. The explanatory usefulness of these variables arises logically from the characterization of the United States in the Pacific economy as a pluralist, liberal regulatory hegemon. USTR most often initiated 301 negotiations against a Japanese, Korean, or Taiwanese "unfair trade barrier" when both circumstances were fulfilled, sometimes initiated 301 investigations if one of the two conditions was met, but never initiated 301 investigations if neither of the conditions was met. These conclusions, based upon the large, longitudinal, market-sector-specific data set, contradict recent analyses of 301 and trade policy implementation in the Pacific. Based upon the 1989 Super 301 initiation decisions against Japan, Michael Mastanduno argues that strategic concerns, industry preferences, and Congressional preferences explain USTR behavior. American export policy is thereby understood to be explained by the idea of strategic trade policy, interest group power in American pluralism, and interbranch politics. Based upon seven cases of US-Japan negotiated trade disputes, Ellis Krauss and Simon Reich argue that competitiveness and high tech vs. non–high tech explains US behavior. Thus, American export policy is understood to be a high-tech, "picking-winners" industrial policy.[48] Though containing grains of truth, both studies mischaracterize American export policy in the Pacific because they overstate the significance of strategic, picking-winners industrial policy and completely ignore GATT regime utility, which is an absolutely crucial factor in the implementation of US export policy in the Pacific. They mischaracterize in this way because their analytic frameworks devote too little attention to the American executive-branch office that conducts US export policy (USTR) and too much attention to American pluralism—examples again of too much use of "society-centered" and "system-centered" explanations and too little use of "institution-centered" explanations. They also mischaracterize because their data is too narrowly drawn: Mastanduno generalizes from the single year 1989 (when the Uruguay Round was a USTR preoccupation), and Krauss and Reich generalize from a few manufacturing-sector cases.

The attention to a systematic, empirical, market-sector-specific investigation of the implementation of 301 by the US executive, rather than to the flame-throwing legislative rhetoric of the 1980s (a preoccupation of Bhagwati and Patrick's volume on Super 301), affords a sober analysis of 301's impact on the world trading system that contradicts previous analyses. Drawing from one case study (the 301 dispute with Brazil over its informatics policies), Peter Evans argues that the reason behind 301 policy is that the United States is a "declining hegemon" in international trade relations, an argument seconded by Jagdish Bhagwati with his characterization of 301 policy as the product of "diminished giant syndrome."[49] The market-sector-specific evidence of 301 implementation shows, however, that the US can be more aptly described as no longer a "benevolent hegemon" in agriculture and traditional manufacturing markets and an "ascending hegemon" in service and intellectual-property-based markets. USTR took many actions against East Asian policies that violated GATT obligations regarding agriculture and manufacturing. USTR took still other actions against nontariff barriers to service and intellectual-property-intensive industries, thus pressing forward with global liberalization in sectors of the world economy not then liberalized under the GATT regime. The prediction of David Lake that a hegemon will use its power to impose a liberal world trade order continues to find support in the evidence of US behavior.[50] Competition is global, and US productivity and competitiveness are high in many market sectors (high tech and non–high tech); hence American business enterprises are no longer ignoring foreign market opportunities, and USTR occasionally presses for the removal of specific trade barriers confronted by American producers of goods and services. American trade power remains sufficient to achieve many of its trade policy goals. Armed with a better explanation of how and why 301 policy is implemented, the empirical findings of USTR's "success rate" (research by Thomas Bayard and Kimberly Elliott), the "limited case" for 301 (research by Alan

Sykes), and the "justified disobedience" defense of 301 (research by Robert Hudec) may be better understood.[51]

The process-tracing case studies emphasize the influence of trade lawyers on the 301 process and further reinforce why 301 trade dispute settlement is often rule-oriented trade diplomacy. Most 301 initiation petitions are filed by law firms in the name of the American business firm or association. Using knowledge of 301 law, of USTR's predispositions, and "inside-the-Beltway trade politics," the trade lawyer helps the business firm design a 301 strategy. At USTR, the lawyers (from the General Counsel's office) chair the interagency Section 301 Committee, thereby coordinating the investigation and negotiation processes. The East Asian governments also hire trade lawyers (often American and Washington-based) to help them design their response strategies in 301 negotiations. The attorneys often frame the terms of the debate and propose final terms of the settlement.

Despite the similarities of the East Asian states as late-industrializing, "weak" bargainers in the Pacific, and thus the fundamental similarity of their responses to 301 (as analyzed by David Yoffie),[52] each of the East Asian states pursues a somewhat different response strategy. The Japanese pursue a "stall" strategy; the Koreans pursue a "crisis capitulation" strategy; the Taiwanese pursue a "clever-concession" strategy; the Chinese pursue a "combative-counterpunch" strategy. The response strategies are explained through analysis of the dependence of the country upon the United States for exports and security and of the governmental institutions that carry out trade diplomacy with the United States.

The process-tracing case studies indicate that USTR pursued rule-oriented and power-oriented trade diplomacy in the Pacific. USTR's rule-oriented trade diplomacy was "settlement by negotiation and agreement with reference to the norms and rules upon which both parties previously have agreed" in the disputes about Japan, Korea, and Taiwan footwear, Taiwan rice, Japan tobacco, and Korea beef. USTR's power-oriented trade diplomacy was "settlement by negotiation and agreement with reference (explicitly or implicitly) to the relative power statuses of the parties" in the disputes about Korea intellectual property, Korea insurance, and Japan semiconductor. Thus, neither realist nor liberal political economy can offer wholly accurate descriptions of trade diplomacy in the Pacific, but both offer stylized descriptions that capture important aspects of 301 negotiation processes: application of GATT rules, use of GATT dispute settlement procedures, and the threat of economic sanction.

The risk of noncompliance is great in a settlement agreement that is the outcome to power-oriented trade diplomacy. The negotiators do not have internationally legitimate rules to serve as a model for the agreement text, and this often leads to ambiguous and/or unimplementable settlement agreements. Without internationally legitimate rules, the respondent government does not feel concern for its reputation of compliance with international laws or the maintenance of international regimes. Disputes settled through a process of rule-oriented trade diplomacy, on the other hand, possess internationally legitimate rules to guide the drafting of the agreement text. Respondent states feel the concern for international reputation and for international regime maintenance. Thus, trade diplomats are likely to get substantial compliance in settlement agreements with the following characteristics: (1) expected trade behavior is clearly specified, (2) expected trade behavior is implementable, (3) effective monitoring procedures are provided in order to detect noncompliance, and (4) positive and/or negative incentives for compliance are offered. Careful rule-oriented trade diplomacy can render impractical the weak-state bargainer's tactic of cheating on treaty agreements.

Analysis of the rule-oriented and power-oriented trade diplomacy carried out by USTR with Japan, Korea, and Taiwan begs the question: after fifteen years of bilateral trade dispute diplomacy, what is the fit between the East Asian political economies and the GATT regime? The fit is generally good under the GATT principle of reduction of trade barriers, not good under the principle of nondiscrimination, manageable under that of fair trade, and getting better under those of multilateralism, reciprocity, and economic development. The East Asian political economies have moved far toward compliance with extant rules of the GATT regime but fall far short of effectively promoting cooperation, minimizing conflict, and settling commercial disputes in the Pacific. Thus, much additional rule creation is needed under GATT/WTO auspices, especially in the areas of services, intellectual property, competition and antitrust, and standards harmonization, and the Uruguay Round has been an important step in that direction.

Minilateral, regional institutions of trade diplomacy may play important future roles in helping promote trade diplomacy in the Pacific and supplementing and correcting for the limitations of multilateralism and unilateralism. Recent analysis by economists takes a dim view of the prospects for regional integration in the form of a free trade area in the Pacific since it "lacks a compelling economic rationale."[53] But, liberal political-economy theory shows that regional integration and institution building constitute a political process that is often motivated more by political goals than by economic goals.

Liberal political economy shows that regional cooperation is best predicted by analysis of three variables—structural conditions (state political-economy structures), process conditions (transactions), and perceptual conditions (cost benefit and salience)—and it is concluded here that prospects for regional institution building through APEC and the Asian Development Bank are favorable but that American leadership is crucial. I have also concluded that regional institutions can supplement GATT/WTO multilateralism by leaving to WTO dispute settlement procedures dispute settlement cases where WTO rules apply and by promoting minilateral cooperation through (1) information gathering and dissemination, (2) the establishment of an appeals body (on the model of the NAFTA body) for antidumping/countervailing-duty decisions pertaining to regional trade, and (3) ongoing consultations for commercial-standards harmonization.

The arguments of this book are presented in the nine succeeding chapters. Chapter 2 explains the initiation decision and describes how USTR is organized to implement 301 trade policy. Chapter 3 explains the response strategies to 301 and examines how the Japanese, Korean, and Taiwanese governments are organized to respond to American 301 investigations. Chapters 4 and 5 explain the processes and outcomes of rule-oriented and power-oriented trade diplomacy in the Pacific, recounting the nine case studies researched for this book. Chapter 6 explains the differing compliance records in the nine case studies. Chapter 7 evaluates the fit of the Japanese, Korean, and Taiwanese political economies with the principles and rules of the GATT regime. Chapter 8 applies the analytic framework employed in the study of 301 diplomacy with Japan, Korea, and Taiwan to China. Chapter 9 explores the potential for minilateral, regional institutions in the diplomacy of the Pacific economy. Finally, Chapter 10 considers the implications of the study for government policymakers and for business managers and suggests new research questions for scholars of international relations and political economy.

CHAPTER 2

Implementing 301 Policy

Though firm trade policy behavior is underresearched,[1] American businesses apparently petition their governments to pursue bilateral trade dispute settlement because their competitiveness is threatened by a foreign competitor. The threat may be from fair competition (as in an escape clause case) or from (allegedly) unfair competition (as in antidumping, countervailing duty, Section 337, or Section 301 cases). Japan, Korea, and Taiwan have been repeatedly accused of "unfair" trade behavior by the United States under the authority of Section 301 of the 1974 Trade Act and then subjected to American trade power: eliminate this unfair trade barrier or face economic sanctions. Because of the asymmetry in the bilateral structures of power, the outcome will be what the Americans want[2] minus the concessions extracted by the strategic, if weak, Japanese, Korean, and Taiwanese bargainers.[3] Given American capability to exact its will, the important research questions for students of American economic policy are the following: Which issues will the American government choose to pursue with the East Asian governments? All or selected issues? Either way, how is "issue" defined? Who defines which issues to take up? When should issues be raised to international disputes? In short, how is 301 policy implemented in the Pacific?

The observed pattern of 301 initiations in the Pacific can be explained by the institutional mission and goals of the Office of the US Trade Representative within the context of the pluralist, liberal-tending, industrialized, hegemonic US political economy. USTR, which leads US government participation in GATT relations, aims to project American interests within the GATT regime. USTR favors cases that allege noncompliance with extant GATT rules or that can be used concomitantly with USTR's multilateral rule-creation negotiation goals, and it shies away from cases that undercut its leadership position within the GATT. USTR aims to preserve the President's prerogatives in the implementation of US trade policy and to ensure that it (not the

Commerce Department) is the executive branch's top agency for trade policy. Thus, USTR takes up the cases of the commercially competitive industries, thereby demonstrating to Congress that it is "being tough with foreign trade barriers." Though few people think that USTR's actions will reduce the trade deficit as a matter of economics, many people think that USTR's actions will reduce protectionist pressures as a matter of trade politics. Taking up the case of a commercially uncompetitive industry squanders precious resources, unless the case involves a GATT regime utility issue of separate interest to USTR. Advised one staff member: "Think of us as like a prosecutor's office. Prosecutors love to win and hate to lose; we look for cases that we can *win*. You don't get ahead around here by losing. The last thing anyone wants around here is another Brazil informatics case."[4] (The United States had little leverage over the Brazilians since their export dependence on the US was minimal. Hence, USTR expended much time and energy only to fail.)

Even the rhetorically charged "Super" 301 was implemented by USTR in just the same way as regular 301. The two variable models presented here explain US behavior under its Super 301 policy as well as regular 301 policy. Super 301, the policy created by Congress with the 1988 amendments to the original 1974 301 law, demands that USTR surveil the world, looking for state trade barriers that limit US business opportunities in international markets, and announce the "priority countries" and "watch countries" that will be receiving USTR attention. Super 301 "priority countries" were announced by USTR as having specific "unfair trade barriers" actionable under Section 301 (and were administratively assigned regular 301 case numbers). Super 301 in 1989 was implemented according to the same logic as regular 301. The robustness of the present framework is further supported by the second year of Super 301: in 1990 (the last year of Super 301 until the Clinton administration decision to carry out Super 301 by executive order), USTR announced that it would not name any new priority countries because completing the GATT Uruguay Round was its highest priority.

A premise of this research is that USTR is an organization composed of individual policymakers who implement 301 trade policy deliberately. Therefore, USTR is capable of being a purposive, goal-directed organization and its behavior indicates its goals.[5] This research, however, does not assume *a priori* that USTR behaves that way, and it recognizes that the patterns of behavior may be random or, at least, that neither goals nor behavior may be consistent. In order to investigate USTR's behavior, this chapter employs the data set of the forty Section 301/302 trade disputes initiated and settled in the 1970s and 1980s between the United States and Japan, Korea, and Taiwan. The data is used to test hypotheses derived from realist political economy and liberal political economy, the two major research traditions in the study of international economic relations. The chapter first offers the political economy explanation behind the goals and behavior of USTR, discusses the operation of USTR and legislative demands of Section 301, then explores theory purporting to explain USTR's implementation of 301. From this theory, hypotheses are proposed and tested against the evidence. The chapter concludes with implications for theory and policy.

PLURALIST, LIBERAL REGULATORY HEGEMON

The United States is the archetype of the weak state. The polity is pluralist: power is dispersed, decision making is fragmented, and resources are allocated through markets. The US Constitution forged a weak state with limited powers and checks and balances that grew without major external security threats and with increasing wealth and relative egalitarianism. The US pursues a liberal regulatory industrial-policy strategy, which asserts that markets allocate resources more efficiently, give incentives to producers to produce what the public wants, give incentives to workers to acquire useful skills, conserve scarce goods by setting their prices high, offer a high degree of economic freedom, and maximize aggregate wealth better than nonmarket alternatives. The strategy admits that markets treat the weak, incapable, or unlucky indifferently, may be unstable, may allow oligopolies or monopolies to exploit consumers, and may produce negative externalities such as water pollution. In general, the government ought not to "decide what should be produced and how or by whom; it does not fix prices itself, nor does it control investment or entry on the basis of its own calculations of how much is economically desirable; the government does not specifically control who should be permitted to do what jobs, nor does it specify the permissible dimensions and characteristics of the product."[6] Government ought to be "maintaining the institutions within whose framework the free market can continue to function, of enforcing, supplementing, and removing the imperfections of competition—not supplanting it."[7]

As markets in America grew from local to regional to national, and as corporate capitalism supplanted proprietary capitalism as a means of industrial organization early in the twentieth century, the federal government expanded its legal reach such that "only the idiot or the powerless goes into the market without a lawyer, and without political clout—something workers learned after most capitalists had."[8] Regulation of business by the state through "enforcing, supplementing, and removing the imperfections of competition," says Theodore Lowi, has gradually expanded in the United States throughout the twentieth century as the pluralist polity has allowed specialized interest groups to pressure Congress to write ambiguous laws to be administered by ever-expanding, ever more intrusive executive-branch agencies.[9] Business in America, contends James Q. Wilson, is schizophrenically regulated at the Federal Trade Commission, at the Antitrust Division of the Department of Justice, at the Food and Drug Administration, at the Occupational Safety and Health Administration, at the Environmental Protection Agency, at the Office of Civil Rights, and at scores of other agencies by lawyers who seek to prosecute every act of regulatory noncompliance and by economists who seek to prosecute only anticompetitive acts.[10] The tension between the American ideological commitments to legalism and to liberalism makes American business-government relations regarding regulation more adversarial and conflictual than in Britain, which is also legalistic, liberal, and pluralistic.[11]

The emergence in the twentieth century of America's growing and increasingly globally competitive corporate capitalism, coupled with America's rise toward great-power status, gradually turned American trade and direct-investment policy from Hamiltonian mercantilist to liberal.[12] It encouraged American policymakers to lead in the creation of the GATT (even if they were unable to get Congress to agree to American participation in an International Trade Organization) and to lead in tariff-cutting and new-rule creation in the Tokyo Round and Uruguay Round multilateral trade negotiations. The American hegemon believed its interests and those of its allies were served by the creation of a liberal-tending, rule-oriented international trade regime, even if its own behavior throughout the post–World War II era would better be described as a "pragmatic liberalism" capable of overt protectionism (e.g., steel and apparel orderly-market arrangements) and covert protectionism (e.g., automobile voluntary export restraints and abuse of antidumping procedures).[13] Because of the structure of the US economy—a competitiveness based upon technology-intensive industries and services—the US industrial policy now recommends that the GATT-based international trade regime grow to govern international economic relations regarding service trade, intellectual-property rights, foreign direct investment, standards harmonization, and competition and antitrust policy.

Despite the emergence of Japanese manufacturing producers in the 1970 and 1980s, the United States remained the hegemon in the Pacific throughout the period—a relatively open economy with 250 million relatively wealthy consumers. In 1974, producers in Japan exported goods worth $12.5 billion to the US, producers in Korea $1.5 billion, and producers in Taiwan $2.1 billion. In 1984, producers in Japan exported goods worth $57 billion, producers in Korea $9 billion, and producers in Taiwan nearly $15 billion. In 1991, producers in Japan exported goods worth more than $91 billion, producers in Korea $17 billion, and producers in Taiwan $23 billion.[14] About 35% of Japanese exports, more than 26% of Korean exports, and nearly 30% of Taiwanese exports went to the United States.[15] The big-ticket items for Japan were automobiles and auto parts, consumer electronics, office machines and parts, telecommunications equipment, and electrical machinery. The big-ticket items for Korea and Taiwan were consumer electronics, footwear, and automobiles and auto parts.[16] Thus, each of the East Asian countries was heavily dependent on access to the US market.

USTR AND 301 TRADE POLICY

According to Section 301 of the 1974 Trade Act, as amended in 1979, 1984, and 1988, USTR has the authority to

(A) suspend, withdraw, or prevent the application of, benefits of trade agreement concessions . . . ;

(B) impose duties or other import restrictions on the goods of such foreign country; or

(C) enter into binding agreements with such foreign country that commit such foreign country to (i) eliminate, or phase out, the act, policy, or practice that is the subject of the action to be taken [by USTR].

USTR is also authorized to take "all other appropriate and feasible action within the power of the President," i.e., even retaliate, against a foreign government to aid a US firm or industry that has been victimized by unfair foreign trade practices. If USTR determines that

(A) the rights of the United States under any trade agreement are being denied; or

(B) an act, policy, or practice of a foreign country

(i) violates, or is inconsistent with, the provisions of, or otherwise denies benefits to the United States under, any trade agreement, or

(ii) is unjustifiable and burdens or restricts United States commerce, then

USTR *must* take action. If USTR determines that "an act, policy, or practice of a foreign country is unreasonable or discriminatory and burdens or restricts United States commerce," USTR *may* take action. Section 301 was amended in 1984 so that "commerce" includes service trade and foreign investment in addition to merchandise trade. The 301 process begins with a petition from an American company or industry and a decision by USTR to initiate an investigation. The statutory language, however, is sweeping, and so USTR possesses much latitude; therefore the research question posed in this paper cannot be answered by mere textual analysis of the statute. Under Section 302 of the statute, USTR is authorized to conduct informal negotiations with a foreign country, thus offering the opportunity for quieter, less overtly coercive diplomacy.[17]

The administrator of 301 law is USTR. Renamed the Office of the United States Trade Representative (USTR) in 1980, the Special Trade Representative for Trade Negotiations (STR) was created by Congress through the Trade Expansion Act of 1962 and implemented by President Kennedy in a January 1963 executive order.[18] President Carter's 1980 executive order authorized USTR to make and administer American trade policy, lead all trade negotiations, represent the US government in international trade organizations such as GATT and UNCTAD, and act as an international agent for American business in Section 301 actions. USTR has never had more than about 250 staff members, so it is a small organization with an ambitious mission and many important tasks to carry out. Thus, USTR must always prioritize its agenda.

The United States Trade Representative, who holds the rank of Ambassador, sits on the Cabinet-level Economic Policy Committee. In addition to serving on Cabinet trade-related committees, the Representative serves as Vice Chairperson of the Overseas Private Investment Corporation (OPIC) and as an ex officio member of the Export-Import Bank. Reporting to the Representative are three Deputy US Trade Representatives and the Chief Textile Negotiator, each with the title of Ambassador, and the General Counsel. One of the Deputy US Trade Representatives serves in Geneva as the American representative to GATT and UNCTAD, while the other two deputies divide administrative and policy responsibilities. The General Counsel advises USTR on US and international trade law.

USTR is composed of four categories of offices: support, multilateral, bilateral, and sectoral.[19] The support staff includes the Counsellor to the USTR, the General Counsel, Congressional Affairs, Chief Economist, Trade Policy Coordination, and Administration. The staff with responsibility for multilateral issues include the offices of GATT Affairs and (since the late 1980s) Uruguay Round Coordination. The staff with responsibility for bilateral issues include the offices for (1) North America, (2) Europe and the Mediterranean, (3) Latin America, the Caribbean, and Africa, (4) Japan and China, and (5) Asia and the Pacific (everything in the region except China and Japan, but primarily Taiwan and Korea). The sectoral offices include (a) industry (such as steel, automobiles, and semiconductors), (b) services, investment, and intellectual property, and (c) agriculture (such as rice, sugar, beef, and tobacco). Each office is composed of three to ten professional staff.

The General Counsel's office, with 12 lawyers on its staff, is one of USTR's largest offices. By early 1990, the Bush administration US Trade Representative—herself a lawyer—institutionalized what had long been the de facto primacy of the General Counsel's office lawyers in 301 bilateral trade dispute settlement. She created the post of Assistant US Trade Representative for Dispute Resolution and gave the position to a Deputy General Counsel, whose title became Principal Deputy General Counsel.[20] In that capacity, but "under the supervision of the General Counsel," she oversees the Section 301 program, leads the US team in the Dispute Settlement negotiating group of the Uruguay Round, and coordinates formal international trade dispute settlement.

The lawyers in the General Counsel's office were educated in American law schools. Since education is a potent socializing force,[21] their extensive legal preparation is not trivial. The law school curriculum emphasizes the application of rules to social relations. Hence, the lawyer who joins the USTR General Counsel's office is predisposed to resolve trade disputes by applying the rules—GATT or other treaty law—to transnational commercial relations. Many other top officials at USTR were educated in law schools, including the Clinton administration US Trade Representative, Mickey Kantor, the Bush administration US Trade Representative, Carla Hills, and her predecessor, Clayton Yeutter (who also earned a Ph.D. in economics). In addition, five senior USTR officials (excluding the General Counsel's office) during the Bush administration were educated as lawyers.[22] Six others possessed their highest educational degrees in public policy, international affairs, or political science. Unlike law schools, public-policy and international-affairs schools usually emphasize in their curricula theory about economics, bureaucracy, decision making, foreign policy, and the history and politics of a particular country. Hence, by way of educational preparation, USTR senior officials are predisposed to resolve trade disputes with reference to international law and to economic principles such as comparative advantage and free trade, with sympathy toward the target state's economic and political position, with comradery toward opposing negotiators who are fellow government bureaucrats, and with sensitivity toward the multiplicity of American foreign-policy objectives. These are, however, educational archetypes at USTR. In 1979, with the objective of being better prepared for negotiations with the Japanese, USTR hired a Japanese-reading lawyer with a public-policy degree for the USTR General Counsel's office.[23] Other staff members have multiple educational preparations as well.

USTR trains its staff members in-house in a training process described by several experienced staff members as an informal apprenticeship or guild system.[24] New professional staff are usually hired on a trial basis for one year to "see how they work out." They are thought of as "apprentices," and if they do not work out, they are returned to their bureaucratic home at State or Commerce or Agriculture. The job requires a variety of special skills and characteristics—intellectual, professional, and personal. The effective USTR staff member must be a leader and a good communicator; he or she must be creative, honest, and smart. At USTR, they believe it cannot be determined whether a person possesses these attributes without time spent on the job. Apprentices are trained within each office and do not receive formal, USTR-wide training. In the beginning, new staff members are given relatively simple, low-responsibility tasks to perform. As their knowledge and skills grow, they are given more demanding, higher-responsibility tasks to perform. Within a short period of time, capable apprentices graduate to more difficult assignments. USTR is an aggressive agency that runs largely on the vitality of relatively young staff members.

When the Reagan administration came into office in 1981, only one Cabinet committee made American trade policy, the Trade Policy Committee (TPC), chaired by the US Trade Representative.[25] The Reagan administration preserved the TPC when it came into office, but also created the Cabinet Council on Commerce and Trade, chaired nominally by the President but usually by the Secretary of Commerce. In 1982, President Reagan added the Senior Interdepartmental Group on International Economic Policy, chaired by the Secretary of the Treasury. The memberships of the three committees differed. The TPC included the US Trade Representative, the Secretaries of the Treasury, Defense, Interior, Energy, State, and Agriculture, the National

Security Advisor, and the Attorney General. The Cabinet Council on Commerce and Trade included the US Trade Representative, the Attorney General, the Vice President, and the Secretaries of Energy, Commerce, State, and Treasury. The Senior Interdepartmental Group on International Economic Policy included the Secretary of State, the Secretary of the Treasury, and the US Trade Representative. Trade policy matters went to the TPC first for a decision. The TPC reported to the Council of Commerce and Trade; Commerce and Trade reported to the International Economic Policy Group. Hence, the Secretary of Commerce could overrule decisions of the US Trade Representative. These interlocking committees managed US trade policy for the Reagan administration until April 1985.

The year 1985 was a watershed for US foreign trade policy as record trade deficits and prominent bilateral trade disputes with Japan led to a crisis atmosphere. The process by which the US carried out its trade policy, including 301 policy, became as important as the substance of the trade problems themselves. Some critics charged that USTR lacked sufficient resources and political clout to carry out its duties effectively. Critics of USTR opined that its staff is too small to do well all that it is asked to do. Some said that the US Trade Representative, who vies with the Secretaries of Commerce and Treasury for control of the creation and implementation of trade policy, lacks the authority to do any of it well. Other commentators contended that the real problem is bigger than USTR alone. Senator Daniel Patrick Moynihan, noting that "when everyone is responsible, no one is,"[26] argued that trade policymaking and implementation responsibility is dispersed too widely in the American government. Some observers compared the apparent success of Japanese trade policy with that of the US and concluded that the structure of US trade policy-making and implementation should be modeled after the Japanese system. During the 1980s, Congress considered and reconsidered bills to reform the structure of American trade policy-making and implementation. The reform proposals often called for the unification of USTR and the Department of Commerce into a "Department of Trade" or even a deliberately MITI-mimicking "Department of International Trade and Industry," a DITI. The Commerce Department Secretary—whose power would be magnified by the plan—politicked vigorously from late 1982 until early 1985 for the idea. Yet the reform movement gradually subsided as reformers failed to garner sufficient support in the administration and Congress to achieve change.

The White House announced in April 1985 a reorganization of the Cabinet decision-making committees.[27] The reorganization plan came only a few weeks after the administration admitted that the plan to create a Department of Trade or a DITI was dead.[28] The reorganization eliminated most of the previous Cabinet committees, supplanting them with two committees nominally chaired by the President: the Economic Policy Council and the Domestic Policy Council. All economic policy matters—both national and international—were managed by the EPC, while all noneconomic domestic matters were managed by the DPC. The Economic Policy Council was chaired by the Secretary of the Treasury and included the Secretaries of State, Agriculture, Commerce, and Labor, the US Trade Representative, the Director of the Office of Management and Budget, the Chairman of the Council of Economic Advisors, the Vice President, and the Chief of Staff. Whenever international policy matters were discussed, the National Security Advisor was invited to attend. The reorganization continued, however, the existence of a trade policy Cabinet committee, the Trade Policy Review Group (TPRG). The TPRG, chaired by the US Trade Representative, reported to the Economic Policy Council. Thus, the line of trade policy authority apparently went clearly from the US Trade Representative to the Secretary of the Treasury to the President.

Especially for trade disputes, however, the organizational chart and process became more confused during fall 1985. President Reagan announced in September 1985 the creation of a Trade Strike Force to target specific unfair trade practices that the US would eliminate. The Strike Force was conjured up not by the Economic Policy Council but by the President's speechwriters.[29] The Secretary of Commerce was hastily put in charge of the Strike Force after the President's speech. For the Secretary of Commerce, who had lost the "Department of International Trade and Industry" bureaucratic struggle, the Strike Force was a way back into trade policy-making.[30] Nevertheless, the Strike Force was an important player in Pacific trade dispute settlement only in the Japan semiconductor case—a case in which Commerce and its Secretary had long been actively involved. Over the course of the late 1980s and into the 1990s, USTR's preeminence in 301 bilateral trade dispute settlement became clear.

Does USTR have adequate staff resources to settle Pacific trade disputes? Does the US Trade Representative possess interagency influence sufficient to settle Pacific Basin trade disputes? The evidence indicates that USTR does possess adequate resources to negotiate a settlement. The US negotiating teams appear to have been adequately prepared to negotiate effectively, though occasionally did not do so. The conclusion, nevertheless, does not preclude the possibility that because of insufficient staff USTR must work excessively hard to prepare for negotiations, as some USTR observers contend. The US Trade Representative generally possesses sufficient political clout vis-à-vis other senior executive-branch policymakers to settle Pacific disputes without debilitating political interference. "Debilitating" is the measure here, for a political system of checks and balances within an open society expects participation by other political players in any important issue of policy implementation.

SECTION 301 PROCESS

Rarely do business firms or industry associations attempt the Section 301 dispute settlement process without the help of Washington trade lawyers, though legally they may do so. Most initiation petitions are filed by law firms in the name of the business firm or association. Trade law is an arcane specialty of law even in a profession not notably less recondite today than during the years after the Conquest, when the Norman lawyers argued in French in the English courts. Trade lawyers learn both US trade law and international trade law but often specialize in certain types of trade law, say, in intellectual property or in countervailing-duty suspension agreements. But it is not only the lawyers' mastery of complex rules that makes them indispensable to the bilateral trade dispute settlement process. The effective trade lawyer is also nimble at "inside-the-Beltway" politics. The best trade lawyers know well trade policymakers at USTR, the White House, the Departments of Commerce and State, the International Trade Commission, and the key Congressional representatives and staff people. They monitor the ebb and flow of Washington trade politics. Especially in the sometimes freewheeling Section 301 process, the effective trade lawyer knows the predispositions and tendencies of the USTR staff and the types of arguments that typically move them to action. The trade lawyer who files a petition buttressed by arguments that USTR has previously refused to accept may not be giving the client good service. On the other hand, long shots can sometimes be worthily attempted, and the bizarre argument may be a brilliant bargaining tactic. In Section 301 cases, timing is often as important as argument to get USTR to initiate an investigation. Capable trade lawyers know when the time is ripe to press a case and when to hold back for the more opportune moment. For these reasons, private trade lawyers often have government experience at USTR, the White House staff, ITC, or Commerce.

All this legal advice does not come inexpensively. Interviews with trade dispute participants revealed that trade lawyers often bill their time out at several hundred dollars per hour. This amount, multiplied by the hundreds of hours needed to initiate and carry the case through to the end, together with the necessity of hiring economic consultants to assist with case preparation, means that the business firm will pay its lawyers one to several hundred thousand dollars, depending on the complexity of the case. Indeed, the legal tab for the Semiconductor Industry Association for the preparation of its case against Japan supposedly came to about a million dollars. This figure does not include the legal fees paid in Washington and New York by the Japanese to defend themselves in the case. A legal scholar has estimated that during the early 1980s American business was paying private trade lawyers about $93 million annually to carry out antidumping, countervailing-duty, Section 337 (copyright), and Section 301 cases.[31] Rule-oriented trade diplomacy is not without its costs. As a matter of corporate strategy, the question is the following: is the expense of such a legal process justified by the outcome? It is a worthwhile research question for business management scholars.

According to statutory dictate, the formal process of taking action under Section 301 begins with a petition to, or a self-initiation by, USTR. The actual process, however, usually begins before a formal petition is filed at USTR; it usually begins with an informal meeting between representatives of the industry, their trade lawyer, and representatives of USTR.[32] USTR representation typically consists of members of the General Counsel's office, the area office, and the sector office. At this informal meeting or meetings, the American firm or industry informs USTR staff that it believes it is the victim of unfair trade practices. For example, the trade lawyer for the Rice Millers Association might arrange a meeting with the USTR Associate General Counsel, a representative from the Asia and Pacific office, and a representative from the agriculture office to complain about Taiwanese rice policies. The trade lawyer would explain the problem and convey to USTR the importance of the issue to the Rice Millers Association. USTR, for its part, explains whether the problem has been discussed with the Taiwanese in the past, the Taiwanese position, the bilateral foreign-policy milieu, and USTR's preferred course of action. USTR may try to resolve a trade problem through informal bilateral discussions with the other government. If the informal bilateral talks do not bear fruit, however, then USTR staff may discuss with industry representatives and trade lawyers the possibility of a formal Section 301 petition filing.

By rule of custom at USTR, trade lawyers for a firm or industry contemplating a Section 301 petition filing send a draft petition around USTR for comments. It is the rare Section 301 petition that arrives at USTR unannounced. For example, USTR staff were not surprised by any of the petitions filed in the cases studied here. In fact, three of the Section 301 cases studied here were initiated by USTR (Japan tobacco, Korea insurance, and Korea intellectual property), while in two other cases, USTR invited petitions (Semiconductor Industry Association against Japan and American Meat Institute against Korea).[33] The particular recipients of the draft at USTR will vary, depending upon the country and market involved. The trade lawyer will often want to get the reaction of the area office and the sector office. But, the trade lawyer will *always* want the opinion of the General Counsel's office, since the USTR lawyers chair the Section 301 Committee.

301 INITIATION DECISION

Realist political economy predicts that USTR will not take up a case against a country over which it has no leverage, a proposition that was presumed to be true in this study and untested. Liberal political economy, arguing that the key to understanding American trade policy is to recognize the pluralist nature of American political economy, predicts that USTR will initiate a 301 investigation if and only if a powerful domestic interest group requests it. Realist political economy, on the other hand, which contends that the domestic sources of foreign policy behavior are irrelevant and that US policymakers are interested in maximizing the relative US position of wealth and power in the world economy, predicts that USTR will initiate a 301 investigation if and only if a commercially competitive domestic industry requests it. Related to (but not entailed by) the realist proposition is the following hypothesis: USTR will initiate a 301 investigation if and only if commercially competitive, high-technology industry requests it.

Liberal political economy, believing that states tend to cooperate and that economic regimes influence behavior, holds that USTR will initiate a 301 investigation if initiation will not injure bilateral diplomatic relations, if the respondent state's policy behavior violates a rule of an international economic regime, and if the respondent state's policy behavior may be exploited in GATT multilateral trade negotiations.

In order to test these hypotheses, three variables were operationalized—commercially competitive industry, high-technology industry, and GATT regime utility. Commercially competitive industry is defined as an industry that on the basis of price and quality, can sell its goods and services in international markets. An industry was coded here as a commercially competitive industry if Commerce Department data showed that it was a significant exporter. High-technology industry is defined by the Department of Commerce as an industry in which R&D is a relatively high proportion of gross sales.[34] An industry was coded as a high-technology industry if it made the

Commerce Department list.[35] GATT regime utility is defined as either (a) rule noncompliance or (b) multilateral trade negotiation rule-creation relatedness. A case was coded as involving GATT regime utility if USTR's General Counsel had specified a GATT rule violation or if the issue was on the agenda of either the Tokyo Round or the Uruguay Round multilateral trade negotiations.

The propositions are tested against the evidence of 301 trade policy implementation in the Pacific. Almost all of the disputes involved industries with powerful domestic interests—pharmaceuticals, wood products, telecommunications, and beef. This finding is apparent evidence in support of the hypothesis that USTR will initiate a 301 investigation if and only if a powerful domestic interest group requests it. The Japan leather, the Japan baseball bat, the Korea steel, and the footwear cases, however, contradict this hypothesis. Neither Japan leather nor Japan baseball bat involved big industries, yet USTR took up their cases. On the other hand, USTR also rejected petitions from the steel and footwear industries, each with substantial political clout, showing that USTR resists even powerful interest groups. Thus, though being big in pluralist America always affords a hearing, it is neither necessary nor sufficient for initiation of a 301 investigation.

The independent variables are plotted against the disputes in Table 2.1.

Almost all of the initiated disputes involved American industries that were commercially competitive in the world economy—baseball bats, satellites, insurance, beer, and tobacco. This finding provides strong support for the sufficiency (though not the necessity) aspect of the hypothesis that USTR initiates 301 investigations if a commercially competitive industry requests it. Indeed, as a matter of international business strategy, it would be nonsensical to discover that commercially uncompetitive industries were expending valuable resources to open markets that they then would be unable to exploit anyway. The 301 process is procedurally expensive in terms of both time and money, firms thus do not take up the process unless they think there will be substantial gain. But a few cases are anomalous: the then uncompetitive footwear and automobile industries did employ 301 as a matter of business strategy. In the footwear dispute, the Footwear Industries Association really wanted USTR to accept their contention that European import quotas diverted East Asian footwear to the US market. USTR rejected Footwear Industries' petition even though the petition arrived just before the November 1982 Congressional elections. When USTR refused to accept that argument, the main purpose of their petition was removed and USTR's efforts on their behalf gained little, from their perspective (i.e., more open markets in East Asia, but meaningless because their products were no more competitive).

Table 2.1   301 Trade Disputes in the Pacific and Independent Variables

Dispute	Commercially Competitive	Hi-Tech Industry	GATT Regime Utility
Taiwan appliances	X		
Japan steel NO ACTION			
Japan thrown silk	X		X
Japan leather	X		X
Japan citrus	X		X
Japan beef	X		X
Japan telecommunications	X	X	X
Japan cigars	X		X
Japan pipe tobacco	X		X
Korea insurance	X		X
Japan baseball bats	X		X
Japan footwear			X
Korea footwear			X
Taiwan footwear NO ACTION			
Korea steel wire NO ACTION			
Taiwan rice	X		X
Taiwan film	X		X
Korea insurance	X		X
Japan wood	X		X
Korea intellectual property	X	X	X

In the automobile dispute with Taiwan, the US auto industry (especially Ford) aimed to void a Taiwan-Toyota contract that offered the Japanese carmaker incentives for certain export performance levels.[36] Since planned production of the Taiwan-Toyota venture greatly exceeded total Taiwanese demand, the dispute was really about protecting US automakers from imports.

To recognize that uncompetitive industries generally do not complain to USTR about foreign trade barriers suggests the problem with asserting that evidence in support of the commercially competitive industry variable is

Table 2.1, continued

Dispute	Commercially Competitive	Hi-Tech Industry	GATT Regime Utility
Japan pharmaceuticals	X	X	
Japan intellectual property	X	X	X
Japan telecommunications	X	X	
Japan semiconductors	X	X	
Japan tobacco	X		X
Taiwan automobile FDI			X
Taiwan insurance	X		X
Taiwan automobile customs			X
Taiwan beer	X		X
Japan legal services	X		X
Japan agriculture	X		X
Japan beef	X		X
Japan citrus	X		X
Korea beef	X		X
Korea cigarettes	X		X
Korea wine	X		X
Japan construction	X		X
Japan satellites	X	X	X
Japan supercomputers	X	X	
Japan wood products	X		

support for the realist claim that the US is seeking relative gains through implementation of 301 policy (such as the contention of Michael Mastanduno, based on the evidence of the HDTV, satellites, and FSX cases).[37] The realist claim is that USTR will initiate investigations (then negotiate toward a settlement agreement) in support of advantages for US producers to the detriment of third-country producers. Evaluation of this claim demands detailed examination of the settlement agreements, which occurs below in succeeding chapters. Nevertheless, cursory examination of the extant nature of global competition indicates that in most of the agriculture and traditional manufacturing sector cases a 301 initiation to support an American industry supported third countries' industries as well (e.g., Japan beef helped Australia and New Zealand; Japan citrus helped Brazil; Japan wood products helped Canada and the ASEAN countries; Japan footwear helped Taiwan) and at least some of the service and intellectual-property-intensive manufacturing cases helped third countries' industries (e.g., Korea and Taiwan insurance helped Japanese insurance companies; Korea intellectual property helped German, Japanese, and Swiss pharmaceutical and chemical companies; Japan construction helped Korean construction companies), though a few cases probably helped US industries exclusively (Japan supercomputer, Japan law, and Taiwan film) because the US firms have no real global competition. This forms considerable evidence against the realist prediction that the US seeks relative gains.

About half (19/40) of the 301 initiations in the Pacific have concerned the manufacturing sector. The East Asian economies have been growing rapidly. Their businesses have been competing aggressively in the American market (thus the demands by some American producers for protection under escape clause, antidumping, and countervailing-duty procedures), and their markets have become more attractive to American producers (thus the demands for market opening under the 301 policy). About a third (13/40) of the cases have involved agriculture markets, while a few involved service markets. Agriculture market distortions have been a persistent international trade problem, while service cases emerged as bilateral trade problems in the Pacific because of the growth during the 1970s and 1980s of international service trade. The evidence, then, does not support the hypothesis that USTR will initiate a 301 investigation if and only if a commercially competitive, high-technology industry requests it. USTR does not implement a high-tech, picking-winners industrial policy strategy through the implementation of 301 policy.

Since good diplomatic relations with Japan are highly important to the United States and those with Korea and Taiwan quite important, the evidence here should be a good test of the hypothesis that USTR will not initiate an investigation if it will injure bilateral diplomatic relations. In the Pacific region, US initiation of bilateral dispute settlement under the 301 policy totaled ten cases in the 1970s and thirty cases in the 1980s. Thus, extensive US initiation of trade dispute settlement with Japan, Korea, and Taiwan contradicts the liberal political-economy hypothesis. Even the most casual observer of trade problems between the United States and Korea, Taiwan, and (especially) Japan knows that these relationships have been testy if still pacific. (On the other hand, US concern for good bilateral diplomatic relations with these East Asian states is shown by how USTR carries out the negotiations and by the settlement agreements that it signs. See Chapter 4.) Since, before the 1974 Trade Act, the US tolerated and even encouraged East Asian trade barriers, what accounts for the policy change? One interviewee remarked to me, "At one time the State Department put so much pressure on us during [the Japanese] elections and such that we didn't even talk to them [about trade disputes]."[38] The very existence of the 301 clause of the 1974 Trade Act, the fact that the law was implemented, and its increasing use demonstrate that trade policy had become important domestic and foreign policy in the United States by the 1980s.

Liberal political economy proposes that initiation depends upon noncompliance of an East Asian government policy with a treaty of the GATT regime, some other multilateral treaty, or a bilateral treaty of friendship, commerce, and navigation. Noncompliance was specified in twenty-six of the forty cases of 301 initiation against Japan, Korea, and Taiwan, with twenty-two being violations of multilateral treaties and four being violations of bilateral treaties. In addition, in two of the three cases in which no action was taken (Japan steel and Taiwan footwear), no action was taken because there was no rule violation. Thus, 301 initiations often involve an allegation of regime rule noncompliance, providing evidence in support of liberal political economy's hypothesis. An American trade negotiator emphasized while talking about a case with a GATT violation, "We had justice on our side; they knew we weren't going away on this one."[39] Indeed, one Japanese official opined: "GATT is key; it may determine win or lose for the US. If the US has a strong GATT case, the case will go differently. The US can use GATT as a very effective tool."[40] Without a clear GATT violation, USTR only reluctantly took up the semiconductor case when cases similar to the semiconductor problem found their way onto the Structural Impediments Initiative agenda, rather than the rule-oriented Section 301 agenda.

Furthermore, analysis of the fourteen cases without GATT rule violations shows that GATT considerations nevertheless were critical in the other initiation decisions. An additional five cases alleged noncompliance with rules that, though not extant, were emerging in the then ongoing GATT Uruguay Round multilateral trade negotiations. The intellectual-property disputes with the East Asian governments arose as multilateral talks were under way, the so-called TRIPs (trade-related intellectual property) talks in the Uruguay Round. The service trade disputes were initiated simultaneously with the Uruguay Round talks toward the GATS (General Agreement on Trade in

Services). The Taiwan auto dispute was initiated as the Uruguay Round agenda was being set to include TRIMs (trade-related investment measures) negotiations.

The five remaining disputes were initiated by USTR despite the absence of an immediate GATT consideration. Many late-1980s disputes involved product standards, an issue that was taken up in the Uruguay Round in the food products sector and is likely to be taken up in some mid-to-late-1990s rule creation activities within the new World Trade Organization. Even the Japan semiconductor case, which often is described as having proceeded with complete disregard for GATT considerations, may possess a long-term relationship with GATT considerations. The dispute was superficially about trade but really about the differing industrial organizations in the United States and Japan. Thus, even these cases may be harbingers of GATT rule creation regarding competition/antitrust policy. Because of the lack of data, uninitiated cases are difficult to analyze, but, one infamous, uninitiated, potential 301 case—the Japan rice dispute—has not been pursued by USTR under the 301 policy because USTR preferred to settle the dispute within the context of multilateral negotiations over agriculture. In sum, then, considerable support is found for the proposition that USTR initiates a 301 investigation if the respondent state's policy possesses GATT regime utility.

The importance of GATT in the USTR calculus also helps explain the puzzle that remained from the discussion above about why USTR takes up the cases of small interest groups. The leather case was initiated by USTR (and subsequently linked with the footwear dispute, since the latter could be seen as a subset of the former) because it possessed precedent value beyond the economic value.[41] It was the first attempt by the US to make the Japanese political economy conform with the rules and principles of the GATT and liberal-market political economy. A US trade policymaker said, "Leather and footwear was [a] medium to attack the Japanese system."[42] Another US policymaker mused: "Nobody would have believed then that it would result in 1990 with the Structural Impediments Initiative. Now we are demanding the complete restructuring of the Japanese economy."[43] Leather products, including footwear, were heavily protected by the Japanese government for domestic social, economic, and political reasons. The Japanese conceded that their leather import policy violated GATT Article XI's prohibition against quantitative restraints, which USTR ultimately demonstrated through a GATT panel finding. The baseball bat case was similarly initiated by USTR because it possessed precedent value beyond narrow calculations of commercial value. It was a medium to attack discriminatory Japanese standards and regulations.[44]

Table 2.2   301 Implementation Model and Findings

	high GATT regime utility	low GATT regime utility
high commercial competitiveness	27 / 37	6 / 37
low commercial competitiveness	4 / 37	0

Note: Total N = 40, but no action was taken in three cases.

Through their precedent value these "small" cases can have impact far beyond the immediate market gains.

The implementation of US 301 policy in the Pacific can best be explained with two variables: the commercial competitiveness of the business firm or association raising the complaint and the GATT regime utility for USTR of the East Asian government policy in question. The argument, with data findings, is summarized in Table 2.2.

USTR most often initiated a 301 investigation when the petitioning firm or industry group was commercially competitive and when the dispute involved GATT regime utility (either a rule violation or a relationship with rule creation activities). USTR sometimes initiated an investigation when the petitioning firm or industry group was commercially competitive, though the dispute involved no relationship with GATT regime rule creation activities. USTR sometimes initiated investigations when the petitioning firm was commercially uncompetitive but the dispute possessed GATT regime utility. USTR initiated no investigations that involved an uncompetitive industry and no GATT regime utility.

The observed pattern of 301 initiations in the Pacific can be explained by the institutional mission and goals of the Office of the US Trade Representative. USTR is the President's top administrator of his trade policy. Since the President's goals include augmentation of the country's national power, the promotion of national economic growth, and constituency support from vital economic interest groups, USTR's goals include all these things as well. Since the President aims to keep as much authority over trade policy as possible as a matter of interbranch domestic politics, an important USTR goal is to demonstrate to Congress that it is being a good steward of American national interests in the world economy. Since the President aims to preserve good bilateral diplomatic relations with the countries of East Asia, an important goal of USTR is to carry out 301 with diplomatic considerations in mind. From the

1970s to the 1980s the salience of these goals shifted, as bilateral diplomacy became eclipsed by changed domestic economic circumstances: persistent recession, eroded competitiveness, and large trade deficits. Thus, USTR increasingly took up the complaints of commercially competitive industries. If USTR could reduce trade barriers in East Asia on their behalf, it could demonstrate to Congress and to the public that it was "being tough with foreign trade barriers" and that US commitment to free trade principles continued to be sound—and better than managed trade alternatives.

USTR is also the President's chief diplomat in GATT regime activities. USTR is charged with promoting US interests in the regime; thus it considers the relationship of the trade problem with the GATT regime. During the 1970s and through the mid-1980s, this typically meant that disputes were taken up involving noncompliance with a rule of GATT. In the late 1980s, it typically meant disputes that could be used concomitantly with USTR's multilateral-negotiation goals in the Uruguay Round. Thus, despite the considerable evidence that USTR takes up cases that allege GATT rule noncompliance, some cases illustrate to the realist that USTR will press forward with initiation when commercial interests and national-power considerations demand it and despite the absence of extant or emerging regime rule violation. These same remaining cases illustrate to the liberal political-economy scholar that US policymakers believed American national interest was served through additional rule creation in the Uruguay Round and even beyond the Uruguay Round, especially in the areas of product standards and competition/antitrust policy. Thus, realist political economy and liberal political economy explain aspects of 301 implementation in the Pacific; liberal political economy synthesizes the strengths of each research tradition and offers the superior explanation.

CONCLUSION

This chapter has provided parsimonious explanation of USTR's implementation of American 301 trade law in the Pacific, thereby showing that there are empirically derivable decision rules to explain the behavior of USTR and that 301 implementation is neither a random exercise in American trade power nor a process driven by big interest groups. The variables—commercial competitiveness of the industry and GATT regime utility—were tested against the evidence of the universe of 301/302 cases involving Japan, Korea, and Taiwan in the 1974–1989 period. USTR most often initiated 301 investigations against a Japanese, Korean, or Taiwanese "unfair trade barrier" when both circumstances were fulfilled. USTR sometimes initiated 301 investigations if one of the two conditions was met, but initiated no 301 investigations if neither of the conditions was met. USTR's implementation of 301 policy is explained by its institutional mission within the context of the US position as a pluralist, liberal-tending hegemon in the Pacific. USTR is and wants to remain the executive branch's chief trade policymaker and negotiator on matters multilateral, minilateral, and bilateral. USTR must manage relations with Congress, with domestic interest groups, with GATT, and with foreign governments. No longer a benevolent hegemon, USTR initiated 301 negotiations with Japan, Korea, and Taiwan that aimed to ensure that in their trade policies they were playing by the rules. A hegemon with an economy of globally competitive service and intellectual-property-based industries, USTR aggressively initiated 301 investigations that aimed to promote multilateral, GATT rule creation activities in the Uruguay Round. In practices that span several administrations, USTR has possessed clear goals and implemented 301 in order to achieve these goals.

These variables will likely predict US 301 behavior in the years to come under the World Trade Organization–based trade regime that has been ushered in by the successful completion of the Uruguay Round. The Uruguay Round "Dispute Settlement Understanding," in the minds of many American trade partners, aimed to rein in US 301 policy (especially Super 301) and establishes that all member disputes that allege rule noncompliance will be settled using WTO panel procedures. Thus, USTR likely will continue to favor 301 initiation in cases that allege rule noncompliance. USTR will continue, however, to take up the cases that involve commercially competitive industries, especially those cases not covered by extant GATT rules. USTR might look especially favorably over the next few years on issues that promote its overall strategy, as in cases involving standards and regulations harmonization, services, and competition policy and cases concerning emerging major markets such as China, India, and Southeast Asia. Cases involving Central and South America must overcome USTR's reluctance to revisit the squandered effort on Brazil informatics but will become increasingly viable as more exports from these countries are sent to the US and as talks progress on enlargement of NAFTA southward. Cases concerning eastern Europe and Russia risk entanglement with security and diplomatic policy considerations, so they may be more difficult to get initiated.

This chapter shows that both realist and liberal political-economy research traditions are needed to explain the implementation of US 301 trade policy and that the analytic frameworks of previous studies of 301 policy have placed too much emphasis on "system-centered" and "society-centered" explanations and too little emphasis on "institution-centered" explanations. Attention to American government institutions affords an analysis that takes account of institutions as mediators of demands by domestic interest groups (as called for by liberal political economy), as projectors of state power of the US in the world political economy (as called for by realist political economy), and as creators and maintainers of international regimes (as called for by liberal political economy). Both realist and liberal political economies are shown in this chapter to be solvers of interesting problems in international relations and thus continue to be progressive research traditions in the study of international relations.

The conclusions of this chapter are drawn from the largest, most systematic, market-sector-specific data set so far presented on US export policy in the Pacific, with the (approximate) universe of completed Section 301/302 investigations carried out by USTR between 1974 and 1989. With forty cases spanning fifteen years, the large, longitudinal, market-sector-specific data contradict recent research analyses of 301 and export policy. Several recent contributions, though they contain grains of truth, have been shown to mischaracterize the implementation of 301 policy by overstating the significance of strategic, picking-winners industrial policy; by ignoring completely the crucially important GATT regime utility variable; and by characterizing 301 policy as the product of a declining-hegemon or diminished-giant syndrome when the market-sector-specific evidence shows that the US can be more aptly described as no longer a benevolent hegemon in agriculture and traditional manufacturing markets and an ascending hegemon in service and intellectual-property-based markets.

CHAPTER 3

Responding to 301

One of the implications of the analysis of 301 initiation decisions is that the East Asian states are not innocent victims of "Japan bashing." Japan, Korea, and Taiwan are the victims of their own positions in the Pacific economy as capitalist developmental free riders on the GATT regime. The East Asian capitalist developmental industrial policies are the shrewd catch-up policies of the late industrializer. To be effective, these policies demand access to foreign markets, especially the wealthy US market, and call for only limited access by foreign competitors to domestic markets in Japan, Korea, and Taiwan. To be implemented, these policies depend upon polities that afford cooperative, collectivist decision-making styles. The East Asian responses to 301 policy logically follow from the structures of their political economies and their industrial-policy strategies, described here as capitalist developmental free riders. But the puzzle that this chapter seeks to explain is why the response strategies of these newly industrialized/industrializing East Asian countries differ in interesting ways.

Japan, Korea, and Taiwan are relatively weaker than the United States in trade dispute diplomacy: they depend upon the United States for their national security, and they depend upon access to US markets to sustain their national-wealth goals. Realist political economy explains well, then, why the East Asian governments carried out deliberate 301 response strategies that negotiated for compensations as part of the settlement agreements. "Losers" within the governments of Japan, Korea, and Taiwan press their chief negotiators for compensations or concessions that they can offer their constituencies. They all hire American trade lawyers to help them with their defense, for they realize that 301 negotiations with USTR often entail rule-oriented trade diplomacy. But their individual strategies are implemented differently because of differences in the degrees of their export and security dependence and differences in the national governmental institutions of trade diplomacy. The

Japanese strategy has been a "stall" strategy, which aims to extend negotiations over months or even years with as little real policy change as possible. The Korean strategy has been a "crisis capitulation" strategy, which aims to put off concessions completely until sanctions are threatened by the US. The Taiwanese strategy has been a "clever-concession" strategy, which aims to settle disputes through concessions designed to appease USTR and American domestic interests without making wholesale change in the Taiwanese policy. The moderate dependence of the Japanese upon the United States affords it a strategy that the extremely dependent Koreans and Taiwanese have been chary to attempt in trade diplomacy with the United States. The primary difference between the Korean and the Taiwanese strategies is that the Taiwanese learned more quickly than the Koreans that American trade politics can be manipulated so that concessions are less costly. Since concessions are inevitable given USTR's determination to "win," the hard bargaining ought to be over the compensations and finding the minimally acceptable concessions, not over whether concessions will happen at all. The explanation lies in the governmental institutions of trade diplomacy: while Korean trade dispute diplomacy has been led primarily by administrators of Korea's industrial policy at the Ministry of Trade and Industry, Taiwanese trade diplomacy has been led primarily by handlers of Taiwan's foreign policy at the Ministry of Foreign Affairs.

This chapter first examines the political-economy contexts in Japan, Korea, and Taiwan for their response strategies, linking explanation of strategy to basic factors of polity and economy. The next section describes the governmental structures for 301 response decision making in the three countries. The final section explores the similarities and differences in the Japanese, Korean, and Taiwanese response strategies.

CAPITALIST DEVELOPMENTAL FREE RIDERS

The Japanese polity is corporatist; the Korean and Taiwanese polities have been statist (though Korea appears to be in transition toward corporatism and Taiwan appears to be in transition toward pluralism). The structures of the East Asian polities make them capable of carrying out the capitalist developmental industrial-policy strategy. The capitalist developmental strategy, first articulated by Japan and carried out as well by Korea and Taiwan, combines central features of the import substitution, liberal, and mercantilist-policy strategies. The strategy recommends that market intervention substitute imported goods and services with domestically produced goods and services through import and foreign direct-investment restrictions. The domestically produced goods, however, are sold on international markets. The strategy aims to ensure that exports exceed imports by a considerable margin and that trade relations are nonreciprocal. Japanese inward FDI and import patterns are well outside the norm among the OECD states and resemble import-substituting India more than an industrialized country.[1]

The strategy recommends that government target certain critical or driver industries for promotion. Japan's capitalist developmental strategy targeted apparel, steel, shipbuilding, automobiles, machine tools, computers, consumer electronics, semiconductors, and telecommunications,[2] though its targeting of pharmaceuticals, chemicals, and commercial aircraft has (so far, anyway) failed. The Japanese state employed import restrictions (quotas and tariffs); subsidies to R&D, production, and export; investment controls; an undervalued exchange rate; export promotion assistance; government and private procurement preferences; and a competition policy aimed at maintaining vigorous, if oligopolistic, competition within particular market sectors, especially among the *keiretsu* groups. The policy strategy picks "winner" industries whose promotion the Japanese government planners believe will benefit the economy disproportionately to the costs of the promotion itself. The capitalist developmental industrial-policy strategy depends upon a structure of polity that is corporatist or statist, for it must possess political capacity adequate to intervene rationally, not politically, into the market. David Friedman argues that the role of targeting by the polity had much less to do with Japanese success than the vigorous nature of competition in the economy and the manufacturing-process innovations made by Japanese firms, and Daniel Okimoto notes that the strategy has had much less to do with the commercial success of Japan's new industries of the 1980s than it did in the 1940s through the 1970s.[3] Despite these caveats, the capitalist developmental strategy lies between independence and interdependence, between markets and planning, and it created new competitive pressures in the US economy and imposed barriers to imports and foreign investment.

Korea and Taiwan adopted the capitalist developmental strategy. The Korean and Taiwanese governments had initially implemented import substitution strategies after the end of Japanese colonialism, but both made their transitions away from import substitution by the end of the 1950s.[4] Both countries were experiencing balance-of-payments problems and were heavily dependent upon US aid, and both were met with US demands that they wean themselves from US aid. The result was transition toward an export-led strategy in order to achieve BOP equilibrium and earn foreign exchange for domestic development.[5] These export-led strategies came to mirror in many respects the Japanese strategy, because the strategy appealed to many in the powerful state structures in Korea (military, single-party rule) and Taiwan (Leninist party rule). In Korea and Taiwan the strategy involved high levels of planning and interdependence, including very high levels of productive investment, more investment in certain key industries than would have occurred without government intervention, and exposure of many industries to international competition.[6] The governments intervened in the markets through land redistribution, financial-system control to put industrial production ahead of consumer spending, macroeconomic stability (price controls, undervalued foreign-exchange rates), wage controls (and union repression), export performance rewards, foreign direct-investment controls, foreign-technology acquisition, and sector-specific subsidies and export promotion assistance through the Korea Overseas Trade Promotion Corporation and the China External Trade Development Council.

Korea and Taiwan are late industrializers, and successful late industrializers are good learners.[7] They visit international expositions, attend international conferences, tour foreign plants, consult foreign suppliers, hire foreign experts, and beg, borrow, buy, and steal foreign designs. Nevertheless, there are differences in the Korean and Taiwanese implementations of capitalist developmental industrial policy-strategies, due in part to the decidedly different industrial organizations prevalent in Korea and Taiwan. The Korean economy has been dominated by massive, privately held, diversified *chaebol*, modeled after Japan's prewar *zaibatsu*. Taiwan's economy has been dominated by publicly held national champions and small entrepreneurial firms. The high growth rates in Korea and Taiwan in the 1960s, 1970s, and 1980s were thus the result of extensive market intervention, not free markets. Yet the market intervention aimed to create globally competitive firms disciplined by international markets. As in Japan, the strategy imposed barriers to imports and foreign investment.

The East Asian industrial-policy strategies, thus, have been considerably at odds with the strategy deployed in the United States. A principle underlying the GATT regime is that trade barriers should be reduced in the world economy. Motivated by the gains from free trade that Anglo-American comparative-advantage theory postulated, the American and British framers of the GATT committed contracting parties to eliminate (with some exceptions) quotas and progressively to reduce tariff levels. The intellectual and policy commitment in East Asia to the reduction of trade barriers in the world economy, however, has been limited. Recalling Meiji Japan, Hunsberger explains that

> Japan did not move very far toward theoretical or doctrinal free trade, which was being practiced by Britain, then the world's greatest trading nation and Japan's leading trade partner. A few doctrinaire free traders appeared in Japan, but even some of these later turned protectionist, and the influence of free-trade ideas was minimal. When a Western economic theory did attract a significant following, it was the theory of Friedrich List, the German economist who stressed protection of infant industries during industrialization.[8]

During the late 1800s and because of the unequal treaties that had been forced on Japan by the West, Japanese tariff rates tended to be low. Since the Meiji government lacked the tariff policy tool, it stimulated industry with low-interest loans, technical assistance, and government procurement preferences. The antecedents of the modern activist Japanese government lie here. Furthermore, beginning in 1899 and until foreign pressures reemerged in the 1950s, Japanese tariffs were progressively raised.[9]

Japan acceded to the GATT in 1955. The United States shepherded the Japanese accession through, despite the opposition of many European states. Europeans feared Japanese exports and criticized Japanese import barriers. The one-third tariff cut negotiated as part of the GATT accession was significant, but it was the first Japanese tariff cut of the century and left many high tariffs. Despite the Japanese 40% cut in the Kennedy Round MTN, tariffs remained higher than the other advanced industrialized countries until 1972. In that year, the Japanese promulgated a unilateral 20% tariff reduction, which made Japanese tariff levels similar to the rest of the OECD countries.[10] By 1987, the overall weighted-average tariff rate was 6.2% in Japan, while it was 3.3% in the United States. By sector, manufactures tend to have low tariffs in Japan. The highest Japanese tariff rates are in food products (28.5%), agricultural products (21.8%), footwear (15.7%), and apparel (13.9%).[11] Quotas, too, remain in agriculture markets. Hence, though some tariff barriers and quotas (in important markets) persist, formal market barriers in Japan generally comply with GATT-established norms in the world economy.

The Korean and Taiwanese experiences with trade protection largely parallel the Japanese experience. The Korean government has employed a number of policy tools aimed at protecting domestic industries, including quotas, tariffs, and special customs duties and taxes.[12] Quotas have been imposed on many manufactured and agricultural goods. In 1980, general tariff levels averaged 25% and manufactures averaged 32%. But by 1989, tariff levels dropped to about 13% generally and about 11% on manufactures.[13] On the other hand, tariffs have tended to be very low on natural resources and other basic inputs for manufacturing. As was the case with Japan, Korea acceded to the GATT under exceedingly generous terms. Until the 1980s, the Ministry of Trade and Industry also demanded that potential importers meet export performance requirements before being granted a license to import, and retail distribution by foreign-owned firms was prohibited.[14] Even now, trade protection lingers. Quotas were removed in 1991 on 243 agricultural products but persist on fruits, grains, beef, pork, and paper.[15]

The Taiwanese government extensively employed import quotas and tariffs in order to protect infant domestic industries. In 1956, about half of import sectors faced tariffs up to 30%, and the other half faced import tariffs between 31% and 165%.[16] Not a GATT contracting party, Taiwan nevertheless responded to American pressure beginning in the 1970s. Overall tariff averages have now been gradually reduced to about 10%, but agricultural-commodity tariffs average more than twice that amount.[17]

EAST ASIAN TRADE DIPLOMATS

Japan: Organizationally, bilateral trade dispute settlement with the United States involves several Japanese government agencies. Because of its institutional mission, the Ministry of Foreign Affairs is usually involved. If revenue or customs issues are at stake (as often they are), the Ministry of Finance is involved. The participation of other agencies depends upon the market sector at issue. Disputes about manufacturing usually involve the Ministry of International Trade and Industry. Those about agriculture, fishing, or wood products involve the Ministry of Agriculture, Forestry, and Fisheries, and those about telecommunications the Ministry of Posts and Telecommunications. Construction disputes involve the Ministry of Construction, and commercial-aviation and maritime disputes the Ministry of Transport. Disputes about pharmaceuticals and medical equipment involve the Ministry of Health and Welfare, and those about legal services the Ministry of Justice. Disputes about technology might attract the interest of the Science and Technology Agency.

The mission of the Japanese Ministry of Foreign Affairs is to conduct Japanese foreign relations, including management of Japanese multilateral and bilateral trade relations.[18] Staff members of Foreign Affairs lead the

Japanese mission to GATT and UNCTAD in Geneva and the Japanese negotiating teams in multilateral trade negotiations and in bilateral trade dispute settlement with the United States. Bilateral trade dispute settlement with the United States also involves staff members from the North American Affairs Bureau, the Economic Affairs Bureau, the Economic Cooperation Bureau, the United Nations (international governmental organization) Bureau, and the Treaties Bureau. The goals of the trade dispute settlement negotiators from the Japanese Ministry of Foreign Affairs are cooperative bilateral relations with the United States, with other governments, and with multilateral institutions. In addition to senior Japanese political leaders, their constituencies consist of fellow diplomats from other countries, for they have no domestic constituency of their own. Indeed, for this reason, Ministry of Foreign Affairs officials, unlike officials from other Japanese agencies, do not "descend from heaven" at retirement to top jobs in the private sector.[19]

Though Foreign Affairs takes the lead in foreign trade relations, it is far from the most influential Japanese government participant. One observer remarked to me, "The Prime Minister does not listen to MoFA on trade issues anymore."[20] The Japanese trade-negotiating teams include representatives from the functional ministries under whose purview the trade issue falls. Since resolution of a bilateral trade dispute often demands domestic policy change in Japan, these functional agencies are the real power centers on the Japanese side. Because so many US-Japan disputes involve manufacturing sectors and because manufacturing exports have been so important to the Japanese economy, the Ministry of International Trade and Industry (MITI) has often been a major participant on Japanese bilateral and multilateral trade-negotiating teams. By administering industrial policy for manufacturing, MITI has been the powerful actor in bilateral trade dispute settlement with the United States. And because of its mission, the needs of the manufacturing sectors dominate politically and bureaucratically the activities of MITI.

MITI's mission is to raise productivity, strengthen international competitiveness, achieve efficiency in the use of finite resources, continually move up the ladder of value-added, improve the general quality of life, and maintain good relations with trading partners.[21] Throughout much of the postwar era, MITI has been able to influence greatly the behavior of Japanese industries and firms through the use of a panoply of policy tools that together have been called "administrative guidance."[22] MITI's power has been far-reaching, greater than the simple regulatory power of American government agencies. Administrative guidance, explains Chalmers Johnson, is the authority of agencies such as MITI "to issue directives, requests, warnings, suggestions, and encouragements."[23] The policy instruments of MITI include financial-capital access, research-and-development subsidies, taxation, import protection, export incentives, demand creation, and government procurement. MITI's mission and influence within the Japanese policy process ensures it close, cooperative relations with Japanese political and industrial leaders. MITI is a prestigious ministry for which to work in Japan and lures many of Japan's brightest university graduates.[24] Agency recruits are guaranteed "lifetime employment," though "lifetime" means *professional* lifetime and life ends for Japanese bureaucrats in their late forties or early fifties.[25] MITI staff members leave government service with only a small government pension; hence the need for a second career. This second career often starts in a senior leadership position in a company that is under the purview of MITI.

International trade matters at MITI are primarily administered by the International Trade Policy Bureau.[26] The chief representative of MITI in trade negotiations usually comes from the Trade Policy Bureau. In the case of high-level negotiations, which involve a MITI Vice Minister, the chief representative may have headed the Trade Policy Bureau during his career. The Trade Policy Bureau administers GATT and other multilateral economic organization activities as well as policy on antidumping, safeguards, and tariffs. The office is staffed primarily by graduates of law programs such as the University of Tokyo Law School, and some have also studied trade and economic law at American law schools.[27] Issues such as export and import controls and COCOM participation, on the other hand, are the province of the International Trade Administration Bureau.

Many American trade negotiators attest to the skill and savvy of the MITI negotiators and have been secure in the belief that MITI negotiators have possessed sufficient power within the Japanese polity to be credible negotiators. As even a Japanese official conceded, however, bilateral trade disputes with the US have increasingly involved industries and agencies over which MITI influence is limited.[28] The Ministry of Finance possessed authority over the tobacco dispute and led the negotiations with the US because the dispute involved the government-owned monopoly and, thus, the dispute was an important revenue issue.[29] By the late 1980s, trade disputes with the United States and Uruguay Round negotiations increasingly came to involve representatives from Japanese agencies other than MITI and Finance, such as the Ministry of Agriculture and the Ministry of Posts and Telecommunications. The mission of the Ministry of Agriculture, Forestry, and Fisheries (MAFF) is mainly to preserve the Japanese farmer.[30] Though it maintains a small GATT affairs office that sends delegates to GATT and to multilateral agriculture forums, MAFF tends to be parochial in its outlook.[31] Similarly, the Ministry of Posts and Telecommunications, originally the administrator of the post office and the telephone system but now also the administrator of telecommunications policy, has traditionally not been involved with international activities.[32] The same may be said of other Japanese government agencies that have occasionally come to be reluctant international-trade diplomats: Justice, Construction, Transport, Health and Welfare, etc.

Korea: Until about 1989, the Korean Ministry of Trade and Industry (MTI) led the Korean government team in bilateral trade negotiations with the United States.[33] Since then the diplomats at the Ministry of Foreign Affairs have taken the lead. But like Japan's Ministry of Foreign Affairs, Korea's Ministry of Foreign Affairs makes and implements foreign policy, not industrial policy. Hence, the foreign-affairs ministry is no better positioned in Korea than is its counterpart in Japan to influence policy toward, and the practices of, industry. The functional ministries in Korea are generally the more powerful members of the Korean negotiation teams.[34] So in the many trade negotiations involving manufacturing sectors, the Ministry of Trade and Industry remains the main participant. As one Korean dispute settlement participant remarked to me, "As the complexity of the issue increases, MoFA drops out."[35]

Korea's MTI is similar to Japan's MITI in mission but less powerful in policy formation within the more president-dominant economic policy-making process of Korea.[36] MTI appears, however, to hold extensive trade policy power through its discretion to implement trade policy.[37] MTI's mission includes being the Korean government's principal representatives to GATT and to multilateral trade negotiations. As two Korean scholars have observed: "Because of its dual responsibilities, the MTI has an inherently split-minded approach to trade issues. It advocates freer trade abroad out of the need to expand Korea's exports, but is more cautious about liberalization at home, given pressure for protection from domestic industry."[38] MTI officials, like those from Japan's MTI, often retire into key positions within their country's industry. Indeed, 25% of Korean industry executives have government experience.[39]

The Economic Planning Board and the Ministry of Finance both can be more authoritative in economic policy-making in Korea than MTI. The Economic Planning Board is a "super" ministry.[40] Its mission is to coordinate all Korean economic policy. Its minister also holds the rank of Deputy Prime Minister. EPB's bureaucratic nearness to the Blue House (the Korean White House) can give it much power. Since the EPB does not implement economic policy, it is largely insulated from direct industry-interest pressures. Hence, it can act with less regard for domestic commercial interests than can MTI. With a staff of technocrats educated primarily in the West, the EPB is by reputation the most free-trade-oriented of Korea's economic ministries. Compared to the more fragmented political system in Japan, the president-dominant Korean government affords influence to MoFA and EPB and can overrule MTI.

The Ministry of Finance possesses important authority over trade policy implementation: it has jurisdiction over import tariffs as well as insurance and financial services.[41] The Ministry of Agriculture, Forestry, and Fisheries makes and implements agriculture policy. It functions similarly to the Japanese ministry of the same name, and has the same mission of looking out for the interests of its country's farmers.

Taiwan: Control over trade dispute settlement with the United States has largely been a tussle within the Taiwanese bureaucracy between the Ministry of Economic Affairs and the Ministry of Foreign Affairs, for trade dispute settlement with the United States simultaneously raises two issues of the highest national interest to Taiwanese policymakers: domestic industrial policy and foreign policy. Taiwan's Ministry of Economic Affairs implements trade and industrial policy in the Republic of China. Economic Affairs sets industrial standards through its National Standards Bureau, inspects agricultural imports through its Commission of National Corporations, and supervises the many large public corporations that were traditionally the backbone of the Taiwanese economy: China Steel, China Petroleum, China Shipbuilding, China Tobacco and Wine.[42] Hence, the Ministry of Economic Affairs includes many who oppose market liberalization in Taiwan.[43]

The office of the Ministry of Economic Affairs responsible for trade policy is the Board of Foreign Trade, which has had a reputation as a supporter of trade liberalization. "[Board of Foreign Trade staff] know how trade is played, so they encourage higher government officials to open markets," said one observer. "It is very hard for [Board officials] to teach other agencies about the world trading situation, about why liberalization is important for [Taiwan's economy]."[44] The Board of Foreign Trade, however, is a peculiar instititution in the Taiwanese bureaucracy. Robert Wade contends that bureaucrats such as those at BFT have typically been educated in the United States as economists.[45] Most other officials in the economic-policy bureaucracy, he points out, have been educated as engineers and are not impressed with economic theories about free trade.

As in the cases of Japan and Korea, Pacific trade disputes during the 1980s increasingly came to involve other agencies. The other ministries, even more domestically based than the Ministry of Economic Affairs, are largely populated with opponents of liberalization. For example, intellectual-property disputes involved the copyright office of the Ministry of Interior, and agriculture disputes the Council of Agriculture. The Council of Agriculture of the Republic of China (which is bureaucratically similar to a ministry) includes an office charged with administering agriculture trade policy. Most Agriculture Council staff have been educated in Taiwan, but at least forty have received Ph.D.s in agriculture or agricultural economics in the United States. The Ministry of Finance is often involved in trade dispute settlement through its authority over revenue issues, including customs and tariffs. Indeed, Finance loomed large in what became for the Taiwanese the watershed trade dispute with the United States, the 1986 dispute over wine, tobacco, and beer. Public corporations possess monopolies over production of these products and are responsible for enormous tax revenue that goes to substate tax authorities.

The Ministry of Economic Affairs' trade policy office, the Board of Foreign Trade, had been by tradition the major player in trade dispute settlement with the United States. Indeed, the Board of Foreign Trade possessed much experience negotiating with USTR and possesses wide discretionary authority over implementation of trade policy.[46] Previous trade disputes had mainly concerned issues within Foreign Trade's expertise and administrative purview. But the wine, tobacco, and beer dispute brought issues onto the agenda that it was poorly positioned to negotiate internally and externally, and Foreign Trade is widely considered within the Taiwan government to have botched both the domestic politics of beer, wine, and tobacco and the foreign politics of handling the Americans.[47] In the dispute, negotiations were said to have become increasingly acrimonious because Foreign Trade neither understood the gravity of the domestic-revenue issue to Finance or the foreign-policy issue of Senator Jesse Helms's dual position as an ally to Taiwan on security issues in the Senate Foreign Relations committee and as the powerful representative of North Carolina, America's largest tobacco-producing state. Agreement came when USTR threatened sanctions in December 1986, but many Taiwanese were dissatisfied with both the outcome of the dispute and the process toward that outcome. Taiwanese government leaders decided that trade dispute settlement was too important to Taiwanese foreign relations to be entrusted to the Board of Foreign Trade and turned leadership in trade dispute settlement with the US over to the Ministry of Foreign Affairs.

Foreign Affairs has long possessed a large, sophisticated staff in Washington and in Taipei to monitor US affairs and project Taiwanese interests in the United States. By 1988, senior foreign policymakers from the Ministry of Foreign Affairs had spearheaded the creation of a high-level interagency coordination committee, the Sino-US Economic Committee.[48] The goal of this institutional arrangement was to ensure that trade disputes would not again be allowed to turn into crises due to mishandling by industrial policymakers and to ensure that industrial-policy considerations do not override diplomatic concerns: the Taiwanese diplomatic relationship with the United States is paramount in Taiwanese national policy-making. Thus, the Ministry of Foreign Affairs in Taiwan has institutionalized routine authority over trade dispute settlement. In organization, the Taiwanese practice contrasts with the Japanese and Korean practices, in which the industrial policymakers maintain routine authority until a crisis in the bilateral relationship.

The episode has had a profound organizational effect on the Board of Foreign Trade. In the late 1980s and in anticipation of future GATT membership, the board established an office for GATT affairs staffed with trade lawyers educated in the United States and opened an office in Geneva. This new office was created, according to interviewees, in order to advise on bilateral trade dispute settlement issues and prepare for eventual GATT membership. Many officials at Foreign Trade have received foreign, especially American, graduate degrees in law, business, and international affairs, in addition to economics.[49] As a result, the Board of Foreign Trade has transformed itself into an organization much more capable at international-trade diplomacy than during the mid-1980s.

STRATEGIC RESPONSES TO 301

The East Asian governments recognize that in American hands, trade dispute settlement is quite legalistic. In most cases, they hire Washington-based trade lawyers to help defend themselves against USTR in the Section 301 process. For example, the Japanese hired the firm of Milbank, Tweed, Hadley & McCloy in the tobacco dispute and Tanaka, Walders & Ritger in the semiconductor dispute. The Koreans hired Arnold & Porter in the insurance, intellectual property, and beef disputes, and the Taiwanese hired Kaplan, Russin & Vecchi in the rice dispute. Indeed, one telephone request by this author to an embassy official for comment on a particular trade dispute was met by the following response: "Call our lawyer; he knows all the details." The Washington-based trade lawyers play prominent roles on behalf of the Japanese, Koreans, and Taiwanese in the 301 investigation. They usually research and author the East Asian government's official written response to the USTR initiation decision, thereby attempting to shape the agenda for the bilateral negotiations. They are active participants throughout the negotiations, gathering information for their East Asian client about the political economy of the case at USTR, and for USTR about the political economy of the case in the East Asian country. They consult with USTR and other participating US executive-branch officials, industry representatives, and key members of Congress and their staffs. They suggest settlement solutions and help with the drafting of the final agreement text.

Since East Asian governments and businesses often find themselves in trade disputes with the United States, some Washington trade lawyers specialize in defending a particular East Asian government, industry, or company. The Japanese especially are noted for the size and influence of their American legal and lobbying team in Washington, which they keep constantly busy.[50] Indeed, some trade policy observers suggest that Japan's Washington team is too influential and opine that the US government should change its laws on permissible foreign lobbying activity in order to diminish the capacity of foreigners to influence American foreign policy.[51] On Section 301 trade dispute settlement in the Pacific, the evidence indicates that the Korean, Taiwanese, and Japanese legal and lobbying teams aggressively defend their clients' interests—as they should. They are unable, however, to run roughshod over powerful, committed USTR officials.

In cases where the settlement agreement was weak from an American industry perspective, it was due to the weak case of the American industry, inadequate international rules, or failures by the US negotiating team, not to the extraordinary political influence of the East Asian teams. For example, from the perspective of the American industries that brought the complaints, perhaps the least successful unilateral actions occurred in the Japan footwear, Japan semiconductor, and Korea intellectual-property cases. Yet, as discussed below, in the footwear case, the Footwear Industries Association failed to articulate the existence of significant unfair trade practices by Japan, Korea, and Taiwan. Similarly, in the semiconductor dispute, the Semiconductor Industry Association failed to specify clear GATT violations by the Japanese government. In the intellectual-property case, the US negotiating team was hampered by the lack of GATT law regarding intellectual property.

Unfortunately for East Asian governments and firms, even if falsely accused of wrongdoing, they must hire expensive legal advice to defend themselves. These expenses add considerably to the costs of doing business in the

United States. All the East Asian countries with long-term trading interests in the legalistic American political economy are increasing their own pools of government and private trade lawyers educated in American law schools and in Washington. (Indeed, this is even true of China; see Chapter 8.) The rules of the GATT can be the refuge of the weak against the strong, but only if the rules are well understood.

The legalism is merely a tactical means dictated by dealing with American negotiators, not the strategy itself. David Yoffie, in his study of East Asian state trade policy strategies, emphasizes that the Japanese, Korean, and Taiwanese bring a commitment to realize long-run gains.[52] They (1) negotiate for ambiguity, (2) demand compensation for policy changes, (3) exploit bureaucratic cleavages within the United States, and (4) cheat on agreements. To the Japanese, the best settlement agreement is no settlement agreement; thus, the pervasive tactic is to stall: deny that there are trade problems; admit that the US perceives a trade problem; urge the creation of a study group to discover what the problem really is; settle in for months of (hopefully inconclusive) negotiations. Nearly all the American trade negotiators with whom I spoke expressed frustration with the implications for them of the Japanese stall strategy—meetings without end, negotiations over the irrelevant, tiring trips to Tokyo without reward. Yet many admitted that the stall strategy worked for the Japanese.

The Korean government strategy is crisis capitulation; the Taiwanese government strategy (after the beer, wine, and tobacco experience) is clever concessioning. The stall strategy, which has worked so well for the Japanese, cannot work for the Koreans and the Taiwanese. The trade and security dependence of Korea and Taiwan on the United States compels concession. Until the 1990s, the Korean strategy had as its settlement goal no concession at all. Korean written and oral arguments emphasized Korea's developing-country status, the importance of US-Korean security relations for northeast Asian peace, and the feelings of Koreans toward Americans as "big brothers." These kinds of arguments were naive in the reality of 1980s Pacific trade relations, and when the inevitable sanction threat was issued by USTR, the Korean government was thrown into crisis and, finally, capitulation.

The Taiwanese strategy, on the other hand, recognizes that concessions will have to be made to USTR; thus, the goal is to offer concessions that settle the dispute as narrowly and incrementally as possible. The negotiating tactics are to work cooperatively and quietly with USTR, suggesting solutions that appease industry and Congressional pressure points upon USTR. The strategy depends upon the ability of the Taiwanese negotiators to gather detailed information about the politics of the dispute on the US side. In this sense, the Taiwanese gain some advantage from their lack of GATT membership, for USTR does not possess the option of taking the Taiwanese government before a GATT panel, as they do with Japan and Korea. Thus, the primary difference in the response strategies of the two countries is that the Taiwanese learned more quickly than the Koreans that American trade politics can be manipulated so that concessions are less costly.

Over the course of the 1980s, Japanese, Korean, and Taiwanese trade diplomats learned that USTR's determination to get a settlement agreement achieving its market access and rule compliance goals meant that the hard bargaining ought to be over the compensations, not over the inevitable concessions. The settlement agreement will produce losers at home in Japan, Korea, and Taiwan, and the second-best deal is to bring compensation back to the losers. As explained in the next chapter, American negotiators prefer and usually do try to offer some compensation, a practice they call "giving them some political cover at home."

CONCLUSION

This chapter has examined the response strategies in trade dispute diplomacy of the East Asian states and has argued that Japan, Korea, and Taiwan are relatively weaker than the United States in trade dispute diplomacy. They depend upon the United States for their national security and upon access to US markets to sustain their national-wealth goals. Realist political economy explains well, then, why the East Asian governments carried out deliberate 301 response strategies that negotiated for compensations as part of the settlement agreements. Losers within the governments of Japan, Korea, and Taiwan press their chief negotiators for compensations or concessions that they can offer their constituencies. They all hire American trade lawyers to help them with their defense, for they realize that 301 negotiations with USTR are often rule-oriented trade diplomacy.

Their individual strategies, however, are implemented differently, and these interesting differences have been the puzzle addressed in this chapter. The stall strategy of the Japanese, the crisis capitulation strategy of the Koreans, and the clever concession strategy of the Taiwanese owe their existence to differences in the degrees of their export and security dependence and upon differences in the national governmental institutions of trade diplomacy. The Japanese stall strategy aims to extend negotiations over months or even years with as little real policy change as possible. The Korean crisis capitulation strategy aims to put off concessions completely until sanctions are threatened by the US. The Taiwanese clever concession strategy aims to settle disputes through concessions designed to appease USTR and American domestic interests without making wholesale change in the Taiwanese policy. The moderate dependence of the Japanese upon the United States affords it a strategy that the extremely dependent Koreans and Taiwanese have been chary to attempt in trade diplomacy with the United States. The primary difference between the Korean and the Taiwanese strategies is that the Taiwanese learned more quickly than the Koreans that American trade politics can be manipulated so that concessions are less costly. Since concessions are inevitable given USTR's determination to win, the hard bargaining ought to be over the compensations and finding the minimally acceptable concessions, not over whether concessions will happen at all. Explanation for the differences lies in the governmental institutions of trade diplomacy: while Korean trade dispute diplomacy has primarily been led by administrators of Korea's industrial policy at the Ministry of Trade and Industry, Taiwanese trade diplomacy has primarily been led by handlers of Taiwan's foreign policy at the Ministry of Foreign Affairs.

CHAPTER 4

Rule-oriented Trade Diplomacy

USTR pursued rule-oriented trade diplomacy and power-oriented trade diplomacy in the Pacific. USTR's rule-oriented trade diplomacy was "settlement by negotiation and agreement with reference to the norms and rules upon which both parties previously have agreed" in the disputes on Japan, Korea, and Taiwan footwear, Taiwan rice, Japan tobacco, and Korea beef. USTR's power-oriented trade diplomacy was "settlement by negotiation and agreement with reference (explicitly or implicitly) to the relative power statuses of the parties" in the disputes on Korea intellectual property, Korea insurance, and Japan semiconductor. In this and the next chapter, the nine process-tracing case studies detail the processes and outcomes of trade dispute settlement diplomacy in the Pacific. The case studies show the decidedly different negotiation processes and settlement agreements that emerge from power-oriented trade diplomacy as compared to those that emerge from rule-oriented trade diplomacy. The processes and settlement agreements in the nine case studies are summarized in Table 4.1.

JAPAN, KOREA, TAIWAN FOOTWEAR

With its Section 301 petition, Footwear Industries confronted USTR with a morass of issues and problems. World footwear markets are huge. Shoemaking is labor-intensive, while start-up capital costs are relatively low. Hence, developing countries, typically labor-rich and cash-poor, have found good investment opportunities in footwear.[1] The large US consumer market invites developing-country footwear exports. As a result, since the late 1960s, US shoe producers have faced ever-growing foreign competition for US footwear retailers. Between 1965 and 1977, imports increased from 12% of the US market to 49%.[2] Imports reached 51% of the market in 1976. Between 1968 and 1983, over 350 shoe factories in the United States closed. Still, the industry failed to get much US government help.

Table 4.1   Case Study Settlement Processes and Agreements

Case	Process	Settlement Agreement
Japan footwear	demonstrate GATT Art. XI noncompliance through GATT panel finding; threaten sanction	end quota; phase in tariff protection; lower tariffs on non-footwear products; raise US tariffs on Japanese leather exports
Japan tobacco	demonstrate GATT Art. III noncompliance through GATT panel finding; threaten sanction	change distribution tax procedures; lower tariffs
Japan semi-conductors	threaten sanction	"recognize" 20% market share goal of US firms in Japan
Korea footwear	allege GATT Customs Valuation Code noncompliance through informal GATT dispute settlement procedures; threaten sanctions	change customs procedures; lower tariffs
Korea insurance	allege noncompliance with bilateral FCN treaty and emerging GATS; threaten sanction	grant licenses to foreign firms; make licensing procedures transparent
Korea intellectual property	allege noncompliance with international IPR treaties and emerging GATT TRIPs; threaten sanction	accede to international IPR treaties; write and enforce domestic IPR laws
Korea beef	demonstrate GATT Art. IX noncompliance through GATT panel finding; threaten sanction	phase in the replacement of quotas with tariffs; US industry technical advice to Korean industry
Taiwan footwear	no action taken (US industry complaint without merit)	—
Taiwan rice	allege GATT Art. XVI noncompliance; threaten sanction	export Taiwanese rice to small-country markets only

The US footwear industry petitioned the International Trade Commission (ITC) for escape clause protection and trade adjustment assistance at least 355 times between 1973 and 1978.[3] Though the footwear industry found some sympathetic supporters in Congress, it failed to generate much support from the executive branch. In 1977, however, on the heels of another escape clause finding by the ITC that footwear imports had, in fact, caused serious injury to domestic producers and thus the industry was entitled to relief, the industry succeeded in getting the Carter administration to negotiate an Orderly Marketing Agreement (OMA) with Korea and Taiwan, the two largest importers.

The OMA, which expired in June 1981, resulted in more competition for US producers (from Brazil, Spain, Italy, and Hong Kong, whose firms exploited the market opportunities created when quotas were placed on Korean and Taiwanese imports), better competition (from Korea and Taiwan, whose firms were prompted to become more efficient and move up-market), an even lower US market share than before, and even lower US employment levels. The industry needed a new strategy, one that promised to provide comprehensive protection. The Section 301 trade remedy provided that range of opportunity.

Footwear Industries filed the Section 301 petition with USTR only days before the November 1982 Congressional elections. The petition was ushered in by identical letters to USTR signed by 50 Senators and 111 Representatives to US Trade Representative Bill Brock. The Senators and Representatives urged USTR to accept the Footwear Industries Association petition, highlighting some of the same issues as did the petitioner: "There is a serious problem facing firms and workers in the US footwear industry arising from restrictive foreign practices which have disrupted the domestic industry and which totally contradict American free trade principles." They noted that "the petition will show that unfair trade practices have had the effect of diverting world exports of non-rubber footwear to the US market, resulting in domestic job and production losses." Senators and Representatives from states with large footwear production capacity, such as Maine, Massachusetts, and Pennsylvania, were especially concerned about the industry's problems.[4] American footwear makers, claimed Footwear Industries, had posted tremendous sales losses both at home and abroad. They contended that these sales had stripped 20,000 American of their jobs in only the period from July 1981 to July 1982.[5] Footwear Industries concluded that "the future of the US nonrubber footwear industry and the approximately 200,000 jobs dependent on US footwear production hang in the balance as the continued existence of these barriers diverts the world's excess capacity to the United States and similarly deprives the US industry of the opportunity to develop its own export markets."[6]

Taiwanese footwear makers, the petition admitted, owed some of their success to efficiency and cost competitiveness. According to the American industry, however, Taiwanese success was also owed to unfair, GATT-violating trade practices that included restrictive import licensing, quantitative export restraints with Britain and France, excessive tariffs, and subsidies. The import-licensing system limited footwear imports into Taiwan to a "miniscule" level[7] and thereby violated both the GATT Article XI prohibition against quantitative restraints and the Tokyo Round Licensing Code. The quantitative export restraints with Britain and France violated both GATT Article XI and the GATT Article I MFN guarantee. Taiwan added tariffs ranging from 30% to 100% on footwear imports—amounts "very high by world standards"[8]—and computed these tariffs with a 15% "customs uplift tax." That is, the ad valorem tariffs were applied only after a 15% tax had been added to the c.i.f. (cost, insurance, freight) price. The customs uplift tax violated GATT Article III (national treatment), GATT Article VII (customs valuation), and the Tokyo Round Customs Valuation Code. Taiwan subsidized its producers' exports with tax benefits that violated GATT Article XVI subsidy rules and the Tokyo Round Subsidy Code.

Attorneys for the Taiwan Footwear Manufacturers Association responded to the Footwear Industries petition by urging USTR to reject the Footwear Industries petition.[9] The Taiwanese makers contended that the American industry could not substantiate any of its allegations that Taiwanese policies were unfair and that American shoemakers simply wanted import relief. The Taiwanese asserted that under their import licensing system, footwear had been on the "free" or "permissible" import list and thus there had been no restrictions on footwear imports. "In truth," the Taiwanese admitted, "Taiwan does not import large quantities of footwear because of the tastes and income levels of the populace. The petition makes assertions as if the footwear market in Taiwan were identical to the US. . . . Styles, tastes, and prices all differ."[10] Taiwan's attorneys reminded USTR that the bilateral restraints on footwear trade with Britain and France had been imposed on the Taiwanese government and were not a freely chosen Taiwanese government policy.

The Taiwanese maintained that the subsidy charge was contradicted by Commerce's own determination that the benefits to the footwear industry were *de minimis*, i.e., negligible and nonactionable. To the charge that their tariffs on footwear imports were excessive, they retorted that their tariffs were significantly lower than the tariffs of many other developing countries. They made no mention of the customs uplift tax. Concluded the Taiwanese footwear makers: USTR's acceptance of the petition would be an American retreat toward protectionism.

The American industry alleged that Korean government policies encouraged Korean makers to export and insulated them from foreign import competition. Korea, like Taiwan, restricted footwear imports with its licensing system, but unlike Taiwan, it restricted some types of footwear to zero. Again like Taiwan, Korea had bilateral restraint agreements with Britain and France. Footwear Industries also charged that like Taiwan, Korea subsidized its footwear manufacturers for export, including tax and financing benefits. Korea imposed at least a high 50% tariff on foreign footwear that was permitted to enter the country and further burdened imports with local currency deposits that ranged to 200% ad valorem.

The Korean government responded to the charges against it prosaically.[11] The Koreans asserted that under its import-licensing system most categories of footwear imports were automatically approved and only a few were "monitor[ed] to analyze the effect of competition between domestic and imported products."[12] They pointed out that the bilateral agreement with France was not a formal agreement between the governments of France and Korea but a "declaration of cooperation between businessmen of Korea and France." The Korean government knew that the lawyers at USTR would be aware that such an agreement could not violate GATT, since GATT applies only to governments. With regard to the Korean agreement with Britain, the Koreans maintained that the quota limits were set higher than actual exports to the UK and hence did not restrain trade.

To the subsidy allegations, the Koreans responded that the programs cited in the petition had already been found by DoC either to be *de minimis* or to proffer general, nonactionable subsidies to Korean industries producing for domestic consumption as well as for export by DoC. To the excessive-tax allegations, the Koreans responded that the import taxes were nearly the same as the taxes imposed on domestic producers. If accurate, the Korean defense would entail for USTR the conclusion that Korean subsidies were not actionable and tariffs were consistent with the national-treatment clause.

Footwear Industries accused Japan of erecting trade barriers that permitted foreign footwear only 1% of the large Japanese market. The American makers complained of policies that prevented them from exporting to Japan. But they emphasized that their overriding concern was that Japanese import policies diverted to the US market footwear that otherwise would go to Japan. Footwear Industries noted that its complaint against Japan on footwear was identical to the 301 petition filed in 1977 by the Tanners' Council of America against Japan for its protection of leather goods. The result, according to the petition:

> Not only have Japan's actions succeeded in effectively depriving US footwear manufacturers of opportunities in what the US Commerce Department labeled as one of the two world markets with "the greatest

potential for export of American footwear," but they have also closed Japan's leather footwear market to all comers, including Taiwan and South Korea, whose Japanese-owned or controlled trading companies have begun to bombard other world markets (especially the United States) with footwear made primarily with very low-priced Japanese leather made in large part from US hides.[13]

The petitioners contended that Japan imposed quantitative restrictions with a MITI-administered import-licensing arrangement that apportioned footwear imports among twenty-six certified importers, most of whom were affiliated with Japanese footwear makers. Footwear Industries pointed out that even the Japanese government had conceded to GATT as early as 1966 that the system violated GATT.

The American industry emphasized that it was the trade-diversionary effects of foreign-market import restraints that concerned it. The industry argued:

> In today's world footwear market, the plethora of trade restrictions in many markets is a prime determinant of where foreign producers target their production and exports. For example, a Taiwanese or Korean leather footwear producer in the process of seeking an export market would naturally look to its neighbor, Japan, one of the largest consumer markets in the world, as a logical target. Since Japan effectively bars imports of leather footwear, however, that firm must search elsewhere. Because of this economic reality, Japan is ignored and the producer focuses on other markets.[14]

According to Footwear Industries, it followed that the US market, the most open in the world, was the target.

Footwear Industries confronted USTR with a morass of issues and problems. If it determined that full investigation was warranted, USTR would examine footwear markets on four continents, scrutinize the trade policies of ten governments, and analyze a score of provisions of GATT and the Tokyo Round codes. In December 1982, USTR announced that it would investigate some, but not all, of the charges.[15] USTR initiated investigations into the trade policies of Brazil, Japan, Korea, and Taiwan but not the Europeans. Furthermore, it largely accepted the counterarguments of Korea and Taiwan when it announced it would investigate only import-licensing procedure questions and the tariff levels in both countries. It announced that it would not investigate the allegations that Korea and Taiwan subsidized exports because DoC had previously found these programs to be *de minimis* and thus not actionable. In rejecting the trade diversion argument, USTR kept its policy consistent with GATT practice: GATT has never accepted the trade diversion argument. Despite intense Congressional and footwear industry pressure, USTR resisted employing the Section 301 leverage under a trade diversion argument to protect the US footwear industry. USTR did agree, however, that there was evidence that the Japanese footwear market was closed to exports from the United States and other countries and that Japanese footwear policies merited investigation. USTR separated the Japan part of the case from the Taiwan and Korea parts; it then combined the allegations of Footwear Industries against Japan with the ongoing leather dispute, which involved overlapping policy issues. Hence, despite political pressure, USTR pursued only those issues where it believed a GATT violation existed.

The USTR decision cut the heart out of the Footwear Industries petition, for the trade diversion issue was critical to its case. Footwear Industries tried again, as is discussed below. Nevertheless, the footwear disputes milieu ensured that solutions would be found neither easily nor without economic, social, and political costs.

USTR requested public comment on the Section 301 petition filed by Footwear Industries. NIKE, a successful American maker of athletic footwear, damaged the position of Footwear Industries with some compelling arguments.[16] NIKE contended that despite having only begun production in 1974, it had become a worldwide leader in the athletic-shoe market through aggressive marketing in all the major markets of the world, an excellent research-and-development staff that constantly improved the quality of its shoes and the efficiency of its production, and diversification of production capacity throughout the world, including Korea, Taiwan, Malaysia, Ireland, and New England. It argued that the supposed dichotomy between domestic and foreign production had become a false, empty dichotomy. NIKE contended that footwear makers competed best when they recognized global production patterns and diversified accordingly. It opined that the export potential to Korea and Taiwan was nil, for both countries possessed highly developed footwear producers with the advantage of low labor rates. Furthermore, NIKE explained that significant undercapacity remained in both Korea and Taiwan, so that any lowering of footwear trade barriers in Japan or Europe would benefit Korean and Taiwanese firms greatly. NIKE concluded that Footwear Industries really aimed at market protection in the United States, not market opening in other parts of the world.

Consultations between USTR staff and Korean delegates were held in Geneva in February 1983 under informal GATT auspices.[17] Similar talks were held with Taiwan in Washington.[18] For its part, Footwear Industries continued to assert that bilateral footwear agreements between the Europeans and Taiwan and Korea as well as the closed Japanese market diverted trade to the US market. Having failed to convince USTR to include these issues in its original investigation, Footwear Industries filed a new Section 301 petition with USTR in June 1983.[19] It accused USTR of dragging its feet on the case,[20] repeated its charges against Europe and Japan, and underscored the significance of the statistics: Japan imported 4% of its leather footwear, while the United States imported 60%. They reiterated that the agreements with the Europeans violated the MFN provision of GATT.

USTR again rejected the arguments of Footwear Industries.[21] USTR indicated that Footwear Industries had failed to demonstrate that *governmental* agreements existed between France or Britain and Taiwan or Korea. (Of course, no *governmental* agreements did exist, for they were private, business-to-business agreements.) USTR also contended that Footwear Industries had failed to show a causal link between decreasing imports by Britain and France and increased imports by the United States. After USTR's announcement, Footwear Industries admitted that the "trade diversion theme is a no-win argument at USTR."[22] The Footwear Industries Association, opined *Footwear News*, was in "disarray" after the USTR announcement.[23]

On the other hand, USTR did pick up again the remaining issues with Taiwan, Korea, and Japan. On the Taiwan part of the dispute, USTR announced that it had concluded that just as the Taiwanese Ministry of Finance customs officials had claimed, the Taiwanese footwear import-licensing system was not restrictive. As a result, negotiators from the American Institute in Taiwan (the American government's unofficial Taipei embassy) were conducting talks with the Taiwanese aimed at lowering their tariffs on footwear. The Taiwanese negotiations continued in September.[24] The two sides reached agreement when the Taiwanese offered to lower typical tariffs from 60–65% to 45–50%. USTR announced in December 1983 that it had terminated the investigation.[25] The agreement was not difficult for the Taiwanese side to sign, for all concerned knew that American makers would still not be competitive in the aggressive Taiwanese shoe markets.[26]

The February and July 1983 GATT consultations between the US and Korea yielded results.[27] Korea assured the US that contrary to Footwear Industries' claim, the Korean government did not require an advance deposit on imports. Korea laid out its administrative plans to bring itself into compliance with the Customs Valuation Code by February 1986. USTR expressed satisfaction with those plans and with the likelihood of eventual Korean compliance. Korea also explained to USTR negotiators that since 1 July 1983, under its import licensing system, all nonrubber-footwear imports had been automatically approved. The only issue in contention, then, was the tariff level. Since the tariff was bound by GATT agreement, it did not represent a GATT violation. Nevertheless, Korea agreed to significant tariff reductions. As a result of these discussions, USTR terminated the investigation in March 1984.

Thus, the 301 cases were not going well for Footwear Industries when, in January 1984, it tried again with the escape clause action, requesting the imposition of global import quotas.[28] In spring 1984, American shoe retailers weighed in heavily against the Footwear Industries Association. Attorneys for the Volume Footwear Retailers of America submitted to USTR a brief arguing that US footwear makers were showing strong profits, that US makers had successfully restructured up-market, and that the great increase in imported shoes since the early 1970s was explained not by the "push" of foreign competition but by the "pull" of American retailers. Hence, according to the retailers, (1) trade diversion had not occurred, (2) US makers had not been injured by imports, (3) US makers had had ample opportunity to restructure toward greater competitiveness and had done so (resulting in worker layoffs and factory closings). Therefore, US makers deserved no more protection from the government. Indeed, in June 1984, the ITC announced that by a 5-0 vote it had determined that the American footwear industry merited no protection under the escape clause. Footwear Industries Association's attempt to get protection neared failure.

Regarding Japan, USTR linked the footwear dispute with the ongoing leather-products dispute. The leather aspect of the case was USTR's dominant concern, despite the fact that leather exports to Japan were modest (about $300 million per year), because the leather case possessed great precedent value.[29] In the minds of the USTR policymakers, it was the first direct attack on the Japanese political economy. Leather products, including footwear, were heavily protected by the Japanese government for domestic social, economic, and political reasons.[30] Most Japanese leather products were made by an ethnic minority who lived together in districts known in Japan as the "Dowa districts." The Dowa people had traditionally been disadvantaged by and discriminated against within Japanese society. Hence, according to the Japanese negotiators, they were poorly educated, dependent on leather production for their living, and not easily transferred to other occupations. For these reasons, the Japanese government restricted leather imports to near zero. The Japanese conceded that their leather import policy violated GATT and that free competition would take Japanese consumer leather markets away from the Dowa. Nevertheless, the Japanese government persisted with its policy of protection of leather products and footwear, despite bilateral negotiations with the United States dating to the 1970s.

The USTR negotiators needed a bargaining strategy that would finally change Japanese policy and could counter the quite effective negotiation strategy that the Japanese government had employed on leather and footwear market opening, a strategy that the Japanese would use in the tobacco and semiconductor disputes as well. One trade negotiator described Japan's strategy during the leather and footwear cases as a "dribble out" strategy;[31] another trade negotiator was thinking of the tobacco case when opining that the Japanese "open markets we can't make any money in and open slowly markets we can make money in. By letting the American industry make more money, they think they can appease it."[32] The Japanese government negotiating tack had become familiar to USTR negotiators during discussions over leather and footwear and would be repeated in bilateral trade dispute negotiations over tobacco and semiconductors. First, they denied for many months that there was a trade problem at all. Second, they admitted that the US government perceived a bilateral trade problem, though it was illusory. Third, a bilateral "study group" was formed to investigate the "problem." After many months, the study group drew ambiguous conclusions and recommended small policy changes. Fourth, they bargained for many months over these minor Japanese policy changes. Fifth, they finally made minor concessions. The result was incremental policy changes that minimized the impact of the negotiations on the Japanese economy, business, and society. In the leather and footwear disputes with Japan, USTR determined that the best strategy was to press the Japanese government hard that its policies violated GATT. USTR policymakers decided that a GATT panel finding against Japan over its leather and footwear quotas would bring international normative pressure to bear on Japan to end the quotas. A GATT ruling against Japan would justify to the world trading community an American use of its trade power against Japan. In addition, a GATT panel finding against Japanese quotas on leather goods could be used as precedent in negotiations over tobacco as well as other products.

This negotiation strategy, however, was opposed by many in the executive branch, especially in the Treasury and State Departments, but in USTR as well. These policymakers opposed "legalizing" bilateral trade dispute settlement. They placed a higher value on the goal of friendly diplomatic relations with the Japanese government and rejected a policy that would cause the Japanese government to "lose face" internationally. The Deputy US Trade Representative, however, argued within the administration that only by legalizing the process could the United States get Japan to open its markets. The "legalize it" argument prevailed, and the General Counsel's office was asked to prepare an "airtight" GATT case against the government of Japan over its leather and footwear policies.

In April 1983, after being pushed hard in bilateral negotiations for months,[33] the Japanese government consented to the creation of a GATT dispute settlement panel.[34] The USTR lawyers successfully argued before the GATT panel, and the panel held against Japan in May 1984.[35] In May 1984, the GATT panel issued its report to the GATT Council. The panel noted its sympathy to the socioeconomic problems of the Dowa people but said the Japanese government policies restricting the importation of leather goods violated GATT Article XI and should be ended.[36] USTR thus had new leverage against the Japanese: Japan had been held before the international trading community by GATT to be in violation of international trade laws.

Despite the moral suasion of GATT norms, another year and a half would pass before a settlement agreement was reached. In November 1985, USTR readied a list of Japanese imports against which to retaliate with sanctions, and President Reagan announced his intention to make good on the threat. A personal plea from Prime Minister Nakasone to President Reagan was necessary to avert the retaliation.[37] Finally, two weeks after the Nakasone plea, the Japanese and American negotiators reached agreement.[38] The agreement was complicated, but included leather-product import barrier reductions. The quota system was replaced with a two-tier tariff system that would be phased in beginning in spring 1986. In addition, Japan agreed to accept a substantial tariff increase on Japanese leather exports and to cut its own tariffs on 149 products, including paper, glass, industrial diamonds, sports equipment, silicon wafers, and scientific equipment. USTR valued the concessions at $300 million.

Back in summer 1985, Footwear Industries had filed yet another escape clause petition with the International Trade Commission. This time, however, the ITC recommended quota protection for the industry.[39] Unfortunately for Footwear Industries, President Reagan decided against the protection. The request came during a period of crisis in US trade politics, and when the Reagan administration put together a major policy position on trade, protection for footwear was not part of the mix. Footwear Industries sensed new opportunity in fall 1986. The US and Taiwan were deadlocked over Taiwanese import barriers on tobacco, beer, and wine. USTR readied a list of products that could be targeted for retaliation. Footwear Industries suggested to USTR that footwear would be a "logical choice."[40] When USTR reached agreement with Taiwan, however, the opportunity was gone.

So, when USTR ordered the Customs Agency to increase import duties on leather products and leather footwear from Japan in March and June 1986,[41] it was the only tangible, positive outcome for the Footwear Industries Association. World footwear imports to the United States amounted to $5 billion in 1984, $5.7 billion in 1985, and increased each year to over $8 billion in 1988. More than half of those totals came from the East Asian countries.[42] Imported shoes had captured 81% of the nonrubber-footwear market in the United States, by May 1987, according to the ITC.[43] In 1986, said the Footwear Industries Association, seventy more footwear factories had closed down in the United States, and employment had declined by 8%. Armed with this information, the industry succeeded in getting both houses of Congress to pass legislation in 1988 that would have restricted footwear imports; President Reagan vetoed the legislation.[44]

The Japan aspect of the footwear dispute was crucial in the history of US-Japan trade relations. USTR's GATT case against Japanese leather-import policies was the first attempt by the US government to make the Japanese political economy conform with the rules and principles of the GATT and liberal market political economy. USTR pressed the GATT case against Japan because a GATT victory would offer the United States additional leverage against the Japanese in trade negotiations on not only leather products and footwear but other products as well. Ultimately, the Japanese government would not change its policy until the United States threatened sanctions, but the GATT victory legitimized the US threat in the eyes of the world trading community and enhanced the credibility of the US threat with the Japanese.

TAIWAN RICE

Lawyers for the Rice Millers Association charged that the Republic of China had violated GATT Article XVI (the subsidy article) as well as the GATT Subsidies Code.[45] The Rice Millers claimed that the Taiwanese government purchased rice from its farmers at significantly more than world market prices, then dumped the rice in foreign markets at prices below world market prices. Furthermore, they charged that Taiwan's price support system, an export subsidy under GATT law, encouraged overproduction of rice in Taiwan. Their economists forecast that Taiwan would export 850,000 tons of rice in 1983, thereby causing the value of US rice exports to fall by $303 million and prompting the US Department of Agriculture to spend an additional $118 million to purchase and store American rice.

Taiwan began large-scale rice exportation in 1977. The Rice Millers had filed a similar Section 301 petition in 1980.[46] USTR had resolved the dispute by negotiating with the Taiwanese an Orderly Marketing Arrangement that limited Taiwanese exports for four years. Negotiations between representatives of Taiwan and the United States during summer 1983 failed to achieve an agreement on new export restrictions. The Rice Millers responded to the failed negotiations by filing the Section 301 complaint. The American administration was divided over how to handle the Rice Millers' complaints. The State Department cautioned that US-Taiwanese relations should not be unduly threatened over the issue, but the Agriculture Department pressed the case of the Rice Millers.[47] USTR considered the political power of the rice industry. The Rice Millers Association drew its membership from the South and the West—Florida, Louisiana, Mississippi, Arkansas, Tennessee, Texas, and California—a region of great political significance to President Reagan in a 1984 reelection campaign. USTR also considered the linkage between the case and the ongoing efforts with the European Community and Japan to end agricultural subsidies. USTR initiated bilateral negotiations toward a negotiated settlement. In August 1983, the Rice Millers agreed to withdraw their Section 301 complaint on the condition that Taiwan limit its rice exports to 550,000 metric tons in 1983 and Taiwan agree to a new multiyear bilateral OMA.[48]

Washington attorneys for the Board of Foreign Trade of the Republic of China's Ministry of Economic Affairs filed with USTR in August 1983 a rebuttal document.[49] The Taiwanese government argued that because its rice support program neither intended nor resulted in increased rice exports, it could not be found to be an actionable subsidy under the GATT and the Subsidies Code. Taiwan maintained that the program had been established in 1974 to ensure a steady supply of rice to domestic consumers, to meet government needs (including military supplies), and to provide temporary income support to a segment of the population that could not readily change occupations.

The Taiwanese negotiators contended that increased rice exports were in part attributable to changes in the tastes of the Taiwanese people, who increasingly favored wheat over rice—*American* wheat, they added. The availability of rice for export was "the result of extremely liberal import policies of the R.O.C. with respect to agricultural products from the United States."[50] They noted that the amount of Taiwanese rice available for export was not excessive, since it amounted to only about 10% of the total rice harvest in Taiwan between 1977 and 1982.[51] They argued that their small position in the world rice market ensured that they were price takers and not, as the Rice Millers claimed, price makers. The Taiwanese concluded that "a few thousand tons of old, poor quality Taiwan surplus rice" had not injured the Rice Millers Association. Furthermore, more rice sales in Taiwan by Americans would mean fewer sales in other agricultural markets. It was a veiled threat and a defensive linkage strategy that would have effect.

Despite the protestations of Taiwan's attorneys that its rice policies were not actionable subsidies, the Taiwanese negotiators knew that the United States had a strong GATT case against them.[52] (As one Taiwanese interviewee remarked to me, "Everyone subsidizes; Taiwan is not exceptional.") The Taiwanese government was divided over the continuation of its rice support system. Land reform in the 1950s had resulted in small rice farms, farms too small to be economically viable without government subsidies.[53] The Ministry of Finance pressed for government policies that would increase farm size, and it urged the phaseout of the price support system. The agriculture policymakers at the Council (Ministry) of Agriculture, however, opposed farm enlargement and demanded continuation of the price support system.[54] The problem for the Taiwanese government was that it was receiving vigorous political pressure for its farmers. Indeed, even the father of the Director General of the Coordination Council for North American Affairs sold rice.

The Rice Millers responded that since, according to its projections, Taiwan would export 850,000 tons of rice in 1983—an amount equal to about 7% of total world rice trade—Taiwan could hardly claim that its exports were inconsequential. Citing a lack of progress toward a new OMA, the Rice Millers refiled the complaint the next month.[55] During December 1983 and January 1984, the American Soybean Association, the US Feed Grains Council, and the US Wheat Associates implored USTR to resolve the rice dispute with Taiwan quickly.[56] They pointed out that the Taiwanese were good customers of theirs and that they did not wish to lose sales because of a mishandled dispute over rice. In contradiction, fifteen members of Congress pressed USTR to "seek and employ the necessary measures to have this settled to the benefit of our rice industry."[57] Senator David Pryor, a representative from rice-rich Arkansas and a member of the agriculture committee, pledged to US Trade Representative Bill Brock that Taiwan's "illegal" rice policies and practices must end or he would press for removing Taiwan's GSP benefits.[58] Pryor's position on GSP was known only too well to the Taiwanese negotiators. The loss of GSP tariff preferences would hurt Taiwanese manufactured-goods exports considerably; it was a credible threat.

Both sides knew that the threatened sanctions would be implemented without a settlement agreement; thus there was little question that the US would win. The question was how much the Taiwanese would lose. The American threat to cut GSP tariff preferences for manufactured-goods imports hit its mark with policymakers at the Board of Foreign Trade, who contended within the Taiwanese bureaucracy that the agricultural interests be set aside in favor of the manufacturing interests. The chief Taiwanese negotiator was the Director General of the Coordination Council for North American Affairs, i.e., the de facto ambassador from the de facto embassy. The negotiations came to be about finding political cover for the Taiwanese government.

Finally, the US and Taiwan reached an agreement to resolve the dispute in March 1984 and RMA withdrew its Section 301 complaint.[59] Taiwan agreed to restrict its exports to 375,000 metric tons in 1984 and decrease its exports each year until 1988, when its limit would be 200,000 MTs. Key to the agreement, however, was that Taiwan agreed to export its rice only to countries whose per capita income was at or below $795.00 This provision gave RMA what it wanted—to end Taiwanese dumping of subsidized rice on the large markets of Japan, Korea, and the EU (all countries with per capita GNPs greater than $795.00), where most of its sales occurred. The provision offered political cover to the Taiwanese government, since the right of the Taiwanese to export subsidized rice was preserved, albeit only to small markets. The diplomats from the Ministry of Foreign Affairs, with a clever-concessioning strategy, helped craft a settlement agreement that offered agriculture policymakers a deal they did not like but could live with.[60] The Taiwanese have complied with the agreement, as their rice exports totaled 240,000 MTs in 1987 and only 100,000 MTs in 1988.[61]

JAPAN TOBACCO

In August-September 1985, the Reagan administration confronted a critical trade policy choice in the midst of a contentious trade policy milieu: the International Trade Commission, in response to another escape clause petition from the Footwear Industries Association, recommended to the President that he impose quota protection for the industry. The Reagan administration decided against quota protection for the footwear industry but announced at the same time a new, aggressive US trade policy.[62] The administration announced it would oppose protectionism both at home and abroad. Henceforth, USTR would surveil national trade policies and, on it own initiative, unilaterally take action against protectionist trade policies. The instrument of this new policy would be the Section 301 trade action. Until this time, Section 301 cases had only arisen as a result of an industry complaint. In September 1985, USTR announced Section 301 actions against Brazil for informatics policies, against Korea for insurance and intellectual-property policies, and against Japan for tobacco policies.[63]

American cigarette exporters had long complained that Japan Tobacco Corporation pursued a number of discriminatory policies that limited their sales to only 2.2% of the Japanese cigarette market.[64] First, Japan Tobacco supplied only 8% of Japan's 250,000 dealers with American brands.[65] Second, in addition to a border tariff, Japan Tobacco imposed an internal tax on the retail price of cigarettes, so that US brands were significantly more expensive than Japanese brands. Third, Japan Tobacco demanded that Japanese tobacco dealers order and pay for American cigarettes in advance, while Japanese cigarettes were to be purchased COD. Also, foreign cigarettes were delivered to Japanese dealers only once each month, whereas Japanese cigarettes were delivered each week.

Before 1980, US exporters had not been privy to the pricing formula that Japan Tobacco used to set the retail prices of American cigarettes.[66] Strong pressure from USTR negotiators led the Japanese government to make the pricing formula known and, in addition, to cut the tariff on foreign cigarettes to 35%. The cut to 35% was, however, immediately preceded by the passage of a law to enact a 90% tariff rate. Hence, when the new excise tax was added, the price of American cigarettes in Japanese tobacco shops *rose*, not fell.

Representatives of the US Cigarette Export Association, all senior executives from R. J. Reynolds, Philip Morris, and Brown and Williamson, requested at April 1982 meetings in Tokyo that Japan Tobacco liberalize the Japanese tobacco market.[67] US tobacco exporters urged Japan Tobacco to allow all Japanese tobacco dealers to sell US cigarettes, and to lower tariffs on imported tobacco. They also requested that restrictions on the advertising and marketing of US cigarettes be removed. USTR representatives pressed the case of American tobacco exporters in bilateral trade negotiations, though the Japanese considered these discussions only "study group consultations," meaning that no specific measures needed to be taken when the talks concluded.[68] At additional bilateral talks in August 1982, the Japanese agreed only that by October they would be prepared to establish a special study group on tobacco industry issues.[69] The stall strategy was being implemented to perfection.

In January 1983, Japan Tobacco again lowered the tariff (to 20%) and raised the excise tax on tobacco.[70] At the same time, Japan Tobacco agreed to permit all tobacco dealers in large cities—except Tokyo and Osaka—to sell foreign brands by March 1983, all tobacco dealers in Tokyo and Osaka to sell foreign brands by October 1983, and all dealers in the rest of the country to sell foreign brands by the end of 1985. The agreement covered cigarettes, cigars, and pipe tobacco. Prime Minister Nakasone personally pledged to President Reagan in a Washington meeting that he would not allow Japan Tobacco to negate these actions with countermeasures. The Prime Minister's bold assurances (in the context of Japanese politics) angered the Japanese tobacco industry. When back in Tokyo, Prime Minister Nakasone faced demonstrations from 10,000 farmers.[71]

In July 1983, American tobacco industry representatives negotiated an agreement for Japan Tobacco to move up the date when all Japanese tobacco dealers could sell foreign cigarettes from the end of 1985 to March 1985. Japan Tobacco also agreed to liberalize restrictions on advertising by cigarette importers.[72] In December 1984, Japan Tobacco announced that it had ordered about 20% of the tobacco-growing area to be taken out of production and that all 250,000 tobacco dealers, not just 20,000, would be allowed to sell US brands of cigarettes.[73] The Japanese announced that government-owned Japan Tobacco would become publicly owned, though at least two-thirds of the stock would remain government-owned. Japanese officials declared that the "denationalization" would offer a final resolution to tobacco trade problems with the United States.[74]

Japan Tobacco, in a 1985 statement filed with USTR by its American law firm, rebutted the charges against it.[75] Japan Tobacco argued that it did maintain a monopoly over domestic tobacco production, but contended that this practice was permitted under the 1953 US-Japan Treaty of Friendship, Commerce, and Navigation and under GATT. Furthermore, while it formally maintained a monopoly over the importation and distribution of tobacco products, the result of policy reforms since 1980 and culminating in the April 1985 creation of the new enterprise was that tobacco markets in Japan had been liberalized. Any foreign importer could sell cigarettes to any of the 250,000 Japanese tobacco dealers.

Japan Tobacco further contended that the test-marketing requirements of new cigarette brands, which included stringent demands, had been eliminated. Regulations for cigarette advertising had been loosened and no longer discriminated between domestic and foreign brands. In addition, tariffs had been reduced to about 20% ad valorem. The Japan Tobacco brief to USTR described the Section 301 investigation against its tobacco policy practices as "surprising and distressing" not only because of the extensive tobacco market liberalization measures that had been taken in the 1980s but also because "the current investigation under Section 301 is legally premised on allegations of some Japanese violation of, or denial of US benefits under, international trade agreements, or on allegations of unjustifiable, unreasonable or discriminatory practices. . . . [T]he word 'unfair' is used to characterize Japan's acts or policies."[76]

Lawyers for the Japanese stressed that the USTR accusations of late summer 1985 had been made only a few months after major Japanese tobacco policy changes, which had been "accomplished despite bitter resistance from affected domestic interests." Furthermore, they charged that since USTR asserted violations of the bilateral FCN treaty and the multilateral GATT treaty, consultation and dispute-resolution procedures provided for by these treaties ought to be employed rather than the unilateral Section 301 process.

Regardless of timing and forum, Japan Tobacco declared that Section 301 actions are to remedy present trade problems, not to penalize for past trade transgressions. Since Japan Tobacco had corrected the transgressions of the past, USTR should terminate the investigation. Japan Tobacco's lawyers were probably correct in their assessment that its client had already taken most of the actions that USTR had been pressing them to over the course of the 1980s.

USTR staff, in order to carry out the President's directive to investigate Japanese tobacco import policies and practices, submitted a questionnaire to Japan Tobacco and five Tobacco Haiso distribution companies. USTR asked Japan Tobacco for responses to twenty-six questions about Japan Tobacco's ownership, finances, contract terms with retailers, sales promotion practices, pricing practices, and distribution practices for both domestic and foreign brands. As discussed above, USTR received a full response from Japan Tobacco prepared by its Washington attorneys. USTR also sought public comment on the investigation. It received in October 1985 a lengthy statement from the US Cigarette Export Association, the lobbying arm of Philip Morris, R. J. Reynolds, and Brown and Williamson.[77] The Cigarette Exporters reiterated the many problems their members had had trying to sell cigarettes in Japan. The brief concentrated on Japanese policy before the April 1985 reforms and recommended ten prescriptions to USTR negotiators:

(1) Eliminate the import tariff.

(2) Eliminate the ad valorem component of the excise tax.

(3) Eliminate predatory Japan Tobacco pricing by requiring it to adopt and implement a pricing policy taking into account labor, material, financing costs, administrative costs, and inflation and to adjust retail prices more frequently.

(4) Eliminate the price approval system but replace it, if necessary, by a price notification system.

(5) Eliminate Japan Tobacco's manufacturing monopoly and permit foreign producers to manufacture in Japan.

(6) Once foreign manufacturing is permitted in Japan, permit foreign manufacturers to import tobacco leaf tariff-free.

(7) Eliminate Tobacco Haiso distribution exclusivity.

(8) Require Tobacco Haiso to promote imported cigarettes.

(9) Provide foreign manufacturers with the same National Excise Tax terms as given Japan Tobacco.

(10) Provide the US Cigarette Export Association with tobacco retail-account data possessed by Japan Tobacco.

Ten days later, Japan Tobacco and the Cigarette Exporters submitted to USTR rejoinders to each other's statements.[78] Japan Tobacco contended that the Cigarette Exporters provided slim evidence and argument to buttress its allegations, that Japanese reform measures had already remedied these problems, and that the Cigarette Exporters had made no attempt to relate their allegations to GATT or other international-law requirements. They opined, "This omission suggests awareness that their allegations, even to the extent that they have any basis in fact, do not meet the substantive requirements of the law."[79] Japan Tobacco noted, for example, that the only evidence offered to conclude Japanese price predation was that cigarette prices had risen slightly slower than the consumer price index; that the Tobacco Haiso distribution exclusivity had already been eliminated; and that no request for retail price change had been turned down by the Ministry of Finance since April 1985. Japan Tobacco caustically concluded:

If the USCEA brief had been presented to USTR as a Section 301 petition, there can be little doubt that it would have been rejected for legal inadequacy, as well as for its distortions and concealments of relevant facts. To the extent that USTR and the President may have been persuaded to self-initiate this investigation on the basis of USCEA's representations, it is clear that they have been done a grave disservice. In light of the actual facts, the proper course of action is to acknowledge that this investigation was instituted on the basis of inadequate information and to terminate it forthwith.[80]

The Cigarette Exporters' rejoinder statement urged USTR to look beyond Japanese claims of de jure tobacco market liberalization to its de facto closed market. They contended that "the Government of Japan and its agencies or instrumentalities have created a market structure that renders US access to the Japanese cigarette market illusory."[81] They cited their own small market share as evidence to support their allegations and also charged that despite Japanese claims, Japan Tobacco remained a monopoly and was "part of an uninterrupted pattern of behavior by the Government of Japan to restrict access to its cigarette market."[82] The Cigarette Exporters responded incredulously to Japan Tobacco's charges that they had failed to adapt their cigarettes and to make a long-term commitment to the Japanese market. They provided evidence that their companies had introduced cigarettes specifically aimed at Japanese consumers since the 1960s and that their filtration systems, packaging, and advertising had been copied by Japan Tobacco. They charged, "[Japan Tobacco] has thus had a practice of targeting promising foreign brands, copying them and marketing them at prices which are 30 to 40% cheaper."[83] The Cigarette Exporters prodded USTR to use its broad powers under the Section 301 law to deal with the "subtle and sophisticated trade barriers at play."[84]

USTR spent the fall of 1985 gathering information from both sides. In November it received from the Japanese Tobacco Growers Association a letter that cut to the heart of the dispute: tobacco growers and local agricultural economies depend on tobacco sales, and increased competition hurt them badly.[85] Nevertheless, USTR representatives had little discussion on tobacco with the Japanese for many months. Clayton Yeutter, Bill Brock's successor as US Trade Representative, explained that his staff and Japanese trade negotiators were preoccupied with leather and footwear negotiations.[86] USTR, however, received a push on the issue in January and February 1986 from Senators Jesse Helms of North Carolina and Mitch McConnell of Kentucky.[87]

Once negotiations on tobacco resumed in earnest during spring and summer 1986, USTR demanded complete tariff elimination. The negotiations dragged throughout 1986 as Japanese negotiators from the Finance and Agriculture ministries refused to concede to the US demand of complete tariff elimination. Japan Tobacco's attorneys reiterated to USTR their contention that since Japan's trade policies then violated neither GATT nor the FCN treaty and since the 301 process should not be used to eliminate GATT-legal home market protection, the investigation should be terminated.[88] They contended that the combination of the April 1985 liberalization reforms, the change in the monetary exchange rate, and the US marketing efforts was having the effects desired by US tobacco sellers. They pointed out that import cigarettes increased their sales by 45% to a total of 3.3% market share in the first quarter of 1986. In the month of July, foreign cigarettes increased their market share to 3.7%.

In August 1986, trade talks between American and Japanese negotiators in Tokyo unhappily made no progress.[89] One USTR official said with frustration: "We are beginning to come very close to the wall, and decisions will have to be made at some point. I only hope that the Japanese realize this." Finally, as the 6 October 1986 deadline for the economic sanctions threatened by President Reagan neared, a last-minute deal was struck.[90] Japan Tobacco agreed to reduce the tariffs to zero, make the price approval system transparent, and, by April 1987, modify the excise tax policy so that Japanese firms paid the tax at the same time as foreign firms.

The Reagan administration called Senator James Broyhill of North Carolina just before the signing of the settlement agreement so that he could make the public announcement.[91] The American cigarette industry praised the agreement as an important improvement in selling conditions that would dramatically increase their sales, but it noted that US cigarettes would still be more expensive in Japan than Japanese brands and that Japan still prohibited US production in Japan.[92] The tobacco sales of American exporters in Japan took off dramatically: 1984—$96 million, 1985—$95.8 million, 1986—$128 million, 1987—$495 million, 1988—$610 million.[93] By 1988, tobacco had risen to be among the top twenty US export items to Japan.[94] US exporters captured 15% of the Japanese market by 1989 and projected 20% by 1991.[95] USTR got its big win and it gave no quarter. Often US negotiators struggle to find political cover for the other side so that the foreign government can sell the policy change at home. USTR extended no political cover to Japan on tobacco.

KOREA BEEF

The American Meat Institute, which represents the meat-packing and -processing industry, in February 1988 petitioned USTR under the Section 301 process to investigate Korea beef policies and practices that it considered unfair and violations of international law.[96] USTR announced in March that it would investigate American Meat's allegations.[97] American Meat alleged that since May 1985, Korea had banned the import of American beef. They contended that the Korean Ministry of Agriculture, Forestry, and Fisheries' import-licensing system, which had once been used to restrict, and implement quotas on, beef imports, had become the government's instrument to ban imports altogether. American Meat argued that the Korean beef import-licensing system and import ban violated GATT Article XI and the prohibition against quantitative trade restrictions and nullified American benefits gained under Korean tariff concessions during the Tokyo Round MTN. They contended that Korea could justify the Article XI violation under neither the Article XI exception to prevent or relieve critical shortages of foodstuffs, the Article XI exception to implement governmental programs involving restricted domestic production of agricultural commodities, nor the Article XII exception to protect balance of payments. American Meat concluded that the "practices described in [our] petition clearly violate international agreements to which the United States is a party," and requested that USTR "vigorously . . . enforce US rights under the appropriate agreements."[98]

American-Korean trade relations worsened throughout 1988 as USTR negotiators pressed the Korean government to open its beef, wine, cigarette, advertising, telecommunications, and financial-services markets, among others, and as intellectual-property rights problems persisted. Bilateral negotiations had made little progress, though in January USTR had tabled its proposal and in March the Korean Agriculture Ministry had offered its counterproposals.[99] USTR requested that (1) the import ban end after the spring 1988 legislative elections or by 1 May, (2) the import tariff be reduced from 20% to 15% and the tariff be bound in GATT, and (3) all Korean restaurants be permitted to buy foreign beef by December 1988. The Koreans proposed that (1) all Korean tourist hotels be allowed to buy foreign beef and (2) the overall quota on the importation of beef be raised.

The 1988 Trade Act's Super 301 provision further poisoned trade relations with Korea. The Koreans lobbied aggressively throughout early 1989 to avoid being named a "priority foreign country." They succeeded, but only after a mass hiring of Washington trade lawyers, lobbyists, and publicists.[100] The Korean government agreed to liberalize over three years 243 agricultural and fishery products, advertising, foreign investment, and pharmaceuticals.[101] Trade problems were accompanied by US complaints that Korea was manipulating its exchange rate with the US to ensure sustained export growth of manufactured goods, and the US Department of the Treasury announced in October 1988 that it would begin negotiations with Korea's Ministry of Finance to effect change in Korean monetary policies.[102] The Korean Embassy responded that the US was giving it too little credit for the extensive trade liberalization efforts it was making.[103] At the same time, the Korean foreign debt was finally nearly gone, the result of several years of large balance-of-payments surpluses.[104] Super 301 fractured further Korean policymakers between those who favored trade liberalization as sound economic and foreign policy and those who opposed trade liberalization as dangerous social and political policy.[105] Yet both Korean and American trade policymakers acknowledge that after this flurry of activity and rancor, the trade relations warmed considerably.[106]

For both the United States and Korea, 1988 was a national election year: presidential elections in the former and legislative elections in the latter. The presidential elections propelled the Republican administration to press for more market liberalization, bilaterally in Korea and elsewhere and multilaterally through the Uruguay Round, especially in agricultural markets. Farmers are an influential lobby in nearly every state in the Union. On the other side of the dispute, Korean farmers would be a formidable political force during the legislative elections. Thus, the Korean and American governments were implacable opponents over beef policy.

The Korean government negotiators contended to the American negotiators that their beef policies aimed to "stabilize cattle prices and guarantee a proper income level for livestock producers."[107] The Ministry of Agriculture, Forestry, and Fisheries admitted that it manipulated the supply and demand of beef on the Korean market for domestic policy reasons and that the manipulation included a ban on imported beef since May 1985. They argued that their policies were justified as a matter of domestic public policy and as a matter of international law. The Koreans maintained that their beef ban was legitimized by GATT Articles XI and XII. Article XI, they explained, allowed temporary quantitative restrictions in order to remove domestic surpluses of agricultural commodities. The Korean ban on beef imports, they claimed, was a temporary action aimed at doing just that. To the charge that a "temporary action" that had persisted for three years was not temporary after all, they argued that the term "temporary" should be defined "relative to the kind of agricultural products affected." "When it comes to cattle, a low calving rate means that it takes approximately three years before cattle are ready for slaughter." Hence, the Koreans concluded, their action was temporary. They found additional legal justification for their actions with the GATT balance-of-payments exception. The Korean Traders argued that GATT had recognized since 1966 that Korea needed to be able to restrict imports for balance-of-payments reasons. They pointed out that GATT in the interim had made "no official ruling" that would contradict this position.[108] In addition, they emphasized that their cumulative foreign-debt obligations had imposed a substantial drain on their monetary reserves. Hence, the balance-of-payments justification remained compelling, in their view. The Koreans conceded, however, that "whether Korea's suspension of beef imports is legitimate or not may be an issue subject to further examination." They went on to recommend that "in light of the existing friendly relationship between our two countries, it is more desirable to pursue a mutually satisfactory solution of the issue through the legal proceedings of the GATT."[109]

The written Korean government comments to USTR declared that potent domestic pressures in Korea vigorously opposed excessive beef imports. The document opined that most of the benefits from Korean beef liberalization would go to producers from Australia and New Zealand, not producers from the United States. The Korean government also commented that any increase in US beef exports to the Korean market would result in sales losses in Korea by US grain farmers due to the corollary reduction of cattle herds in Korea. It was attempting to show that policy calculations as well as legal judgments would have to be made by both sides in order to settle the dispute. The Koreans further argued that they were not alone in the world community in restricting beef imports, since Switzerland, Norway, Finland, the European Community, Japan, and the United States did so as well. To a logician, it was a tu quoque argument, to be sure, but nevertheless a defense of a kind that carries political force with policymakers.

The Koreans announced in May 1988, however, that they would resume the importation of limited quantities of foreign beef in June.[110] But they actually did not permit foreign (US, Australia, New Zealand) beef imports until September, for use at the Seoul Olympic Games.[111] The move was not enough to mollify either American Meat or USTR. USTR wanted to press forward with the case not only because of the pressure from the beef industry but because it saw in the beef quotas a clear GATT Article XI violation and so the beef dispute could be an instrument to test before GATT the durability of Korea's balance-of-payments exception.[112] The precedent of Japan's loss at GATT over leather quotas was fresh on the minds of USTR staff, but as a reminder, American Meat's attorneys filed a copy of the GATT panel report on Japan with their Korean beef petition. USTR wanted to take this case to GATT. The GATT Council, upon request by the United States, Australia, and New Zealand, authorized in May 1988 the establishment of a GATT dispute settlement panel to investigate the dispute and issue recommendations on its resolution. The Koreans had blocked the creation of the panel at the April GATT Council meeting, saying all other means of achieving agreement had not been exhausted.[113] Bowing to the inevitable, however, Korea withdrew its objection in May. In May, the Korean government also announced that it would expand the quotas, beginning in June.[114] In fact, the quotas were not opened until September and then only for use at the Seoul Olympic Games.[115] In July 1988, Korea announced a 14,500-metric-ton quota for beef imports for the second half of 1988.[116] The quota for 1989 was set by the Koreans at 50,000 metric tons. US beef exports to Korea in the second half of 1988 were valued at $25.6 million; in the first half of 1989 they were valued at $41.1 million. The Korean hope that expanded quotas would satisfy USTR was, of course, not going to be realized, since USTR had a more ambitious set of negotiation objectives.

In May 1989, a GATT panel issued a report that concluded that Korea's beef import restrictions violated the GATT Article XI prohibition against quantitative restrictions.[117] The GATT panel determined that the Korean balance-of-payments situation was too strong to allow continued invocation of the GATT exception. The panel recommended that Korea promptly establish a timetable to phase out the beef restrictions. The Korean government, knowing all too well that this GATT judgment would likely strip it forever of the balance-of-payments exception, refused to allow adoption of the panel report at both the June and July 1989 meetings of the GATT Council. Yet both USTR and GATT officials expected Korea to capitulate in practice, even if they continued to reject publicly the panel finding.[118]

In September, the American Meat Institute pressed USTR to name Korea formally as an unfair trader and threaten it with sanctions.[119] USTR also was deluged with letters supporting the beef lobby: the California-Arizona Citrus League, the California Cling Peach Advisory Board, the California Avocado Commission, the Western States Meat Association, the Blue Diamond Growers, the Welch's Company, and the National Cattlemen's Association. Clearly beef was only the beginning. USTR announced that effective 28 September 1989 (its statutorily imposed deadline), as a result of the Section 301 investigation and the GATT panel report, it had determined that "rights to which the United States is entitled under a trade agreement are being denied by Korea's restrictions on the import of beef." USTR announced that it would not, however, retaliate immediately with economic sanctions but would instead offer a last opportunity for a negotiated settlement—a Washington meeting between Korean President Roh Tae Woo and President George Bush was only two weeks away. At the meeting, President Roh pledged to open more Korean markets, but no agreement on beef was made.[120]

Finally, in November, as USTR was readying a list of products for retaliation, agreement was reached. The agreement, formalized in April 1990, followed the precedent established by the settlement in the US-Japan beef dispute.[121] The settlement agreement called for gradual opening of the Korean beef market by 1997 and the replacement of the quotas with tariffs. It also established an American-industry-to-Korean-industry dialogue aimed at rationalizing beef production in Korea, thus offering to the Koreans something in return for their concessions. These American concessions were the political cover that brought a bitter, protracted negotiation to an end. Nevertheless, by persisting with its GATT case, USTR dealt the Korean government trade negotiators a weak bargaining hand for many years to come in markets protected by quotas.

CONCLUSION

This chapter has argued that although rule-oriented trade diplomacy involves dispute settlement qualitatively different from power-oriented trade diplomacy (to be presented in the next chapter), bilateral power relationships are nevertheless present in the negotiations.

Realist political economy offers the following explanation of the process and outcome of bilateral trade dispute settlement: (1) believing that a domestic commercial interest is confronting a foreign trade barrier, a more economically powerful state initiates a dispute settlement against an economically weaker state; (2) the trade diplomacy consists in the threat by the stronger state of economic sanctions against the weaker state; (3) the settlement agreement conforms to and promotes the economic interests of the stronger state without concession to the interests of the respondent state; (4) unless threatened by sanctions, the respondent state noncomplies with the settlement agreement; (5) the dispute renews. Liberal political economy, on the other hand, offers the following explanation: (1) believing that a domestic interest is confronting a foreign trade barrier, a state initiates a dispute settlement against another state regardless of the structure of international power; (2) the trade diplomacy consists in the initiator's demonstration of GATT regime rule noncompliance by the respondent; (3) the GATT regime mediates settlement of the dispute; (4) the settlement agreement conforms with GATT regime rules, though with concessions to the respondent state; (5) the respondent state complies with the settlement agreement. Each of these stylized descriptions from international-relations theory captures important aspects of international trade diplomacy as experienced in the Pacific.

Bilateral trade dispute settlement in the Pacific under US 301 policy consists in the initiation by the economically stronger state against the weaker, as realist political economy predicts. (Though by definition of research design in this study, since East Asian-initiated trade disputes were not studied.) After deciding to initiate investigations against the alleged East Asian trade barriers, USTR trade diplomats designed negotiation strategies. Rule-oriented trade diplomacy was conducted in six cases: Finding no GATT rule violation and thereby concluding that the complaint was without merit, they took no action in Taiwan footwear. USTR General Counsel lawyers demonstrated GATT rule noncompliance through the formal GATT panel dispute settlement process in Japan footwear, Japan tobacco, and Korea beef. The US negotiators alleged GATT rule noncompliance through informal GATT dispute settlement procedures in Korea footwear. Since Taiwan was not a signatory to the GATT and panel dispute settlement procedures were not available to the negotiators, USTR lawyers bilaterally argued with Taiwanese negotiators that the Taiwanese policy violated GATT rules (which Taiwan had pledged bilaterally with the US to observe). In these cases of rule-oriented diplomacy, USTR threatened sanctions to exact settlement agreement.

Power-oriented trade diplomacy was conducted in three cases: Despite the absence of GATT rule violations in Korea intellectual property, Korea insurance, and Japan semiconductor, USTR pressed forward with negotiations. In the intellectual-property disputes, USTR trade diplomats argued that Korean policy ought to be made to comply with extant international treaties and emerging GATT regime rules on intellectual property. In the insurance dispute, they argued that Korean policy ought to be made to comply with the extant bilateral treaty of Friendship, Commerce, and Navigation (which offered national treatment to services) and with emerging GATT regime rules on international service trade. In the semiconductor dispute, with the Commerce Department investigating and taking primary responsibility for the dumping allegations, USTR trade diplomats argued that though there were no apparent GATT rule violations, there was a pattern of exclusionary business practices by Japanese electronics manufacturers that the Japanese government condoned and must remedy. In the cases of power-oriented trade diplomacy, USTR threatened sanctions to gain settlement agreements that considered the GATT regime and its rules.

As liberal political economy predicts, the US demonstrates regime rule noncompliance when it can. But liberal political economy does not predict the extensive use of American trade power. As realist political economy predicts, the US 301 policy, as written by Congress and as implemented by USTR, always at least implicitly threatened economic sanction, and indeed USTR threatened Japan, Korea, and Taiwan in all the negotiations. Thus, realist political economy is quite correct in predicting that the US will bully Japan, Korea, and Taiwan with its 301 policy. Nevertheless, the threat always came after lengthy negotiations, often after the demonstration of GATT rule violation through regime dispute settlement procedures, and it sometimes aimed to encourage regime rule growth.

The settlement agreements changed East Asian trade policies on compliance with regime rules in Japan footwear, Korea footwear, Japan tobacco, and Korea beef: quotas were eliminated and tariffs phased in, and customs valuation procedures and distribution and tax procedures were changed. In Taiwan rice the two sides agreed to cut a deal (agreeing to export to small-country markets only) and leave as an open question whether Taiwanese policy truly violated complicated GATT rules on agriculture subsidies. In Korea intellectual property, new patent, copyright, and trademark laws were to be written and accessions to international treaties were to occur. In Korea insurance, licensing procedures were to be made transparent and were to be granted to foreign insurance companies. In Japan semiconductor, the Japanese government agreed to "recognize" the "expectation" of the US government that US firms would gain a 20% market share in the Japanese market.

Realist political economy predicts that America's trade power allows it to get what it wants minus the concessions exacted by the strategic, if weak, East Asian bargainers. John Odell aggregated US-initiated trade disputes with Korea for the period 1960 to 1981 to argue that the settlement outcome was usually closer to American policy preferences than to Korean policy preferences. John Conybeare employed game theory and a small number of case studies, ranging from medieval Anglo-Hanse trade wars to Depression-era Smoot-Hawley tariff wars to post–World War II US-European Community agriculture and US-EC-Japan steel trade disputes, to contend that power predicts winner. Realist political economy offers a parsimonious explanation to the research problem of predicting dispute settlement outcomes.[122]

Yet research has shown that weaker states can negotiate much better trade dispute settlement deals than gross measures of power would predict. David Yoffie, in his study of East Asian state strategies with the Americans, emphasizes that weak bargainers must bring a commitment to realize long-run gains.[123] They must (1) negotiate for ambiguity, (2) demand compensation for restrictions, (3) exploit bureaucratic cleavages within the opponent, and (4) cheat on regulations and agreements.[124] William Mark Habeeb offers a more general logic behind weak state capabilities. He explains that conclusions about state interactions drawn from a modeled structure of a static, aggregated power relationship ignore the dynamic of process. Power, he explains, is deployed through interaction. Outcome is explained by issue-specific power deployed through savvy exploitation of alternatives, commitment, and control.[125] Big states may have awesome power, but they also have overwhelming ranges of commitments and unwieldy bureaucracies. The committed and nimble can outmaneuver the distracted and ponderous.

Weak-state bargaining power cannot be explained by realism, but it can be explained by liberalism's assumptions that states possess multiple foreign-policy goals, that substate actors matter, that power resources are issue-specific, and that linkage of issues is difficult. In these case studies of 1980s disputes, the East Asian negotiators did not do as well as they had done in Yoffie's case studies which predated the 1980s: the US government in the 1980s was much more focused on its trade interests than it had been in the past.

Realist political economy, denying the possibility of cooperation in international relations, predicts that in international trade dispute settlement the more powerful will only inadvertently grant concessions to the weaker country. Liberal political economy, on the other hand, optimistic about the likelihood of cooperation, predicts that the more powerful will grant concessions to the weaker respondent country. The experience in the Pacific shows that liberal political economy's prediction is the more accurate, for the settlement agreements often included political cover for the East Asian government. Political cover means, in the jargon of the trade negotiator, that the American chief negotiator seeks for the opponent chief negotiator some rationale for, or (modest) benefit from, agreement. East Asian states find political cover in being able to explain to their affected business communities and citizens that they conceded to international regime rules, not to American power (which confers little political cover to East Asian state policymakers). East Asian policymakers can explain to domestic interest groups that trade policy must change for the good of the state's international reputation, for the good of reciprocity within the regime, and for the good of the international trade regime itself. Said one US negotiator about the Japan leather and footwear case: "We said to the Japanese, 'You are wrong; you will lose.' A GATT loss would allow them to sell it at home."[126] Indeed, the USTR lawyers successfully argued before the GATT panel, and the panel held against Japan. One participant remarked, "The Japanese knew they were beaten; they didn't even put up a defense in GATT."[127]

In addition to GATT as political cover, USTR and East Asian negotiators found political cover in several other case studies. In Korea insurance, the agreement granted a gradual licensing of foreign firms; in Korea footwear, the agreement called for customs valuation procedure changes but only modest tariff cuts; in Korea beef, it called for only a phased elimination of quotas, their replacement with tariffs, and American beef industry technical support to the Korean industry; in Taiwan rice, it called for only a limitation of markets in the world in which (allegedly subsidized) rice could be sold; in Japan semiconductor, the public agreement asserted only an ambiguous expectation of US producers to larger market share in Japan, and the confidential side letter asserted a still ambiguous expectation that might be an import quota. Only in Japan footwear, Japan tobacco, and Korea intellectual-property cases were the settlement agreements without political cover for the East Asian government. Political cover is anomalous for realist political economy, which predicts that the more powerful United States bullies the East Asian governments without attention to their domestic political problems. But political cover is a kind of negotiation concession, and such concessions are an important part of building cooperative bilateral trade relationships.[128] Trade negotiators realize that, after the dispute of the day is resolved, the game continues to be played on another day. In the jargon of game theory, trade negotiators cooperate with one another because the game is iterated, not single play. Political cover brings to daily experience the game theorist's abstract explanation that the players "cooperate." As liberal political economy predicts, cooperation is the rule, not the exception, in international trade diplomacy in the Pacific.

The bilateral dispute settlement outcomes delineate gains and losses for the United States and each East Asian state as a whole (as well as gains and losses for domestic interest groups, producers, consumers, legislators, and bureaucrats). All the case studies resulted in gains for domestic consumers in Japan, Korea, and Taiwan as measured by increased competition in the marketplace, and in losses for domestic producers in Japan, Korea, and Taiwan as measured by the increase in competition from foreign producers. All the case studies resulted in gains for the American producers who got USTR to take up their cases and expand their market opportunities in Japan, Korea, and Taiwan. These judgments are matters of economics. As a matter of international relations, however, the question is, Does the United States seek to better its position in East Asian markets even to the exclusion of third countries? That is, does the US seek "super-most-favored-nation treatment" as is sometimes alleged?

In international-relations theory, this is the question of relative versus absolute gains. Realist political economy predicts that USTR will negotiate agreements that better the positions of US producers only, not third-country producers. Thus, the agreements would allow only US companies a bigger share of a quota, lower import tariffs, revised standards and regulations, or licenses to do business. Liberal political economy predicts that USTR will negotiate agreements that benefit third-country producers as well as US producers. the agreements would be carried out under MFN terms. The evidence of the case studies shows that in the eight cases in which outcomes offered gains, six cases (Japan footwear, Japan tobacco, Korea footwear, Korea insurance, Korea IPR, Taiwan rice) resulted in outcomes that advantaged third-country producers as well as US producers. Only in Korea beef, which offered a grudging, modest quota increase that benefited US producers, and in Japan semiconductor, which offered US firms an import target share and design-ins, did USTR negotiate agreements that resulted in relative gains for the United States. Thus, the evidence is mixed but tending toward the liberal political-economy assumption of absolute gains. Additional research is needed on this point.

The conclusion was also drawn in this chapter that though the evidence is mixed, the liberal political-economy prediction that the US will seek absolute, not relative, gains with its trade dispute diplomacy finds more support than does the realist proposition for the "super-most-favored-nation" treatment of relative gains.

CHAPTER 5

Power-oriented Trade Diplomacy

USTR pursued power-oriented trade diplomacy in the disputes on US trade with Japan in semiconductors and with Korea in services and intellectual-property-intensive market sectors. American power-oriented trade diplomacy was domestically the product of an American semiconductor industry with the wrong industrial organization and corporate strategies for global competition and of American service and intellectual-property-intensive industries that were well positioned for global competition. It was power-oriented diplomacy in international relations because the extant GATT regime, as a result of inadequate rules, was incapable of settling the disputes. Since there are no explicit international rules on competition policy and since the GATT Article III national-treatment obligation leaves much ambiguity, neither international dispute settlement procedures nor international norms could mediate the semiconductor disputes. Since the GATT treaty explicitly limits the coverage of its rules to traded goods, not traded services, and since no multilateral regime existed for service trade, neither international dispute settlement procedures nor international norms could mediate the conflict over insurance. Since intellectual-property protection varies considerably across national boundaries and since extant international treaties on patents, trademarks, and copyrights had only been signed by industrialized countries, neither international dispute settlement procedures nor international norms could mediate the conflict over intellectual property.

USTR policymakers were nonetheless committed to seeking bilateral settlement agreements that would enhance the competitive opportunities of these American industries. The challenges were great because American trade power was being employed entirely without authoritative international institutions as mediators and legitimizers. In semiconductors, the United States was hamstrung by a liberal regulatory political economy that had no policy means to encourage corporate alliances and mergers (save the "discipline" of the dog-eat-dog marketplace, but in this case, the Japanese companies were the big dogs), and so trade policy would have to do. In services and intellectual property, the United States in the late 1980s was an ascending hegemon, doing what it had done in the late 1940s—creating international regimes. The US strategy was to pursue multilateral rule creation in the then forthcoming Uruguay Round MTN, bilateral rule creation through the US-Canada Free Trade Agreement (and later minilateral rule creation through the North American Free Trade Agreement), and unilateral pressure through 301 initiations.

JAPAN SEMICONDUCTOR

The Semiconductor Industry Association 301 petition to USTR was unprecedented in scope. SIA contended that the Japanese government had identified semiconductors as an industry essential to its national development and targeted it as an industry to be promoted. SIA accused the Japanese of a wide range of unfair practices, not limited to overt barriers such as quotas and tariffs but including more subtle nontariff barriers. They contended that even as the Japanese government was apparently taking actions to open its semiconductor market in response to US pressure in the 1970s, it was simultaneously implementing "a series of liberalization countermeasures designed to create a market structure capable of withstanding the effect of import and investment liberalization."[1] The Japanese government, said SIA, had encouraged a small number of large, integrated electronics firms—Hitachi, NEC, Matsushita, Fujitsu, Toshiba—to interlink their research, development, production, and sales of semiconductors so that US firms' sales in Japan were limited to types of semiconductors not produced by Japanese firms and to filling in spot market shortages. Despite aggressive marketing efforts by US firms and despite its dominance of American, European, and all other semiconductor markets, their market presence in Japan in 1985 remained stuck at the same 10% share they had in 1975. They charged that Japanese government policies had encouraged Japanese firms to create "massive production capacity" that periodically resulted in "surges of low-priced Japanese exports." That is, SIA contended that Japanese firms often dumped their chips on the US market and were safeguarded against financial risk by the certain profits of the secure Japanese market and their bulky corporate treasuries. As a result of Japanese government policies, SIA claimed, US firms had lost sales and revenue in both the US and the Japanese markets—sales and revenue sufficient to threaten their very existence.

SIA sought to achieve two objectives: it called on USTR to "dramatically improve" US sales in Japan "within a short period," and on DoC to prevent dumping by Japanese firms in the US market. In order to achieve these objectives, SIA urged USTR to negotiate commitments from the Japanese government to encourage their firms to purchase a significantly higher proportion of their semiconductors from US companies. SIA requested that USTR encourage the Japanese government to investigate whether their firms were violating Japanese antimonopoly laws and to make long-term policy reforms to ensure that the Japanese semiconductor market responds to market forces freely. If negotiations failed, SIA recommended that (1) USTR initiate a GATT dispute settlement proceeding against the Japanese government, (2) DoC unilaterally enforce US antidumping laws against Japanese firms, and (3) the US Department of Justice investigate Japanese firms to determine whether they had violated US antitrust laws. USTR, then, was confronted by SIA with a complicated complaint that involved investment and antitrust policies as well as import and export trade policies.

US-Japan conflict over semiconductors began in the early 1960s when Texas Instruments, then the world's largest semiconductor maker, applied to the Japanese government for permission to produce in Japan.[2] TI only gained permission to manufacture semiconductors in Japan on the conditions that it license its patents to Japanese firms and that it not take more than 10% of the Japanese market. By the end of the 1970s, Japanese firms controlled a large segment of the US market in 16K DRAMs. US firms claimed that the Japanese obtained their market share by dumping. Only when US makers threatened an antidumping action did the Japanese raise their prices on the US market (and lower prices a bit on the Japanese market).[3] In 1980, Japanese firms were first onto the market with 64K DRAMs (with the exception of IBM, which did not sell on the open market) and announced the first prototype 256K DRAM.[4]

Beginning in 1981, the US and Japanese governments discussed the semiconductor industry nearly continuously. At the prompting of American semiconductor-maker complaints regarding Japanese semiconductor practices, a US-Japan Working Group was established to discuss the problem in June 1982. The Working Group comprised a US team led by USTR and Commerce but including the Council of Economic Advisors, the National Security Council, the Office of Management and Budget, and the departments of State, Labor, Treasury, and Defense.[5] Commerce and USTR wanted to negotiate a guaranteed Japanese market share for US firms and a bilateral monitoring system that would collect monthly data on shipments and prices in order to prevent dumping, but the other US agencies opposed both positions; thus, the US sought neither from the Japanese government.[6] The Working Group reached agreement in November 1982, then again in November 1983. The first semiconductor agreement committed Japan to "develop possible concrete measures to promote imports of manufactured goods in high technology" and created a Joint High Technology Data Collection Task Force that would gather shipment data but not price data. Thus, the Japanese commitment to promote semiconductor sales by US firms was ambiguous, and the data collection system could not monitor dumping. The second agreement addressed market access: "For the purposes of increasing US participation in the Japanese market, the Government of Japan should encourage Japanese semiconductor users to enlarge opportunities for US-based suppliers so that long-term relationships could evolve with Japanese companies." The Japanese commitment to market access was expanded in a protocol attached to the agreement, the "Chairman's Note." The Japanese government agreed to encourage Japanese users of semiconductors to become long-term partners with US suppliers by including US firms more closely in their design and procurement processes. One of the negotiators explained that the American team pressed their demand by arguing that GATT required national treatment and that this is what US firms wanted.[7] For its part, the US committed itself to "strengthen its sales and marketing efforts" and "increase its understanding of the Japanese market." On data collection, the two governments agreed to continue with the existing system.

At the time of the filing of the Section 301 petition, SIA represented fifty-seven American producers of semiconductors, including "captive" producers such as IBM and AT&T, which manufacture semiconductors for internal consumption, and "merchant" producers such as LSI Logic and VLSI Technology, which manufacture semiconductors for sale to other semiconductor-user firms.[8] The Semiconductor Industry Association had been formed in 1977 to confront growing Japanese semiconductor competition but did not adopt a protectionist public-policy preference.[9] The semiconductor makers determined that protection would lead to higher component costs for US users of semiconductors, thereby threatening the viability of these American industries. SIA believed that if the US electronics industry perished, the US semiconductor would perish with it. SIA adopted four basic policy positions on high technology: (1) goods should flow freely, unhindered by tariff or nontariff barriers; (2) technology should transfer freely throughout the West; (3) intellectual-property rights should be extended to new information areas; and (4) investment should move freely. These positions were deduced from SIA's assessment that states that adopted mercantilist policy positions would find their firms falling behind. SIA recognized Japan as the exceptional winner with a mercantilist strategy. Thus, while in principle SIA opposed protectionist trade policies, some in the Association argued for laying the principle aside with regard to Japan. SIA attorney Alan Wolff warned three months before the 301 petition filing, "There may still be time to continue to press for the first best solution of market liberalization, although there is recognition that if this fails, second best solutions may have to be adopted." But, the warning included an important caveat: "Whatever these solutions may prove to be, they must be in the interests of US computer and telecommunications firms if the solutions are to be of value."[10] SIA well understood its industry's place in the high-technology "food chain."

In June 1985, lawyers for Micron Technology, a non-SIA semiconductor maker, filed an antidumping complaint with DoC and ITC against Fujitsu, Hitachi, NEC, Oki, Toshiba, Mitsubishi, and Matsushita, sellers of 64K DRAMs.[11] The dumping petition charged that the named Japanese firms were selling their chips for about 75 cents per unit, despite production costs alone that Micron alleged to be about $1.25 per unit. The AD filing further complicated USTR decision making on the pending Section 301 petition: Now DoC and ITC would be conducting investigations separately from any USTR might carry out. Also, the AD process, as statutorily mandated, offers much less discretion to administrators than does the Section 301 process, and it imposes firm deadlines.

The Section 301 petition filed on behalf of SIA did not have the full support of all the membership. Some members strongly advocated the imposition of quotas. Members that were users of semiconductors, such as IBM, and that manufactured semiconductors in Japan, such as Motorola and Texas Instruments, reluctantly supported the petition and opposed the imposition of quotas on Japanese imports as a petition outcome.[12] Some members objected to the estimated $900,000 legal cost of the case. Related American industries reacted to the Section 301 petition differently as well. American manufacturers of the equipment that makes semiconductors repudiated the SIA petition. An official of the Semiconductor Equipment Manufacturing Institute pointed out that US industry was being kept in business by Japanese semiconductor makers who, unlike their US counterparts, were expanding production.[13] On the other hand, the Telecommunications Group of the Electronic Industries Association praised SIA's intentions but scorned its timidity; it recommended quotas.

Senior Reagan administration officials also reacted to the petition differently. Leaders at Commerce, CIA, and the Defense Science Board supported the petition: they saw a vital American industry threatened. Leaders at State, Treasury, Defense, and the National Security Council contended that the Japanese government had dropped barriers to semiconductor imports back in 1975 and that the semiconductor industry was simply poorly managed.[14] Caught in this political vortex, US Trade Representative Clayton Yeutter announced in mid-July 1985 that his office would investigate SIA's charges.[15] The investigation was really three investigations about three separate disputes: (1) access to the Japanese market, (2) Japanese dumping in the US market, and (3) Japanese dumping in third-country markets.[16] USTR led the investigation on market access; DoC led the investigation on alleged dumping.

USTR negotiators discussed the allegations with MITI officials in July and August. MITI denied that its firms dumped semiconductors, or that the Japanese government had promoted its industry unfairly, and it asserted that US firms possessed about 20%, not 10%, of the Japanese market.[17] At the end of the summer, the Washington and New York attorneys for the Electronics Industries Association of Japan filed with USTR their formal response to SIA's charges.[18] Electronics Industries submitted a thick, tightly reasoned, heavily footnoted document to USTR. The document offered considerable evidence aimed at rebutting SIA's allegations and presented an alternative picture of the state of the semiconductor industry. Electronics Industries argued that SIA was misusing the Section 301 process. It alleged that SIA provided no evidence that Japanese *government* actions in 1985 violated international law. SIA did not demonstrate the existence of specific trade barriers but, rather, alleged that an entire market structure "functions to exclude foreign participation." Furthermore, SIA asserted that Japanese firms violated Japanese and American antitrust laws, but provided no evidence to support its claim and even failed to enumerate the specific laws that had allegedly been breached, said Electronics Industries.

Electronics Industries contended that SIA misled USTR with market data based on faulty assumptions fallaciously applied. It laid out a formula that included direct and indirect imports and subsidiary production and divided this figure over total market demand, including captive consumption. With this formula, Electronics Industries concluded that the US share of the Japanese market was 19.1% and the Japanese share of the US market was 9.6%, rather than the 11.4% and 17% computed by SIA.[19] Electronics Industries disaggregated SIA's market share numbers in order to allege that US and Japanese end user industries were quite different and that US and Japanese producer firms made quite different chips to meet these special needs. Japanese end users, they said, tended to be makers of consumer electronics, while American end users tended to be makers of computers, telecommunications equipment, and defense products. "The complaint of failure to gain a larger share of the Japanese market," they declared, "rings somewhat hollow when it is recognized that US companies do not emphasize the types of semiconductors that are in most demand in Japan." Electronics Industries also alleged that US firms provided poor service and lower-quality products than Japanese firms. They provided anecdotal evidence from Japanese end users of poor service provided by US firms and cited US industry data that indicated more quality control problems with US makers' semiconductors. Electronic Industries accused SIA of manipulating the facts with its claim of a "buy Japanese" practice in Japan. They charged that SIA's claim that Intel lost the Japanese market for 8080 microprocessors when NEC increased production of the item was misleading. They explained that NEC sales of 8080 microprocessor declined just as Intel's did and declined because end users replaced the 8080 model with Intel's 8085 model, which NEC coproduced. Hence, "the decline in use of the 8080 microprocessor was due to a change in models, not to displacement by NEC," and the "disappearing market syndrome" is "a self-serving illusion apparently created to mask the reality of the underlying competitive process."

Electronics Industries of Japan, then, presented a picture of the industry at odds with the picture presented by SIA. The Japanese contended that industries related to semiconductors, including computers, consumer electronics, telecommunications, and automobiles, have become increasingly integrated. End user firms in the US, Europe, and Japan have been systematically increasing cooperative ties and expanding their own semiconductor production capacities in order to ensure themselves a constant supply of quality components designed precisely for their needs. Accordingly, the SIA petition represents the interests of US merchant semiconductor producers. These merchant producers, which were poorly positioned for changing market conditions, sought protection of the US market and guaranteed market shares in Japan to keep themselves in business. SIA wanted "super-national treatment," opined Electronics Industries:

> The petitioners seek to make Japan a scapegoat for the problems of the US merchant producers. Those problems cannot be solved by launch-

ing an attack against alleged Japanese market barriers. The barriers do not exist, and the SIA is only tilting at windmills. . . . In the long run, the solution lies in transition toward a more integrated market structure in the United States—a process which is already well underway. . . . The semiconductor industries in Japan and the United States are not, and should not, be antagonists. Manufacturers in both countries should devote their energies toward advancement of technology and should avoid diversion into irrelevant and divisive trade disputes.[20]

The ITC announced in late July that it preliminarily determined that Japanese firms had dumped 64K DRAMs.[21] In late September, the fracture within SIA widened when Intel, Advanced Micro Devices, and the National Semiconductor Corporation filed a dumping case against eight Japanese makers of EPROMs. The Intel petition asserted that market prices in 256K and 128K EPROMs had declined from $17.00 and $7.50 each in January 1985 to $4.00 and $2.50 each by August 1985. The petition asserted that by August Japanese firms had seized 60% of the US market. A supplementary petition fielded on behalf of Intel by William Finan, a well-known industry analyst, charged that Japanese producers had flooded the American EPROM market in 1985.[22] Finan cited MITI data indicating that Japanese firm inventories went from 30 million units in January to 97 million in June—while their cash registers were ringing unprecedented sales.

Intel's general counsel explained the AD petition:

We have invested heavily in new plants and equipment and have proved ourselves vigorous competitors in the $1.1 billion worldwide EPROM market. . . . This record is irrelevant, however, when we face Japanese competitors equipped to gain market share at any cost. . . . They can afford to engage in predatory pricing because they are part of giant Japanese conglomerates prepared to subsidize their semiconductor operations for as long as it takes to gain control of the market. . . . There is a violation of US law here and we want it to stop.[23]

As part of his new aggressive unilateralism trade policy, President Reagan announced in September the creation of an interagency Trade Strike Force, chaired by the Secretary of Commerce. The Strike Force apparently had to strike at least once; hence, it struck against Japan with an unprecedented DoC self-initiation of a dumping investigation on 256K and defined the product under investigation as 256K DRAMs and *all succeeding genera-*

tions of DRAMs. As a result, the investigation would continue as technological change moved on to more advanced chips. The difference was important, for the wider definition prevented Japanese firms from being content in the knowledge that technological advance could outpace the yearlong dumping-investigation procedures.

Just as in the case of acceptance of the SIA petition, however, the Reagan administration was of many minds about the strike against Japanese semiconductor exports. At the crucial interagency meeting, the NSC (National Security Council) representatives opposed the strike on grounds that it might threaten Japanese support for the Strategic Defense Initiative. The State Department representative opined that the US semiconductor industry had followed the wrong track in product development and that to help it would be tantamount to an industrial policy. The Treasury Department, with two representatives present in the meeting, presented two viewpoints: one senior official agreed with the State Department position and added the economic argument that dumping benefits the society receiving the dumped goods; a second official supported the DoC position. USTR, perhaps with its own pre-eminence in trade policy in mind, contended that the action was prematurely aggressive. Without consensus, President Reagan did not officially authorize the strike until December 1985. The Trade Strike Force never struck again.

In October 1985, SIA submitted to USTR a document aimed at "correcting" "misleading statements and inaccurate factual assertions" contained in the Electronic Industries brief. SIA prefaced the document with the following: "In our view the proper role of the US Government is not that of an impartial adjudicator, but of an advocate of legitimate commercial interests. SIA notes that the Japanese Government has adopted such a role with respect to its own industry."[24] It is ironic that USTR was being criticized by the Japanese for acting as prosecutor, judge, jury, and hangman.

In the brief to USTR, SIA cited US makers' low market share in Japan, despite sustained efforts by US firms, as the best evidence in support of its case. They rejected Japanese anecdotal claims about poor US service, noting that a few anecdotes are "inadequate to explain gross disparities in market share in a multi-billion dollar industry characterized by tens of thousands of individual transactions." SIA matched Electronic Industries with anecdotes of US users who had quality and service problems from Japanese companies. They rejected the contention that differences in end users (consumer products in Japan, computer and industrial uses in the US) accounted for the small US share in Japan, calling it "misleading and a distraction." Said SIA:

"Competitiveness in semiconductors is determined by reference to circuit application (e.g., MOS logic, MOS memory) not the particular end product—8 bit microprocessors, for example, are used interchangeably in consumer, computer, and industrial end products."[25] SIA argued that Japanese claims that its great expansion in production capacity was "farsighted investment behavior" were contradicted by industry analysts who predicted world demand growing at 16.5% per year while Japanese industry expanded production at a rate of 40% per year. SIA concluded that Japanese producer capacity expansion, coupled with Japanese dumping on US and other markets, indicated Japanese intent to dominate global semiconductor markets. SIA focused in on Japanese government behavior, saying that "Japanese protectionism and subsidies—deliberate government policies indicative of industrial targeting—had nullified and impaired benefits of the US under the GATT" and that the "anticompetitive activities by Japanese producers" were actionable under Section 301. SIA charged that the practices of Japanese producers, taken together, indicated collusive interfirm behavior excluding foreign firms and that the Japanese government had not only tolerated the behavior but encouraged it, thus nullifying US benefits under GATT. SIA's lawyers were mapping new GATT ground by arguing that Japanese competition policy was nullifying US benefits under the GATT.

Within three weeks, Electronics Industries issued a written reply.[26] The arguments remained the same; the tone grew more vitriolic. Electronics Industries accused SIA of "a crude attempt to revive simplistic US notions of 'Japan Inc.,' an argument both discredited and offensive": "SIA's view as to what evidence is needed to show existence of a cartel seems confined to what the police look for in their initial search for murder suspects: motive and opportunity."[27]

USTR led negotiations on market access in Japan throughout the fall and winter, but without progress. In a typical negotiating session,[28] the Americans would demand an open Japanese semiconductor market. The Japanese would respond that it was already open. The Americans would ask rhetorically, "Then why do we still have only 10% of your market?" The Japanese would answer, "How much do you want? 11%? 12%?" The American negotiating position was not to specify market share targets. Hence, USTR negotiators would not respond to the MITI question with a specific market share figure.

The dumping investigations, however, were grinding along according to statutory dictate. During the fall, the two sides nevertheless attempted, through a negotiated settlement, to resolve the dumping dispute without an AD investigation. The Japanese were proposing a floor price mechanism, i.e., an agreement that Japanese firms would not offer their chips at less than an agreed price. DoC opposed this solution and favored a nonnegotiated, routine investigation ending with the imposition of dumping margins.[29] It maintained that some Japanese firms had significantly higher manufacturing costs than others. If each Japanese firm were required to sell at a price that exceeded its costs, some Japanese firms would be pushed out of the market and thereby out of business. A floor price, if set sufficiently high, allowed all Japanese firms to make profits. The Japanese Embassy criticized the 6 December DoC antidumping-case initiation (the Strike Force action) and recommended that the USTR-led 301 discussions aimed at a floor price agreement would better resolve the problem.[30] Indeed, the Japanese producers probably felt more secure in the nurturing hand of MITI negotiators than in the legalistic grip of the AD investigation.

In March, DoC determined preliminarily that Japanese firms had dumped EPROMs and 256K DRAMs. The ITC preliminarily determined that American industry had been injured by the dumping.[31] The negotiations on market access, however, were still at an impasse. On 27 March 1986, the two sides suspended negotiations over semiconductors. On the same date, fifty US Senators sent a letter to President Reagan urging him to emphasize trade problems in his upcoming mid-April summit with Prime Minister Nakasone. They impressed on the President that he should not allow his desire for a warm, friendly meeting with the Prime Minister to allow "unwarranted" trade concessions by the US. The Senators also threateningly reminded the President that pending trade legislation would be strongly influenced by their perception of the state of US-Japan trade relations. The summit meeting, however, led to no breakthrough in the semiconductor dispute.

Political pressure was mounting. In May, the House of Representatives passed a resolution 408 to 5 recommending that the President retaliate with sanctions if a settlement agreement was not signed soon.[32] The 31 July 1986 deadline was quickly approaching when dumping duties would be levied. In late June, a Deputy US Trade Representative threatened economic sanctions if a satisfactory agreement was not soon reached.[33] The threat achieved its desired effect: the (third) Semiconductor Arrangement was signed on 30 July, one day before the final dumping determination was due to be announced.[34] The Semiconductor Arrangement, formally signed in September 1986, addressed all three trade problems—dumping in the US market, dumping in third-country markets, and access to the Japanese market.

On dumping in the US market, the US and Japan agreed to negotiate suspension agreements on the dumping cases. In order to ensure that dumping did not occur (which the Japanese had never admitted), MITI agreed that it would monitor the costs and prices of certain specified semiconductor products. The burden then fell on US government administrators, despite not being provided with cost data by Japanese firms, to act if they suspected US market sales at "less than company-specific fair value." On dumping in third-country markets, the Japanese government similarly pledged to monitor prices and costs of Japanese exports. The Arrangement provided that "if the government of the United States of America believes that exports or sales by any firms in the US market at prices less than company-specific fair value and the Government of the United States of America provides the Government of Japan with information to support the belief, immediate consultations may be requested." They agreed that the consultations would have a 14-day limit. The Japanese government then was responsible to "take appropriate actions available under laws and regulations in Japan to prevent" dumping. Nevertheless, the US explictly retained the right to initiate AD investigations under its own laws.

On market access, one participant remarked, "We could never find the smoking gun; we could never find the GATT violation, but we knew we should have had a bigger share of [the Japanese] market."[35] In the beginning, US negotiators sought to open Japanese markets for American (and all foreign) semiconductor makers, in addition to pursuing dumping issues. Without clear evidence of GATT-noncompliant market barriers and without GATT rules for competition policy, USTR opted for results: "Give us twenty percent of your market."[36] The Semiconductor Arrangement[37] explicitly recognized the signers' complementary expectations: "The Japanese producers and users of semiconductors anticipate substantially increased supply by and usage of foreign-based semiconductors. The United States of America anticipates substantially improved opportunities for foreign semiconductor sales in the Japanese market more reflective of the competitiveness of the US industry." The Japanese, in order to help the United States realize its anticipation, committed itself to "impress upon the Japanese producers and users of semiconductors the need to aggressively take advantage of increased market access opportunities in Japan for foreign-based firms which wish to improve their actual sales performance and position." The US, in order to help itself, committed itself to "impress upon the US semiconductor producers the need to aggressively pursue every sales opportunity in the Japanese market." Both agreed "that the expected improvement in access should be gradual and steady over the period of this Arrangement." There was no guaranteed market share figures, only cautious commitments to "anticipate," to "impress," to "improve gradually and steadily."

A once confidential letter from Ambassador Matsunaga to Ambassador Yeutter, however, was attached to the public treaty.[38] Its contents leaked to both the Japanese and the American press. The letter explicitly recognizes a 20% target for foreign semiconductor market share. It states: "The Government of Japan recognizes the US semiconductor industry's expectation that semiconductor sales in Japan of foreign capital-affiliated companies will grow to at least slightly above 20 percent of the Japanese market in five years. The Government of Japan considers that this can be realized and welcomes its realization."

A "recognition" of an "expectation" may not be a commitment, however. Also, the letter continues, "the attainment of such an expectation depends upon competitive factors, the sales efforts of the foreign capital-affiliated companies, the purchasing efforts of the semiconductor users in Japan and the efforts of both Governments." This clause leaves much room to maneuver if the target market is not met—and it would not be for quite a long period of time. The market access provisions of the agreement were mere political ruse, and the Japanese government really conceded only to take some actions to help the American semiconductor industry do business in Japan.

The Semiconductor Arrangement was harshly criticized by industrialists, economic journalists, and economists in the United States, Japan, and Europe. Critics charged that the treaty abrogated the principle of free trade and would lead to higher semiconductor prices, driving many small US users out of business. Furthermore, since Japanese firms increasingly dominated world semiconductor markets, they would reap the windfall profits from higher prices. Yet Japanese firms saw the outcome differently. *Nihon Kenzai Shimbun*, Japan's *Wall Street Journal*, editorialized that the agreement would increase semiconductor production competition from South Korea and other nations.[39] Indeed, even some American semiconductor makers complained that the terms of the Arrangement weakened them against new South Korean competitors.[40]

The European Community, which had criticized the Arrangement consistently throughout the summer as news of its terms leaked out, charged that the agreement violated GATT law.[41] The EC took the agreement before GATT under Article XXII consultations. When this effort failed, the EC requested and received during spring 1987 a GATT dispute settlement panel under Article XXIII on Japanese implementation of the terms of the treaty, not the Arrangement itself. The GATT panel issued a report, adopted by the GATT Council in March 1988, that determined that the export-licensing scheme designed by MITI to prevent third-country dumping violated the GATT Article XI prohibition against quantitative restrictions. The panel, however, rejected the EC contention that the Japanese market access measures favored US products and thereby violated GATT Article I's MFN obligation.[42] The Semiconductor Arrangement language (excluding the "confidential" side letter) was too ambiguous to violate GATT MFN requirements. In June 1989, MITI reformed the third-country dumping monitoring system so that it would comply with GATT. The European Electronic Components Manufacturers Association filed an AD of its own against Japanese producers before the EC Commission in October 1986.[43]

Within weeks of agreement, several American semiconductor users complained to Secretary of Commerce Baldrige that DRAM prices were rising steeply—as much as 600%. By the end of September, American semiconductor makers alleged that at least one Japanese maker was dumping EPROMs in third-country markets.[44] Regarding DRAMs, in October DoC announced new "fair market" prices, taking 256K DRAMs from about $8.00 per unit to $2.50.[45] Regarding EPROMs, a consensus was building that Japanese dumping was common. Furthermore, US sales totals in Japan were not improving.

In January 1987, a senior official from USTR threatened the Japanese government with sanctions if its firms were not in full compliance with the Arrangement by 1 April 1987.[46] A month later, a sub-Cabinet-level interagency committee reporting to the Economic Policy Council recommended the imposition of trade sanctions if Japanese noncompliance with the Arrangement persisted.[47] At the end of March, the Economic Policy Council recommended and the President announced trade sanctions in retaliation against Japanese noncompliance with the market access and third-country dumping provisions of the Semiconductor Arrangement.[48] Valuing the noncompliance at $300 million, the President imposed 100% tariffs on Japanese television sets, laptop computers, disk drive units, stereo equipment, and other consumer goods. Some of the sanctions (described as $51 million worth) were removed before the Venice Group of 7 summit meeting during the summer.[49] In November 1987, convinced that third-country dumping had ceased, the Reagan administration removed another $84 million in sanctions.[50] The remaining sanctions were not removed until August 1991, when a new Semiconductor Arrangement was negotiated.[51]

US sales in Japan in the fourth quarter of 1989 amounted to only a 12.9% market share. Bilateral discussion mandated by the 1986 Arrangement, the US-Japan Semiconductor Trade Talks, were held in April 1990.[52] The US negotiators complained about the low market share. The Japanese government's view was that it had implemented the terms of the Arrangement. Since it denied the existence of the side letter, it needed only comply with the modest terms of the Arrangement itself. Seeking to deploy the stall strategy yet again, the Japanese proposed that a study group be created to suggest ways of increasing sales in Japan. In summer 1991, the 1986 Arrangement expired. By then, American semiconductor sales in Japan (according to the US formula) had risen during the five years of the treaty from 10% to 13%.[53] Bilateral negotiations resulted in a new five-year agreement, which reiterated the goal of a 20% market share.[54] But the emphasis in the new agreement was quite different. The two governments emphasized private-sector cooperation in the form of "design-ins" by Japanese users of American chips. The important negotiations were really between the old opponents—the Semiconductor Industry Association and the Electronics Industries Association of Japan—and the governments were mere surrogates. They agreed to cooperate toward long-term buyer-supplier relationships. The 20% market share target was met briefly in the fourth quarter of 1992, only to decline each quarter in 1993 to 18.1%.

KOREA INSURANCE

In 1985, as an element of President Reagan's new unilateral trade policy, USTR self-initiated Section 301 investigations against the Republic of Korea for its policies on insurance and intellectual property. USTR announced that it was taking the action because "the Government of the Republic of Korea has restricted the ability of foreign insurance providers to offer their services in the Korean market under the same terms and conditions as those applicable to Korean insurance providers."[55] Two American insurance companies (American International Group and Cigna)[56] charged the Koreans with violating the national-treatment clause of the Treaty of Friendship, Commerce, and Navigation between the United States of America and the Republic of Korea.[57] They alleged that Korea had failed to comply with bilateral agreements reached in 1981 on access to Korean insurance markets[58] and had "engaged in systematic harassment [of the American companies], hindering [their] business activities in Korea." The American companies claimed that Korean government regulations prohibited them from competing in the life, compulsory, and fire insurance markets. They claimed that they had possessed licenses to carry on business in Korea since the 1960s but had been denied licenses to sell life insurance. They asserted that life insurance accounted for three-quarters (about $70 billion in 1985) of the total Korean insurance market. Similarly, the American companies claimed that they had been denied licenses to sell nonautomobile compulsory insurance. They contended that compulsory insurance, i.e., insurance required of Korean citizens as a matter of national public policy, was in itself a significant portion of the total Korean insurance market. Furthermore, because compulsory and noncompulsory insurance are generally purchased together, "few Koreans are willing to purchase their compulsory insurance from an indigenous Korean company and then separately purchase their additional non-compulsory insurance from [American firms]." "Therefore," the American insurers concluded, "a license to issue any particular type of non-compulsory insurance is not terribly valuable as long as [the American firms] are prohibited from writing compulsory insurance." The American companies noted that the Korean government had agreed in the 1981 agreement to end the Korean firm monopoly on the sale of fire insurance. They complained that the liberalization had been thwarted by the close business relationships among Korean insurance companies and banks. Korean banks, according to American firms, "directed" their customers to purchase fire insurance on their property from Korean companies. The American firms charged that the Korean government had tolerated this discriminatory business behavior, and requested that USTR promptly initiate "diplomatic consultations with the Korean government in order to resolve this matter in an expeditious and amicable fashion."

The American insurance companies doing business in Korea had filed a Section 301 complaint with USTR against the Korean government in 1980.[59] The companies withdrew the complaint only after bilateral government-to-government agreement. As time went on, however, they were satisfied neither with the business climate that remained after the agreement nor, indeed, with Korean compliance with the agreement. The American insurance industry pressed USTR and the administration hard on Korean barriers.[60] In the highly charged US domestic trade policy milieu that enveloped the White House and USTR in late summer and early fall 1985, USTR self-initiated Section 301 investigations against Korea for policies and practices regarding insurance and intellectual-property rights. At the time of the decision to self-initiate, US and Korean trade negotiators were also discussing Korean trade policies and practices regarding textiles, cigarettes, computers, beef, aviation, tariffs, and general market access. In the eyes of many Americans, Korea had come to be seen as a second Japan, a "Korea Inc." A former Assistant Secretary of State for Economic and Business Affairs, Robert Hormats, captured the mood of the time:

> The incorrect feeling on the part of some people is that we can't do too much about Japan now, but we're going to hold down some of the smaller countries to prevent them from becoming the Japans of the twenty-first century. In a very tragic sense, a lot of smaller countries are getting caught up in US-Japan bilateral trade tensions. But, unlike Japan, the smaller East Asian countries are not striving for self-sufficiency in manufacturing.[61]

Only days before the USTR announcement of the self-initiation, the Korean Ministry of Finance announced that it would gradually open the fire insurance market to foreign firms, though it admitted that a detailed liberalization plan would not be announced until the end of the year.[62] The Finance Ministry also noted that it would send representatives to the Philippines, Hong Kong, and Singapore to investigate the impact in those countries of foreign insurance company activity.

A delegation representing the Korean insurance industry, including Finance Ministry officials, firm executives, and Washington attorneys, met in Washington with USTR and American industry representatives about a month after the Section 301 announcement.[63] The American industry representatives pointed out that the Korean practices violated bilateral national-treatment obligations, and stated its position: national treatment for nonlife insurance by 1986 and for life insurance by 1987 or 1988. The US industry also raised the possibility of a US company purchasing equity in a Korean insurance firm to gain additional market access. The USTR representatives stressed to the Korean delegation that domestic political pressures about trade problems were strong and that the Koreans risked loss of merchandise if they failed to open their insurance markets to US trade and investment.

The Korean delegation urged a quick end to the investigation because their insurance markets were small and unprofitable. They maintained that too much competition would be "destructive" to the infant Korean insurance industry and that if USTR pushed them to open insurance markets further, more competition would come not only from American firms but from Japanese firms as well. In a written submission, the Korean negotiating team (with the help of its Washington-based trade lawyer) argued that the Korean government had already taken extensive measures to open its merchandise markets, despite domestic political opposition and foreign exchange needs to service its foreign debt. They emphasized that Korea remained a developing country in need of capital for investment and that Korea's insurance industry supplied an important portion of the country's capital needs. They pointed to extensive foreign-investment policy liberalization and cited evidence that American companies had profited by these policy changes. They noted that the Ministry of Finance had begun to liberalize its service sectors, including banking. But, they also asserted that further Korean service trade policy change should take place in the multilateral GATT Uruguay Round MTN forum, not in USTR's Winder Building home.[64] They reminded USTR that the Korean government had instituted several insurance market liberalization policies since the 1981 bilateral agreement, including allowing US insurance firms already selling on the Korean market to sell marine insurance, noncompulsory fire insurance, noncompulsory automobile insurance, and, as of July 1985, compulsory automobile insurance.

The Koreans urged USTR to consider the US security relationship with Korea:

> Korea remains threatened militarily by the forces of North Korea—a nation that spends approximately 25 percent of its GNP to maintain a 750,000 man army that outnumbers the forces of the Republic of Korea by nearly 50 percent. As a result, working in close cooperation with the United States, Korea shoulders a heavy burden for regional security requirements, devoting fully 6 percent of its GNP to defense expenditures.[65]

All of the Korean arguments were ad hominem policy defenses, for the Korean government had no legal defense for its policies. On the other hand, the Korean rebuttal that service market concessions should be made in the multilateral GATT forum, not bilaterally, was arguably meritorious. Nevertheless, American insurance companies' desire to expand their Korean (and generally their East Asian) operations, the charged milieu of the dispute, and USTR's ambitious multilateral agenda for services rule creation made the demand for Korean trade policy change of high salience to the American negotiating team. USTR, justifying its action by contending that the Korean practices violated bilateral national-treatment obligations under the FCN treaty and that governing GATT rules would be under negotiation in the Uruguay Round Multilateral Trade Negotiations, threatened the Korean government with the loss of American manufactured-goods export sales.[66]

By summer 1989, ten US and third-country insurance firms had opened joint ventures in the Korean market, a market by then valued at over $200 billion and growing at a 40% per annum pace. By 1991, thirteen foreign insurance companies from five countries were doing business in Korea, including the American companies Prudential, Aetna, Metropolitan Life, Allstate, Connecticut Mutual, and Mutual Benefit.[67]

KOREA INTELLECTUAL PROPERTY

Simultaneously with the Section 301 self-initiation against Korean insurance policies, USTR self-initiated negotiations on Korean intellectual-property policies and practices. The protection of intellectual-property rights had become by 1985 an important priority for trade policymakers in the executive branch and the Congress. They believed that foreign infringement of American copyrights, patents, and trademarks stripped US firms of their primary competitive advantage—their ideas—and reduced both American exports and domestic employment. The trade bills that proliferated in the Congress during this period extensively addressed intellectual-property issues. Indeed, the 1984 Trade and Tariff Act conditioned GSP benefits to developing countries on the protection of US intellectual-property rights. Later, IPR was placed high on the Uruguay Round agenda at the behest of USTR, and the 1988 Trade Act's "Special 301" provision would mandate even greater scrutiny of foreign intellectual-property practices by USTR.

At the prompting of industries injured by inadequate intellectual-property protection, such as pharmaceuticals, motion pictures, and book publishers, USTR negotiators conducted bilateral discussions over intellectual property with a number of developing countries, including Brazil, India, and Mexico, in addition to Korea. In August 1985, the Intellectual Property Alliance had submitted to USTR a comprehensive, country-by-country report on intellectual-property protection problems in developing countries and urged USTR to act to solve them.[68] In the Uruguay Round multilateral trade negotiations, the American objective was to draft new international law on intellectual property and to obtain developing countries' accessions to the new treaties. Hence, the negotiations with Korea were important both in themselves and as precedent for bilateral and multilateral negotiations with other developing countries.[69]

American pharmaceutical and chemical manufacturers asserted to USTR that a number of Korean government policies injured their business.[70] They complained that for chemical compounds, foods, and medicinal products, Korean patent law only protected the specific process for making the product, not the product itself. Since many pharmaceutical products can be readily manufactured by different processes, the patent protection was greatly reduced. They complained that the term of protection under Korean patent law was only twelve years from the time of publication and that since in the pharmaceutical industry the development period from discovery to market approval takes 10–12 years, the Korean patent term offered was "tantamount to no protection at all."[71]

American pharmaceutical and chemical manufacturers also complained that Korean trademark law protected only products that had been licensed to a Korean firm in a joint venture. Furthermore, some products, such as pesticides, were ineligible for trademark protection. American firms explained that the Korean courts offered little hope of redress for trademark infringements, as Korean judges employed a "famous in Korea" test for trademarks. The courts typically held that a trademark merited protection only if it was a trademark well known to Korean consumers. Hence, products new to the Korean market but already well known in other parts of the world were denied trademark protection. The Pharmaceutical Manufacturers Association pointed out that Korean court interpretation of Korean trademark law violated the Paris Convention for protection of industrial property, a treaty to which Korea had acceded in 1980.[72]

American industry expressed concerns about Korean policies and practices regarding technology transfers.[73] Technology transfers had been contingent on the approval of the Ministry of Finance. Finance had regularly rejected technology imports if they involved obsolete technology, right of monopoly sales, or licensing arrangements leading to excessive competition among domestic producers. A new Korean law had recently changed policy so that foreign technology importers would only have to report to, but not seek the prior approval of, the Ministry of Finance. American industry urged USTR to ensure that the de jure policy change would not be de facto thwarted by Finance's retained power to review each notification and to order an investigation.

USTR also received complaints about extensive copyright piracy of books, records and cassettes, films and videocassettes, and computer software.[74] The International Intellectual Property Alliance, a consortium of associations representing the publishing, music, motion picture, and software industries, charged that Korean copyright law offered little protection of foreign copyrights. These American industries asserted that they were losing in total about $150 million annually in Korean markets to pirated products and that the losses were increasing each year as the markets grew and as pirating practices became more prevalent. They pointed out that Korea was not a signatory to any multilateral treaty or to a US bilateral treaty that would protect foreign copyright holders. USTR was urged by the Alliance to press Korea to pass a new copyright law and to accede to international copyright agreements.

Bilateral US-Korean negotiations over intellectual property had been going on since 1983. The Korean negotiating position was that they had not yet reached a level of economic development sufficient to make intellectual-property protection a cost-effective government policy. Strong Korean domestic opposition to the enhancement of intellectual-property protection constrained the Korean government's flexibility in the negotiations.[75] The Korean book-pirating industry was large and possessed an extensive distribution network throughout Korea, and the government was especially sensitive to the political threat posed by college students, who would be seriously impacted by rising textbook prices if the pirating was curtailed.[76] The pharmaceutical and agricultural chemical industries opposed intellectual-property protection as well.[77] The large Korean conglomerates, the *chaebol*, took no visible position on the issue. But it is possible that some *chaebol* leaders agreed with the economic-development strategists in the government and in academia that Korea had to strengthen its intellectual-property policies if it was to remain internationally competitive in the long run, if not in the short run.

Because the Korean position had not wavered after two years of negotiation, USTR decided that the extra leverage of the Section 301 process was needed to resolve the dispute.[78] USTR announced the insurance and intellectual-property investigations against Korea on a Thursday; talks began at USTR the following Sunday.[79] The Koreans persisted then and for many months in their claim that their level of development remained too low to permit reform of their intellectual-property policies. The dispute became linked with the negotiations over insurance, and USTR threatened sanctions on Korean exports of footwear, tires, and electronics and the loss of GSP benefits. Nevertheless, in July 1986 and simultaneously with the insurance dispute, Korean and American trade negotiators settled the intellectual-property dispute.[80] The Ministry of Trade and Industry led the negotiations with USTR and within the Korean bureaucracy, with extensive involvement by the Patent Office of MTI. The agreement covered copyrights, patents, and trademarks.[81] The US threat was persuasive to MTI officials, whose constituency sold manufactured goods in the United States.

On copyrights, the Korean government agreed to draft and submit to its legislature a comprehensive copyright bill and to "exert its best efforts to ensure that the legislation is enacted so as to become effective no later than July 1, 1987." The Koreans also agreed to accede to the Universal Copyright Convention and the Geneva Phonogram Convention within 90 days of the effective date of the new copyright law, which would cover all the types of works enumerated in the UCC and explicitly recognize copyright protection for computer software. The new law would protect sound recordings for twenty years and publications for the life of the author plus fifty years. The Korean government pledged to "strengthen" penalties against copyright infringement, though "such penalties will be consistent with the nature and severity of penalties for other offenses under Korean law." For computer software, the Koreans pledged to implement simultaneously with the new copyright law a "Computer Program Protection Law." The software law would afford protection consistent with that offered other works. In addition, the Korean government agreed to "study the feasibility of extending copyright protection to data bases as compilations," "study the feasibility of extending protection to semiconductor chips," and "study satellite telecasts and cable TV, with a view toward protecting them under the new copyright law."

On patents, the Korean government committed itself to amend its extant patent law for chemical and pharmaceutical products. It pledged to introduce the new bill to the legislature by the end of September 1986 and to "exert its best efforts to secure enactment of the bill by the end of 1986." The new legislation would protect patents for fifteen years from the date of publication of the patent application. The Korean government also pledged to accede to the Budapest Treaty in 1987. The US and Korean negotiators addressed the crucial issue of retroactive coverage of chemical and pharmaceutical patents by agreeing that "through administrative guidance," i.e., bureaucratically but not legally, the Korean government would prohibit the manufacture and the marketing of "certain products" that had been patented in the United States after 1 January 1980, but not before the effective date of the new patent law. The treaty provided that the United States and Korea would agree on the products to be covered by this provision before the effective date of the new patent law.

On trademarks, the Korean government noted that it had already adopted and implemented guidelines prohibiting domestic firms from registering for trademarks that are identical to, or resemble, those owned by foreign firms, "regardless of whether the foreign mark is 'well-known' in Korea." The Koreans noted that September 1985 Ministry of Finance guidelines had ended the export requirement practice on trademark licenses. The Koreans stated that they had amended the Foreign Capital Inducement Act to remove the technology inducement as a condition for accepting applications for trademark licenses.

In the agreement, the Korean government pledged to enforce strictly protection for, and impose "effective penalties" against, violations of intellectual-property rights. It also agreed to make all administrative rules and regulations on intellectual-property rights transparent to the public. The two sides agreed to consult through the Korea-US Economic Consultation Trade Subgroup on the implementation of the agreement. With the signing of the agreement, USTR agreed to terminate the Section 301 investigation.

In February 1987, USTR announced guidelines that had been negotiated with the Korean government for the implementation of the treaty provisions on US pharmaceutical and chemical patents that predated the new Korean patent law.[82] American companies could have process patents pending with the Korean patents administrators amended to include product patent claims. Pharmaceutical and chemical products patented in the US between 1 January 1980 and 1 July 1987 (the effective date of the new Korean patent law) but never sold on either the Korean or the US market would be manufactured or marketed by Korean firms only with the permission of the US patent holder.

Despite Korea's intellectual-property laws and its accession to multilateral treaties, American pharmaceutical companies remained dissatisfied until early 1990 with the record of compliance with the 1986 US-Korea agreement. Squibb and Bristol-Myers filed Section 301 complaints with USTR.[83] They charged that Korean companies were pirating their products, often with the help of a Korean government-funded research center. European companies made similar complaints to their governments. A British company that held the patent rights to the AIDS drug AZT cried foul when a South Korean pharmaceutical company doing only US$4 million in sales per annum announced that it had independently developed AZT in less than a year.[84] The *Far Eastern Economic Review* reported that officials of the Korean company admitted privately that they "may have taken development shortcuts."

In June 1988, USTR announced that in lieu of a new Section 301 investigation into intellectual-property rights, it would carry out a fact-finding study jointly with the US Patent and Trademark Office on Korean intellectual-property policies and practices.[85] USTR took this action in order to permit Korea five months to resolve the problems with the pharmaceutical companies. It threatened that if Korea failed, it would reinitiate a Section 301 case.[86] The patent situation in Korea was continually monitored by USTR, the American Embassy in Seoul, and the American industries. Extensive copyright violations continued in Korea until late 1989/early 1990, according to the International Intellectual Property Alliance.[87] Korean attorneys hired by the Alliance, for example, discovered that Korean pirate publishers had put $2 million worth of textbooks on the Korean college market in February 1988. Pirating also continued unabated in videocassettes, records, and computer software. Korean enforcement efforts appeared to the Alliance to be minimal, and it urged USTR to pressure the Koreans to enforce the laws that had been promulgated to implement the 1986 agreement. As a result of this pressure, in May 1989 USTR placed Korea (along with Brazil, India, Mexico, China, Saudi Arabia, Taiwan, and Thailand) on its priority watch list of violators of intellectual-property rights under the Special 301 provision of the 1988 Trade Act.[88] Korea responded by creating an interagency enforcement coordination task force, by assigning special enforcement teams of police and prosecutors, and by vigorously raiding violators. The Korean government increased enforcement against violations of US copyright holders of films, records, pharmaceuticals, books, and software. In addition, the government submitted to its legislature intellectual-property reforms for enactment into law and pledged to submit semiconductor mask legislation in 1992. USTR, in recognition of these actions, downgraded Korea in November 1989 from a priority watch country to only a watch country, thus removing the immediate threat of trade retaliation.[89] By early 1990, patent compliance seemed to have improved considerably because of the actions of the interagency task force.[90] Book pirating appeared to have declined substantially by early 1990, but pirating of other items persists.[91]

CONCLUSION

For USTR, the leather, footwear, and tobacco disputes with Japan were about being an effective advocate for American industries that confronted barriers to export and about demonstrating to Congress and the public that the President was being "tough on unfair trading partners." The investigations and negotiations were about changing the Japanese political economy from capitalist developmental to something closer to liberal regulatory. The means to achieving that end were the elimination of quotas, the lowering of tariffs, and the elimination of distribution barriers. Success was achieved because the barriers were precisely identifiable, because governing GATT rules were clearly specifiable (thus indicating what Japanese policy ought to be), because the Japanese government possessed the capacity to change the policy, and because USTR possessed the power and the will to compel Japanese policy change. The semiconductor dispute was also about changing the Japanese political economy but not about the elimination of quotas and the lowering of tariffs. The barriers were not precisely identifiable, the GATT rules were ambiguous or nonexistent and the Japanese government may not have possessed the capability to change the behavior. American power and will were not in themselves enough.

The semiconductor dispute between the United States and Japan was not about government trade policy but industrial organization and corporate strategy. The Japanese producers of semiconductors were large, integrated firms that not only produced but also used semiconductors as inputs. They were multinational enterprises with global resource bases in capital, technology, and organization. As David Methe explains, the Japanese firms articulated and implemented a corporate strategy of self-sufficiency.[92] Self-sufficiency meant production vertically integrated into all aspects of DRAM production, and it meant multiple applications for every project. The result was superior transfer of product and process technologies across related products, shorter intervals between successor DRAM introductions, more reliable revenue streams, and lower risk. The philosophy behind the Japanese strategy was, When a new technology emerges, how vulnerable are we if we fail to enter the market? American firms, on the other hand, articulated and implemented a corporate strategy of specialization, with a focus on a single aspect of semiconductor production and with narrow applications for every project. The result was poorer transfer of product and process technologies across related products, longer intervals between successor DRAM introductions, less reliable revenue streams and higher risks. As the capital needs for competing in the industry skyrocketed in the 1980s, the Japanese firms were better positioned than the American firms to continue to innovate and produce. Since the half-dozen Japanese producers were linked closely with the users in the Japanese market either through the internal markets of intrafirm exchange or tight external markets of *keiretsu* relationships and since they possessed more or less equal market shares in the Japanese market, there was little room for any new competitor (foreign or domestic) unless the new competitor was producing a superior product—and the American firms were not. When the Japanese producers all greatly increased production in order to gain scale economies in their battle with each other, American and third-country markets were flooded with high-quality, lower-priced chips. American producers could not match the prices cuts, for they needed the revenue to fund R&D for production of the next-generation chip. Without the deep pockets of a Matsushita, a Toshiba, a Fujitsu, or an NEC, the American producers were doomed. For the Americans, it was "one bad quarter and you're out." The philosophy behind the American strategy was, When a new technology emerges, how much risk is there if we enter the market? Yet the irony was that the American strategy was a very risky strategy. The analysis of the Electronics Industries Association of Japan as presented to USTR in the 1985–86 negotiations was quite accurate.

USTR, then, was confronted with solving the competitive problems of a vital American industry without the policy means to do the job. The solution to competitive problems in the American industry involved industrial organization and corporate strategy, but USTR possessed only trade policy tools. It is easy to criticize the Semiconductor Arrangement for its inadequacies, but it is probably unfair to do so. Many of the negotiators for the semiconductor dispute also negotiated the well-drafted and successfully implemented settlements to the leather/footwear and tobacco disputes. In the leather/footwear case, USTR demonstrated that Japanese policy violated GATT, and certain of the legitimacy of its position, it pushed the Japanese government hard. In the tobacco case, USTR, having pressed the Japanese government for years to change their GATT-violating policies and having finally achieved most of these objectives, demanded national treatment with regard to a few remaining distribution and tax regulations and the elimination of a tariff. With the government regulations and the tariff, USTR could point to a "smoking gun." In the semiconductor case, USTR could point to no smoking gun. Hence, USTR could do no better than fashion an agreement that *might* enhance the commercial competitiveness of a vital US industry, even if it violated the spirit of the GATT.

In insurance, USTR was unilaterally attempting to strip the Korean government of an important financial policy of its capitalist developmental strategy. The Korean negotiating team on insurance was dominated by representatives of the Finance Ministry, with little role played by the Ministry of Foreign Affairs. A small number of Korean companies had for many years been a cartel, and both these companies and the Ministry of Finance wanted to maintain the cartel because of the tremendous capital reserves and investment power that these companies controlled. Yet behind the scenes, the Economic Planning Board, an economic-policy planning staff reporting to the President, asserted control over the insurance dispute in 1986.[93] The EPB representatives, representing views of the Ministry of Trade and Industry (which administered policy toward the manufacturing *chaebol* whose interests would be damaged severely by the threatened trade sanctions), forced policy change on the recalcitrant Finance Ministry. The Korean negotiators agreed in July 1986 to grant licenses to sell all types of insurance to American insurance companies and to ensure transparency of Ministry of Finance regulations on insurance.[94] The Korean policy change resulted from fear of American economic sanctions against Korean manufactured goods.[95] I could find no evidence that Korean policymakers were motivated by the noncompliance of their policies with the bilateral FCN treaty. This may be because the diplomats of the Ministry of Foreign Affairs played only marginally in the policy process in the dispute. (Indeed, the Foreign Affairs Ministry has taken the lead in bilateral trade negotiations only since about 1989.)[96] It is also possible that Korean policymakers truly did not want to open service markets unilaterally but only as part of reciprocal concessions in the then forthcoming Uruguay Round MTN. But all Korean interviewees emphasized to me that the Korean government had no GATT specialists during the mid-1980s and gave little consideration to GATT when making policy. During the late 1980s, the Korean Ministry of Trade and Industry established a GATT office and in 1992 increased the size of the office staff greatly.[97] The references in the bilateral negotiations to the Uruguay Round service negotiations were apparently mainly the work of the Korean government's Washington-based trade lawyers.

Though there were substantial problems with implementation and compliance in the intellectual-property dispute (see the next chapter), the agreement resulted in several multilateral treaty accessions by Korea and in Korean domestic intellectual-property rights policy becoming substantially compliant with the international intellectual-property rights regime. As a Korean government official remarked at the time of the insurance and intellectual-property agreements announcement, "Since there are few established rules in international trade covering service trade and protection of intellectual property, the issues . . . were extremely complex and technical when compared to the regime covering trade in goods."[98] The Korean government also attempted to sell the IPR agreement at home by contending that the agreement would enhance Korean economic growth by encouraging the development of innovation-based industries.[99] Nevertheless, many political and business leaders resented an agreement that they believed premature for Korea's level of development and that they believed they were blackmailed to accept.[100]

American power-oriented trade diplomacy will likely be a regular feature of international trade relations in the years to come, for the US is an ascending hegemon that seeks to transform the political economies of its trading partners to make them liberal regulatory, and it will take a good deal of unilateral trade diplomacy as well as bilateral, minilateral, and multilateral trade diplomacy to effect that end.

CHAPTER 6

Compliance with 301 Agreements

The East Asian states will comply with 301 settlement agreements, according to realist political economy, because they fear American trade power. The essence of the realist analysis of the problem of settlement agreement compliance is captured by Hobbes's statement that "covenants without the sword are but words." That is, states comply with or act in defiance of their international commitments as a matter of rational self-interest, and only threat or actual deployment of sanction can compel recalculation of that self-interest. In these cases within the Pacific economy, the East Asian states are always threatened by the American sword and ought, it follows, comply with 301 settlement agreements. But the puzzle addressed in this chapter begins with the empirical finding that two of the eight case studies did not receive substantial compliance with the settlement agreements (Korea intellectual property and Japan semiconductor), where "substantial compliance" means that the state completely or nearly completely implements the terms of the agreement. How can the variation in the outcomes be explained? Since the disputes were all negotiated at approximately the same time and supervised by the same Deputy US Trade Representative, we must explain why the same negotiators wrote agreements that would receive substantial compliance and agreements that would not.

RULE-ORIENTED TRADE DIPLOMACY AND COMPLIANCE

Liberal political economy, in contrast to realist political economy, predicts that substantial compliance occurs in cases of rule-oriented trade diplomacy and that there is great risk of noncompliance in cases of power-oriented trade diplomacy. The evidence of the nine case studies offers support for these propositions, for the two examples of noncompliance are cases of power-oriented trade diplomacy.

Liberal political economy explains the relationships between rule-oriented diplomacy and compliance and power-oriented diplomacy and noncompliance by pointing out that states comply for the same reasons that they generally comply with international laws in the first place. Louis Henkin explains that nation-states comply as a matter of routine with international law because compliance confers the benefits that led the state to sign the treaty and that states fail to comply when they determine that the benefits of noncompliance exceed the costs of noncompliance.[1] Robert Keohane adds that states routinely comply because regimes reduce the transaction costs of carrying out interstate relations.[2] These benefits confer incentives for reciprocity and a reputation for compliance. "A good reputation is like a capital asset: it will make it easier to enter future international agreements, at lower cost. States with bad reputations—like businesses with bad credit ratings—will have to pay more to enter into agreements."[3] Furthermore, states realize that since regimes are difficult to create, policymakers must take care not to allow regime decay or even ruin.

Nevertheless, experience shows that sovereign states assert noncompliance with international law as a necessary foreign-policy option. But international regimes can tolerate occasional violations of international law. When the noncompliant act leads to no injury or to only minor injury internationally, other states ignore the violation. For example, the Korean import ban on beef long violated the GATT Article XI prohibition against quantitative restraints. The Korean policy was not an international problem, however, until American, Australian, and New Zealand beef producers decided that they wanted to sell more beef on Korean markets. Beef exporters felt injured and asked their governments for help.

Compliance with international law may be divided conceptually into two forms: to comply with the law; to comply with the dispute settlement agreement. The first type of noncompliance, noncompliance with the law, is called first-order noncompliance by Roger Fisher.[4] The second type of noncompliance, noncompliance with the dispute settlement agreement, is called second-order noncompliance. Unless first-order noncompliance is so widespread that one wonders whether the law remains in force, this type of noncompliance poses no substantial problem for a regime. Evidence of second-order compliance, on the other hand, can be a significant problem for a regime because it leaves a regime participant injured, unhappy, and perhaps questioning the legitimacy of the regime. For this reason, second-order noncompliance is the more pressing policy problem of the two and, hence, for international-relations scholarship the more pressing research problem of the two.

Second-order compliance with international law is a special kind of social cooperation. Robert Axelrod, in his widely cited *Evolution of Cooperation*, finds that it is the iterative nature of social relations that prompts social actors to cooperate with each other.[5] When the game is to be played and replayed, actors find it in their self-interest to cooperate. When the game is to be played but once, they may find it in their interests not to cooperate. Axelrod and Keohane specify four crucial factors that lead national decision makers to calculate cooperative decisions: long time horizons, regularity of stakes, reliability of information about the others' action, and quick feedback about changes in the others' action.[6] International institutions—laws and governmental organizations—explains Harold Jacobson, create a more stable and predictable milieu for state decision making.[7] Indeed, they do so even for those who do not know well the other actors with whom they will interact and for those who doubt a "shadow of the future" exists for their interactions. In *Rules, Norms, and Decisions*, Friedrich Kratochwil explains that

> we need norms precisely for the reasons that many actors face each other in single-shot rounds and/or in the absence of sufficient information concerning each other's payoff structure. In other words, the interacting parties can often neither rely on a common history nor expect future gains. . . . Precisely for this reason, it is the function of norms to fortify socially optimal solutions against the temptations of individually rational defections. And it is precisely the internalization of the norms' generalized validity claim which bridges the gap among actors who know very little, or virtually nothing about each other. It is therefore more this generalized attitude—obviously counteracted by the incentives of defection—than specific utility calculations which explain why socialized actors follow rules.[8]

For Kratochwil, international laws and settlement agreements regarding laws influence national decision makers to comply, to cooperate.

AGREEMENT DRAFTING AND SURVEILLANCE

In bilateral trade dispute settlement in the Pacific, USTR negotiators seek a written, government-to-government agreement that states the terms of settlement. Text drafting is not mere "field cleanup by the lawyers" after the game is over; it is the crucial, decisive quarter of the game. The drafting of the agreement must be understood as the outcome of bilateral negotiations

Table 6.1   Trade Diplomacy Orientation and Settlement Agreement Compliance

	Compliance	*Noncompliance*
Rule-oriented Diplomacy	5	0
Power-oriented Diplomacy	1	2

Note: N = 8; there was no agreement in Taiwan footwear case.

between USTR and East Asian trade diplomats. In the eight cases studied here in which settlement agreements were drafted, six received substantial compliance. As summarized in Table 6.1, the settlement over footwear with Japan called for Japan to eliminate the import quota and phase in and lower tariffs, and it permitted the US to raise tariffs on Japanese leather exports as compensation. In the tobacco dispute with Japan, the agreement called on Japan to change distribution and tax procedures as well as lower tariffs on imported cigarettes. In the footwear dispute with Korea, the agreement called for customs procedure changes and the lowering of tariffs. In the insurance services dispute with Korea, the agreement called for granting licenses to foreign insurance companies to sell in Korea and for making the licensing procedures transparent. The agreement in the Korea beef dispute called for the Korean government to replace quotas with tariffs and for the US beef industry to offer technical advice to the Korean beef industry. In the rice dispute with Taiwan, the agreement stated that Taiwanese rice exports could go to small-country markets only. Five of the cases (all except Korea insurance) involved, or at minimum alleged, noncompliance with definitive rules of GATT: the Article XI prohibition of quantitative restraints, the Article III national-treatment demand, the Customs Valuation Code, and the Subsidies Code. The negotiators thus had internationally legitimate text to look toward for the drafting of the final settlement agreements. The settlement agreements were, in this way, the result of rule-oriented trade diplomacy and did not depend upon the American sword to ensure compliance.

Liberal political economy takes a lesson from the arms control treaty experience. The purpose of both trade dispute settlement negotiation and arms control negotiation is to change the vital national policies of a sovereign state. In both trade dispute settlement and arms control, negotiators aim to ensure that agreed-upon policy changes actually do occur. The arms control experience suggests that a treaty that meets with substantial compliance will possess the following characteristics: (1) the clear specification of expected behavior, (2) the adequacy of verification procedures in order to detect non-compliance, and (3) the existence of incentives for compliance.[9] An unstated premise of the arms control experience—the capacity of a government to implement its settlement commitments, i.e., its expected behavior—must be explicitly added as a condition for substantial compliance in bilateral trade dispute settlement agreements. The lessons on how to draft arms treaties that will receive substantial compliance have primarily been constructed on the experience of the Soviet Union and the United States. The governments of the Soviet Union and the United States in the post–World War II era have possessed the capacity to implement their settlement commitments. Bilateral trade dispute settlement, on the other hand, involves a greater risk of non-compliance by the governments involved than Soviet-American arms control; trade policy changes truly challenge national political capacity. (The breakup of the Soviet Union and end of the Cold War perhaps makes arms control more akin to trade dispute settlement: political capacity to implement agreement commitments cannot be assumed any longer.) Thus, the application of the arms control experience to bilateral trade dispute settlement agreements suggests that substantial compliance will likely be achieved under the following conditions: (1) expected behavior is clearly specified, (2) expected trade behavior is implementable, (3) effective monitoring procedures are provided in order to detect noncompliance, and (4) positive and/or negative incentives for compliance are offered.

The first condition—clear specification of expected trade behavior—was met by seven of the eight settlement agreements. For example, the Japanese government committed itself in the settlement agreement on tobacco to eliminate a tariff. The Korean government, in settling the insurance dispute, agreed to license foreign firms to sell certain types of insurance in Korea. The Taiwanese government committed itself to ensuring that Taiwanese rice would be exported only to small countries. Even the agreement that settled the dispute with Japan over semiconductor market access clearly specified the expected behavior. Only in the Korea intellectual-property settlement—a case in which substantial compliance did not occur—was expected behavior inadequately specified.

A trade negotiator explained "clear specification": "Clarity demands that you say 'two years,' not 'over a reasonable period of time.'"[10] The agreement between the United States and Korea on intellectual property, however, fails to meet that standard in some of its important provisions. On protection for sound recordings, the agreement states: "Protection of sound recordings . . .

against unauthorized reproduction, importation and distribution will be *strengthened* through *stricter enforcement* of Korea's Phonogram Law. . . . The ROKG will *strengthen* penalties against copyright infringement. . . . Through *administrative guidance*, printed materials copyrighted in the United States . . . will be prevented from unauthorized reproduction, publication, and distribution."[11] The agreement's treatment of patent and trademark issues is similarly ambiguous. Noncompliance occurred.

The second condition—expected trade behavior that can be implemented, i.e., the government possesses the political capacity to do what it has committed itself to doing—was also met in seven of the eight agreements. For example, in the footwear case the Japanese government committed itself to eliminate a quota, and in the tobacco case to eliminate a tariff. The expected trade behavior was implementable by the Japanese government. The agreement commitments in the other cases were also implementable by the East Asian governments. In the semiconductor dispute, however, the Japanese government ambiguously committed itself to helping US semiconductor producers garner 20% of the Japanese market. It is unclear whether the Japanese government possessed the authority to implement its commitment, for even its vaunted administrative guidance may be unable to force Japanese companies to change their purchasing and design-in practices by such a great amount. What is clear is that noncompliance occurred.

Because trade dispute settlement typically demands a policy change that creates domestic losers, governments may have strong incentives for noncompliance. Noncompliance can occur at lower levels of the government despite the best intentions of senior leaders. It is a phenomenon that Robert Keohane has called "involuntary noncompliance."[12] Although the government bureaucracies in Japan, Korea, and Taiwan are large and hierarchically ordered, the lower levels of the bureaucracy and the provincial and local government policymakers have ample discretion when implementing orders from the top.[13] Cases such as Korea intellectual property illustrate that even when political leaders intend compliance, a large bureaucracy must still be moved in support of the new policy.

The third condition—effective monitoring procedures for detecting noncompliance—was met in all cases. Even in the Japan semiconductor and Korea intellectual-property settlements, effective monitoring was provided. In arms control, the US government itself took primary responsibility for monitoring Soviet compliance with bilateral treaties through national technical means. It did so because it did not trust the multilateral institution, the International Atomic Energy Agency, to verify compliance competently. In much the same way, the US government must undertake responsibility for monitoring compliance with trade agreements. The GATT, in theory charged by its members with providing surveillance of national trade policies and compliance with GATT rules, in reality possesses weak surveillance and enforcement capability. Hence, in trade policy as in arms control, the United States provides unilateral surveillance to ensure treaty compliance.

USTR, unlike the Department of Commerce, has no staff officers whose mission is to ensure implementation of, and compliance with, trade agreements. Commerce has one person who does nothing but monitor Japanese compliance with the antidumping portion of the Semiconductor Arrangement. Nevertheless, even the relatively large Commerce Department relies heavily on US industry for monitoring help. For example, the Semiconductor Arrangement requires industry monitoring to ensure compliance; Commerce lacks access to information to guarantee compliance on its own. Thus, American business must actively monitor compliance with agreements that affect it. USTR has relied on the Semiconductor Industry Association, the Pharmaceutical Manufacturers Association, and the International Intellectual Property Alliance to detect noncompliance with the applicable settlement agreements.

The fourth condition—positive and/or negative incentives for compliance—was met to some degree in all cases. Because of the political and diplomatic asymmetry in the relationships between the East Asian governments and the United States, the East Asian governments in bilateral trade disputes always have a positive incentive to improve overall bilateral relations with the United States by signing and complying with a settlement agreement. They also have a negative incentive to sign and comply with an agreement: the threat of losing US markets. The East Asian states need unfettered access to large US consumer markets; thus, loss of these markets is a credible economic sanction. Furthermore, the East Asian states share with the United States the milieu goal of a strong, GATT-based liberal international trading system, because export-led economies depend upon open international markets. Thus, the East Asian states strengthen the GATT regime when they settle and comply with terms of agreements that put their trade behavior into compliance with GATT—second-order compliance. Yet, as Yoffie points out, cheating can be an effective tactic. Careful drafting can render cheating an impractical tactic.

Thus, two power-oriented trade diplomacy cases (Korea intellectual property and Japan semiconductor) did not receive substantial compliance because clear specification of expected trade behavior was not offered in the first instance and because the expected trade behavior could not be implemented in the second instance. The intellectual-property negotiations were difficult because there were no definitive GATT rules on intellectual property to serve the negotiators as internationally legitimate models. The semiconductor negotiations were difficult because there was no allegation of noncompliance with a GATT rule. The negotiators drafted a settlement agreement that was ambiguous enough for both sides to claim victory. They deliberately "papered over" a politically acceptable settlement agreement. One case (Korea insurance) did not involve GATT noncompliance (though it did allegedly involve noncompliance with a bilateral Treaty of Friendship, Commerce, and Navigation). Power-oriented trade diplomacy was more successful in the Korea insurance dispute, where the negotiators drafted an agreement that met all the conditions of good agreement drafting.

CONCLUSION

The risk of noncompliance, this chapter has shown, is great in a settlement agreement that is the outcome of power-oriented trade diplomacy. Since the negotiators do not have internationally legitimate rules to serve as models for the agreement text, the final settlement agreement may be ambiguous or unimplementable, and the respondent government does not feel concern for its reputation of compliance with international laws or the maintenance of international regimes. Disputes settled through rule-oriented trade diplomacy, on the other hand, possess internationally legitimate rules to guide the drafting of agreement text. Respondent states feel concern for international reputation and international regime maintenance.

Trade diplomats likely will get compliance with their settlement agreements if they draft agreements with the following characteristics: (1) expected behavior is clearly specified, (2) expected trade behavior is implementable, (3) effective monitoring procedures are provided in order to detect noncompliance, and (4) positive and/or negative incentives for compliance are offered. Careful rule-oriented trade diplomacy can render impractical the weak-state bargainer's tactic to cheat on treaty agreements. Thus, the puzzle of the compliance records in the eight cases studied here can be explained. It was not that some trade diplomats were incompetent drafters or that the same trade diplomats were sometimes incompetent.

Nevertheless, within rule-oriented trade diplomacy, research questions remain. The evidence here offers some support for the proposition that when GATT rules exist but are themselves ambiguous, the settlement agreement may be characterized by compliance patterns akin to power-oriented settlement agreements. Disputes such as the Japan tobacco case persisted over many years and were settled incrementally. The tobacco case concerned the demand for national treatment and allegations of unfair treatment in marketing and advertising and of noncompliance with the ambiguous obligations of GATT Article III. Additional research with larger data sets is needed to understand more fully the relationship between rule-oriented diplomacy and settlement agreement compliance.

CHAPTER 7

East Asian Political Economies and the GATT Regime

Some observers of international trade relations contend that the GATT regime is poorly suited to organizing trade between the political economies of East Asia and the rest of the world. They contend that the East Asian political economies operate fundamentally differently from the national political economies of North America and Europe and that the liberal GATT regime should be replaced with a managed-trade regime. Indeed, the rule-oriented and power-oriented trade diplomacy carried out by USTR as described in the previous chapters begs the question: what is the fit between the East Asian political economies and the GATT regime? In this chapter, analysis shows that the East Asian political economies have moved far toward compliance with extant rules of the GATT regime but that the extant GATT rules fall far short of effectively promoting cooperation, minimizing conflict, and settling commercial disputes between the East Asian political economies and the other countries of the world political economy. Nevertheless, since competitive advantage in East Asia today lies more in firm strategy and industrial organization than in state policy and since global interdependence is changing East Asian state policy preferences, the conclusion here is that the East Asian political economies are converging with the industrialized countries and that the GATT regime—with much additional rule creation—can adequately govern trade relations with Japan, Korea, and Taiwan.

The norms, rules, and procedures of the GATT regime are guided by six underlying principles: reduction of trade barriers, nondiscrimination, fair trade, multilateralism, reciprocity, and economic development. These principles guide the rules and operating procedures of the GATT regime. They date to the very founding of the regime at the Bretton Woods and Havana conferences of the 1940s, though their meaning and content have changed with the institution over the succeeding half century. They have afforded the enlargement of the regime to more than 100 members and growth of the regime rules. The GATT members wrote new rules on nontariff barriers in the Tokyo Round and on intellectual property, foreign direct investment, standards harmonization, and trade in services in the Uruguay Round. Nevertheless, the GATT regime's underlying principles bear the stamp of the original framers: American and British policymakers educated in neoclassical economic theory and steeped in internationalist commercial and diplomatic traditions. The East Asian political economies challenge these assumptions.

A principle underlying the GATT regime is that trade barriers should be reduced in the world economy. Motivated by the gains from free trade that Anglo-American comparative-advantage theory postulated, the American and British framers of the GATT committed contracting parties to eliminate quotas (with some exceptions) and to reduce tariff levels progressively. As discussed above in Chapter 3, however, the intellectual and policy commitment in East Asia to the reduction of trade barriers in the world economy has been limited. Still, as measured by quotas and tariff levels, overt trade barrier discrimination in Japan, Korea, and Taiwan has been reduced to levels generally consistent with industrialized-country practice. Barriers persist, especially in agricultural markets, but neither European nor North American policymakers can claim open agricultural markets.

Analysis of the Japanese, Korean, and Taiwanese political economies is made here with respect to the six GATT principles, and conclusions are drawn in this chapter with particular emphasis upon the evidence of the Super 301 (including satellites, supercomputers, and wood products), construction services, telecommunications, and Structural Impediments Initiative (SII) dispute settlement negotiations.

NONDISCRIMINATION PRINCIPLE

The nondiscrimination principle of the GATT regime is established in a number of rules, but most importantly in the Article I most-favored-nation (MFN) commitment and the Article III national-treatment commitment. The MFN and national-treatment commitments establish that GATT contracting parties will treat each other equally and will treat foreign business enterprises doing business in their markets no less well than they do domestic firms. But these are general commitments difficult to implement.

Unlike a commitment to eliminate a quota or lower a tariff, a commitment to offer national treatment runs afoul of national laws, government administrative acts, business norms, and cultural traditions. Nondiscrimination in trade policy is not achieved by the stroke of a pen on a multilateral treaty. The conflict between GATT multilateralism and national political economy is nowhere greater than in the nondiscrimination principle. Bilateral and multilateral trade conflict in the world economy often centers on issues associated with the nondiscrimination principle and rules. Since the Tokyo Round, the GATT contracting parties have attempted rule growth in order to minimize conflict in this area, including import and export licensing procedures, government procurement, health and safety standards and regulations, tax policies, state trading practices, and multiple exchange rate systems. Nevertheless, GATT members are currently challenged to extend the nondiscrimination principle through new rule making into trade in services. GATT/WTO negotiators likely will take up foreign direct investment and competition/antitrust policy later in the 1990s. Indeed, efforts regarding nondiscrimination will continue for a very long time: the reconciliation of differences in national political economies challenges policymakers intellectually and politically.

It is in health and safety standards and regulations, government procurement, service trade, investment, and competition/antitrust issues that the Japanese political economy poses the greatest challenge to the GATT regime. Health and safety standards and regulations in Japan have become an infamous symbol of Japan's resistance to imports. American makers of aluminum baseball bats tried without success in 1980 to get the Japanese baseball leagues to approve their bats for use in Japan.[1] The leagues refused, explaining that baseball conditions were unique in Japan and that Japanese players and spectators objected to the sound made by an aluminum bat making contact with a baseball. Negotiations including industry and government representatives from both countries left the dispute unresolved. A more recent US-Japan bilateral dispute—about wood products—highlighted similar problems.

Section 1302 of the 1988 Omnibus Trade and Competitiveness Act demanded that in 1989 and 1990 the Office of the US Trade Representative name priority countries imposing trade barriers that, if eliminated, "are likely to have the most significant potential to increase United States exports."[2] The legislation, the so-called Super 301 provision, prompted USTR to name Japan as an unfair trader (along with Brazil and India) in its policies on wood products, satellites, and supercomputers.[3] The dispute about wood products mainly concerned Japanese Ministry of Construction building codes and product standards, which discouraged the use of wood in Japanese homes and buildings, subsidized Japanese mills, and restricted access to distribution networks.[4] The American wood products industry is perhaps the world's most competitive. Despite the barriers it faced in Japan, American exporters nevertheless did more than $4 billion in sales in Japan. The Japanese response emphasized the volume of American wood products exports to Japan, which were described as "robust," "extraordinary," and "a shining star in the bilateral relationship."[5] The Japanese message was clear: The American industry already made a lot of money in Japan. What more did they want? The American response was equally clear: American wood products exporters could and should make much more money in Japan. Nearly a year of negotiations yielded a settlement agreement. The Japanese government agreed to change building codes to permit the use of wood products, to accept US wood-grading and product standards, and to change the tariff classifications of wood products from high to low tariff classifications.[6]

Product standards and regulations in Korea have similarly challenged the GATT regime. But again, American unilateralism has pushed Korean government policy toward nondiscriminatory policy. A May 1989 bilateral agreement (which resulted from Korean efforts to stay off the Super 301 priority unfair-trader list) requires Korean government ministries to accept internationally recognized standard and certification marks and to notify GATT of all new or amended trade-related standards and regulations that differ from international norms.[7] American and Korean negotiators have specified in some detail transparency requirements for regulations of the Ministry of Health and Social Affairs.

Discriminatory and/or nontransparent standards and regulations have become apparent in Taiwan as well and have recently been added to the agenda for US-Taiwan bilateral negotiations. Any Taiwanese accession to the GATT will also likely lead to Taiwanese policy change. Nevertheless, discriminatory regulations will likely become increasingly apparent as more foreign companies attempt to do business in Korea and Taiwan. Problems over standards and regulations, however, are not so vexing as to be unmanageable by the GATT regime. GATT rules are simply inadequately developed in this area. The general Article I commitment to provide national treatment is ambiguous; the Article X commitment to make standards, regulations, and administrative procedures transparent is insufficient. Though it will be an ambitious undertaking, the GATT members can write new rules concerning standards and regulations. (Uruguay Round negotiators took up food standards and regulations.) The negotiators may draw lessons from the experience of the European Community states, who have employed a mix of regulatory harmonization with mutual recognition.

Government procurement is similarly a problem area, despite the Tokyo Round Code. The Super 301 dispute on supercomputers and satellites, however, indicates solutions. USTR complained to the Japanese government that despite an 80% share of the world supercomputer market and a few sales in the Japanese private sector, American companies had sold only two supercomputers to Japanese government agencies.[8] Japanese government agencies, contended USTR negotiators, had grown accustomed to receiving deep discounts from Japanese supercomputer makers (as much as 80%). These agencies did not find it in their interests to change the bidding process such that they would be paying full price. The Japanese position in the dispute was predictable: The Japanese market for supercomputers was open and had been since 1975, when computer trade was liberalized.[9] On the other hand, admitted the Japanese, it was "true that government procurement prices, particularly those for universities, are low. This is principally due to budgetary constraints on and special characteristics of universities, whose purposes are education, research, and academic development."[10] The Japanese contradicted USTR's market share figures, claiming that of thirty-seven supercomputer purchases by government organizations (including NTT) and national universities, seven (19%) had been American machines. The Japanese charged that on the contrary, it was the American market that was closed to Japanese supercomputer makers. They cited government policies that prohibited non-American supercomputer purchases by the Defense Department, and government pressure that forced "a private university" (MIT) to cancel an agreement to purchase a Japanese-made supercomputer.

Both sides were right: there was no free trade in supercomputers. After much bitter negotiation, a settlement agreement was signed in March 1990.[11] The Japanese government agreed that its agencies would "throw out excessively low bids." Furthermore, the Japanese government agreed to publish the names of companies that made these low bids. The US government, for its part, made no commitment to change it policies on supercomputer procurement.

The satellite dispute was similarly a government procurement dispute. The American negotiators charged that Japanese government agencies and public corporations did not purchase foreign-made satellite equipment. But there was an important difference from the supercomputer case: the Japanese Ministry of Posts and Telecommunications had publicly announced in April 1984 that it would not permit the purchase of foreign-made satellites.[12] This prohibition included the two largest satellite users in Japan—the quasi-government NTT and NHK, the public radio and television network. Furthermore, MPT would not grant new licenses to foreign firms desiring to sell in the Japanese private market.

Conflict between the American and Japanese industries and governments over the latter's telecommunications policies had by the late 1980s become a hardy perennial, just as leather and tobacco had been during the 1970s and until the mid-1980s liberalization. The American telecommunications industry complained that NTT compliance with the bilateral agreement signed under the auspices of the MOSS (Market Oriented, Sector Specific) talks was low. In spring 1989, Motorola submitted a Section 301 petition to USTR alleging that MPT had not complied with the MOSS agreement.[13] The petition resulted in telecommunications being named as a priority practice in the Super 301 announcement of May and in a June concession by MPT to expand access to the mobile-telephone market in Japan.[14]

In April 1990, agreement was reached to bring Japanese satellite procurement policy into compliance with the GATT Tokyo Round Government Procurement Code and other GATT provisions.[15] The agreement opened NTT and NHK to American and foreign bidding on satellite procurement and provided for transparency in bidding procedures. The negotiators also agreed to meet to review implementation of the agreement annually. Hence, the satellite case shows that GATT rules merit more credit than they sometimes receive: noncompliance is a manageable problem for the GATT regime. The supercomputer case, on the other hand, illustrates that Japanese business practices differ from North American and European norms. Business practice issues receive more discussion below.

Trade in services was not covered by the GATT until the recent Uruguay Round General Agreement on Trade in Services (GATS). GATS fills a critical gap in the GATT regime, for services have become by many measures a significant portion of the world economy. State policies on services, however, present substantial barriers to international service businesses. Building on rules and norms extant in bilateral treaties of friendship, commerce, and navigation and in multilateral OECD and UNCTAD agreements, GATS follows the model of the GATT, including the underlying principles, the rules of behavior, and dispute settlement procedures. The GATS negotiators have been especially challenged to resolve problems in national treatment, transparency of regulations, government procurement and public monopolies, market access, and dispute settlement. All this must be done in terms of the different competitive characteristics and policy milieus of the various service sectors—financial, insurance, telecommunications, transportation, construction, etc. It is an ambitious undertaking.

Bilateral US-Japan negotiations have contributed to this process. As the result of negotiations with USTR, legal-services markets in Japan began to be opened in the late 1980s.[16] Also, Congress demanded in Section 1305 of the 1988 Trade Act that USTR initiate an investigation of Japanese government policies on American architectural, engineering, and construction services.[17] In November 1988, USTR formally initiated an investigation and negotiations with the Japanese government regarding construction (as well as architectural and engineering) services.[18] Complaints from the American construction industry, however, were not new, and USTR and Commerce Department negotiators had discussed the issue with Japanese Ministries of Construction, Transportation, and Foreign Affairs officials before the November initiation. A previous round of negotiations had ended in May 1988 with a bilateral agreement, known as the Major Projects Arrangement, aimed at providing greater transparency in bidding procedures for the $7 billion Kansai International Airport construction project as well as other large projects.[19]

The May 1988 agreement was only a beginning, not an ending, of a process to widen access to public construction projects in Japan. Negotiations in 1989 led to Japanese government commitments to curtail collusive bidding and facilitate the issuance of architectural licenses, as well as to other policy changes.[20] But complaints to the Department of Commerce and USTR from American construction, architectural, and engineering firms continued, especially about the airport project.[21] Formal consultations on the implementation of previous agreements were due to begin in December 1990. American bargainers came to these meetings with enhanced credibility, provided by two pieces of legislation, passed by Congress during 1990, that demanded retaliatory sanctions if construction services access problems continued.[22]

In December 1990 and January 1991, negotiators made little progress, but President Bush and Congressional sponsors of the legislation agreed to extend the deadline as a quid pro quo for a Japanese commitment to provide financial support for the Gulf War.[23] Negotiations continued throughout the spring, with a settlement finally coming shortly before the midnight, 1 June 1991, deadline, when sanctions would be imposed. Representatives from the Ministries of Foreign Affairs, Construction, and Transportation agreed to open seventeen extant and six future public construction projects to American company bidding. American negotiators noted that the agreement doubled the number of public projects in Japan upon which American firms could bid.

Many Korean government procurement policies are also inconsistent with GATT rules. Korean negotiators have agreed with representatives of the US Trade Representative's Office to open government procurement to foreign bidders. Negotiations have been coordinated with the June 1990 pledge made by the Korean government to accede to the Tokyo Round Government Procurement Code. Within the context of the GATT negotiations, Korean negotiators have agreed to open some (but not all) telecommunications procurements of the Ministry of Communication and the Korean Telecommunications Authority.[24] Taiwan, on the other hand, overtly contravenes GATT rules: Taiwanese laws require all ministries and public corporations to buy domestically when possible.[25] This policy will be an important issue on the agenda in a GATT accession negotiation.

Concomitantly with the Super 301 investigations against Japanese policies on supercomputers, satellites, and wood products, USTR announced that it would carry on long-term, wide-ranging bilateral negotiations with the Japanese government, to be called the Structural Impediments Initiative.[26] The Structural Impediments Initiative (SII) was a sea change in American trade unilateralism and bilateral dispute settlement. It was an unprecedented attempt to resolve fundamental issues of national political economy. The US-Japan Working Group said its mission was to "identify and solve structural problems in both countries which stand as impediments to trade and balance of payments adjustment."[27] SII was an American initiative, but the effort became a forum for both sides to press for policy changes in each other.

Initial meetings in fall 1989 resulted in the identification of two sets of issues for negotiation. The Japanese named a broad array of American policies: savings and investment patterns, corporate investment activities and supply capacity, corporate behavior, government regulations, research and development, export promotion, education and workforce training. The Americans named a broad array of Japanese policies: savings and investment patterns, land use, distribution systems, exclusionary business practices, keiretsu relationships, and pricing mechanisms. Both sides identified quite specific policies. For example, the Japanese pointed to the benefits to the US economy and business competitiveness of a lower capital gains tax, the reform of certain antitrust laws, the reform of product liability laws, and the adoption of the metric system. The Americans identified suggested reform of the consumer credit system in order to spur domestic consumption, reform of the land taxation system, rationalization of the official assessment of land values, which inflated their values, and deregulation of distribution under the Large-Scale Retail Store Law, which preserved the dominance of small, mom-and-pop retailers throughout Japan. Unlike previous bilateral dispute settlement, the negotiators neither alleged that a domestic industry needed protection from foreign competition nor that a foreign government was violating GATT law with protectionist domestic policies of its own. Officials at USTR understood the step that had been taken by the two countries:

> We should emphasize at the outset, as we always have, that SII is a unique bilateral undertaking between sovereign governments and is an iterative process. It has, therefore, no set patterns of benchmarks. Many changes will take time to implement; and many changes, when implemented, will take time to show up in the trade balance. The results of these improvements in market access, however, should be felt relatively quickly by US industries.[28]

In summary, the Americans agreed to reduce the size of their government deficit, lower the capital gains tax, liberalize import restrictions on steel and machine tools, encourage private savings and reduce consumer debt, increase spending on education, and maintain liberal FDI (foreign direct investment) policies. The Japanese, in summary, agreed to reform their land policies, make their standards and certification procedures more transparent, increase spending on infrastructure (such as housing, roads, airports, and customs processing centers), modify distribution systems, and ease FDI laws. Each offered to the other an ambitious wish list that, if implemented, would please many people on *both* sides of the Pacific. The American "commitments" have been urged by many Americans, and the Japanese "commitments" have been urged by many Japanese.

Thus, bilateral and multilateral efforts are slowly leading the service policies of the East Asian states toward emerging norms of behavior in the world economy. The GATT regime, with the commitment of the GATT membership, appears to be capable of ensuring that service sector policy in East Asia substantially meets the demands of international service business.

Japan was by state policy substantially closed to foreign direct investment before 1980.[29] The 1980 Foreign Exchange and Foreign Trade Control Law, however, liberalized foreign investment to allow wholly owned subsidiaries as well as joint ventures. Before 1980, Japanese law forbade investment unless special, case-by-case governmental approval was offered; after 1980, Japanese law accepts investment with only case-by-case governmental disapproval. Of course, Japanese ministries, e.g., Ministry of Finance and MITI, possess broad discretion to review, impede, or deny particular foreign direct-investment transactions. But though the horror stories of the 1960s and 1970s chilled the desire of many outsiders to attempt investment into Japan, it appears that investment regulations are not a major barrier to access. A recent study by the American Chamber of Commerce and A. T. Kearney Company, management consultants, indicated that the chief problems confronted by investors doing business in Japan were (1) the high cost of business, (2) staffing problems, (3) business complexity, (4) the time needed to become profitable, and (5) the lack of understanding of Japan.[30] Indeed, some American firms—Avon, Chrysler, General Motors, CBS, Honeywell— have *sold* Japanese investments not because they were losing money but because their corporate parents needed the cash.[31] Investors, however, do complain about "business complexity" in Japan, which means the *keiretsu* business networks and the arcane morass of distribution networks.

The *keiretsu* business networks are descendents of the massive prewar conglomerate *zaibatsu* business enterprises. The *zaibatsu* were large, privately owned enterprises that conducted business in many different markets, from banking to all types of manufacturing. This handful of companies dominated the prewar Japanese economy with guidance from the state. General MacArthur and the American occupiers took steps to break up the *zaibatsu* in order to introduce more competition into Japanese markets.[32] The breakup did introduce more competition, but old relationships persisted in external markets as they had in internal markets: The *zaibatsu* became the six major horizontal *keiretsu* networks: Mitsui, Mitsubishi, Sumitomo, Fuyo, Dai-ichi Kangyo, and Sanwa.

Each horizontal *keiretsu* network includes several dozen company members. The members include a large bank, financial institutions (such as insurance companies), large manufacturing companies, and a big general trading company. The companies are linked with each other through equity ownership, interlocking directorships, capital flows, and firm-to-firm communication and cooperation. Roughly 30–40% of the capital needs of the large manufacturing firms are met by the financial institutions of the *keiretsu*.[33] The *keiretsu* relationships in Japan are vertical as well as horizontal. The large manufacturing enterprises, such as Toyota, Nissan, Sony, and Hitachi, carry out most of their downstream and upstream business transactions with distributors and suppliers with whom they have long conducted business. Together, horizontal and vertical *keiretsu* networks still dominate the Japanese economy. Explains Michael Gerlach:

> The majority of these firms rank among Japan's largest industrial, financial, and commercial enterprises. While representing only about 10 percent of the industrial firms listed on the Tokyo Stock Exchange, as of

the late 1970s, firms formally affiliated with one of the big-six groups controlled between 43 and 56 percent of total sales in natural resource sectors (oil, coal, and mining), in primary metals (ferrous and non-ferrous metals), and in cement, chemicals, and industrial machinery. Among financial institutions, commercial and trust banks affiliated with these six groups controlled 40 percent of total bank capital, and insurance companies 53–57 percent of total insurance capital. In real estate, 55 percent of total business was controlled by group members, while in distribution 67% of sales was accounted for by formal *keiretsu* member companies, primarily through general trading companies. These percentages exclude financial and industrial firms in smaller city-bank groups, such as Daiwa, Kyowa, and Tokai, as well as the many companies affiliated with the Industrial Bank of Japan. In addition, they ignore the share of sales accounted for by the extensive network of satellite and subsidiary firm group companies control that are not consolidated in their own sales figures. Toshiba alone has about 200 related companies in Japan and below those are another 600 "grandchild" companies.[34]

Thus, concludes Gerlach, "the reality of contemporary Japanese industrial organization is neither complete openness nor complete insularity. Rather, it is a complex middle ground based on *preferential* trading patterns which rely on probabilistic rather than deterministic measures and models."[35] The *keiretsu* networks advantage Japanese business enterprises by (1) minimizing the risk of outside takeover (as T. Boone Pickins discovered),[36] (2) affording easier access to capital with less concern for quarterly profits or quick return on investment, (3) promoting intragroup cooperation and coordination in R & D, new ventures, and marketing, (4) ensuring markets, and (5) providing insurance against failure or bankruptcy (such as the recent de facto takeover of Subaru by Nissan).[37]

These established relationships, it must be stated, are hard for *any* business firm—foreign or Japanese—to break into. The barriers to entry in the Japanese market are high. And competition amongst the *keiretsu* is vicious. Thus, government policy in the form of competition policy cannot offer an easy, satisfactory fix. Nevertheless, government policy can create more competition in specific ways. In order to determine precisely how, we must delineate the three types of *keiretsu* relationships—horizontal, vertical production supply, vertical consumer distribution.

Antitrust law was unknown in Japan until the American occupying force imposed it in 1947. Cartels and monopoly behavior were, until that time, not only tolerated but even encouraged. The new law was enforced for about five years, resulting in the breakup of the *zaibatsu* and the fostering of aggressive competition among the horizontal *keiretsu*. But antitrust law lapsed into disuse until the mid-1970s, and other competition problems emerged.[38] There was little commitment to free-market ideology and to consumer interests but much commitment to the capitalist development state within global markets and to producer interests. Conflict between MITI, the institution of industrial policy, and the Japan Fair Trade Commission, the institution of competition policy, was invariably won by the former.

Vertical control of the consumer distribution networks by the automobile, consumer electronic, cosmetic, pharmaceutical, camera, and newspaper industries ensures that everyone in the supply distribution chain of a *keiretsu* makes a profit. The arcane laws on retail distribution ensure that competition for the consumer's yen does not become too intense. Furthermore, distribution system control by the Japanese manufacturers ensures that imported consumer goods are introduced only as exotic luxury goods with extraordinarily high markups.[39] "[T]here is little doubt," says Kozo Yamamura, "that the control exerted by large manufacturing firms has been and continues to be an effective means to force Japanese consumers to subsidize the international competitiveness of large manufacturing firms."[40] As a result, firms up and down the vertical-supply *keiretsu* are assured of profits.

Enforcement of Japanese competition policy could help promote more competition in both the vertical-supply *keiretsu* relationships and the vertical consumer distribution *keiretsu* relationships. Deregulation of consumer distribution would force more price competition on the manufacturers, thus compelling cost reductions throughout the vertical-supply networks and encouraging new competition throughout the chain. On vertical-supply *keiretsu*, Article 19 of the Antimonopoly Law prohibits unfair business competition that unjustly discriminates against other entrepreneurs, unreasonably induces or coerces customers to deal with oneself, unreasonably uses bargaining power in dealing with another firm, or unjustly advantages transactions between firms that share officers or shareholders.[41] The policy tools of change, therefore, do exist but must be used and developed judicially and administratively.

Yet, as Ken-Ichii Imai opines, outsiders can and do break into these vertical production supply *keiretsu* relationships. Masahiko Aoki points out the central logic of supplier relationships: Bargaining power depends upon the control of information, the control of technology.[42] The controller of information can bargain effectively within the *keiretsu*. Foreign firms must understand this logic and act upon it. The solutions to the problems posed by Japanese industrial organization lie more in American industrial organization and corporate strategy than in government policy.

The Korean government has substantially opened its markets to foreign direct investment. By January 1992, about 98% of manufacturing sectors and 62% of service sectors had been opened.[43] Much of this trade policy change came in the 1989 Super 301–motivated bilateral agreement with the United States. And, since 1989, local-content, transfer, and technology-licensing performance requirements are no longer a condition of investment. Indeed, the case-by-case FDI investment approval process will be phased out in January 1993 and supplanted with a notification requirement.[44] Taiwan has similarly removed many FDI barriers and abolished export performance and local-content requirements.[45] Some market sectors remain protected, including power generation, petroleum refineries, railroads, trucking, telecommunications, defense, securities, and insurance.

The Korean *chaebol* (*zaibatsu*-like, i.e., similar to the predecessors of the Japanese *keiretsu*) are coming under increasing scrutiny in the world economy and in Korea. Foreign companies will increasingly seek to sell to companies within *chaebol* and may find that it is quite difficult to break in. An American-inspired Monopoly Regulation and Fair Trade Act exists in Korean law but is not enforced.[46] Despite the lack of *keiretsu*-like business relations in Taiwan, we can expect that the nationalistic business culture in Taiwan will increasingly lead to complaints from foreign companies that marketing in Taiwan is difficult. We can expect, then, that Taiwanese and Korean business practices will challenge international rule writers. Ultimately, however, corporate strategy and industrial organization will, as in the case of Japanese *keiretsu*, do more than government commercial diplomacy can.

FAIR-TRADE PRINCIPLE

Fair trade is a principle underlying the GATT regime. The principle is probably rooted in the Anglo-American common-law notions of equity, of fair business practices, and of property rights. Equity is a concept traceable through medieval European law to Aristotle, who said it meant a "correction of legal justice."[47] He pointed out that the law is not always fair. "The reason is that all law is universal but about some things it is not possible to make universal statement which shall be correct." That is, a legal rule—such as the law of GATT—aims at generalizing for an indefinite number of cases and does not permit the exception. The fair-trade principle of GATT offers equity in the form of exceptions to GATT rules such as balance of payments (Article XII), security (Article XXI), emergency safeguard (Article XIX), and general (Article XX). The fair-trade principle also encompasses a notion of fair business practices, for example, that it may be (under certain circumstances) unsporting for firms to dump goods in foreign markets at less than normal value and for governments to subsidize their firms. Finally, the fair-trade principle affords the opportunity to write rules on intellectual property within the GATT regime. Intellectual-property rights rules were negotiated in the Uruguay Round.

Some academic, business, and public-policy leaders, however, contend that the East Asian political economies challenge the fair-trade principle of the GATT regime. Japan especially, some say, is a mercantilist state employing a deliberate industrial policy of targeting that contravenes the spirit and rules of the GATT regime. States Marie Anchordoguy:

> Whether it is government subsidization of Japanese firms in the form of financial aid, protectionism, or the encouragement and tolerance of cartels, or it is the transfer of wealth from Japanese citizens to industry in the form of high consumer prices or saver-subsidized low-cost capital, the effect is the same: Japanese producers are given powerful weapons to compete in international competition, weapons that handicap the battle in Japan's favor.[48]

Anchordoguy concludes:

> If Japan sees the maintenance of the free-trade system as in its self-interest (and it should as long as the United States and Europe are key markets), it must change some of its policies and institutions. Their comprehensiveness and consistency work in ways that create an uneven playing field. This sense of unfairness makes it increasingly difficult for the United States to get popular support to stave off protectionist sentiment in the country and to support the liberal economic order.

Indeed, Japanese government targeting is not the fiction of a hack writer. The industrial policy of the Japanese developmental state has targeted apparel, steel, shipbuilding, automobiles, machine tools, computers, consumer electronics, semiconductors, and telecommunications.[49] This is true even if the targeting of pharmaceuticals, chemicals, and commercial aircraft has (so far, anyway) failed[50] and even if (as I believe) Japanese competitiveness ultimately owes to industrial organization and corporate strategy, not government policy. The Koreans and the Taiwanese have followed the Japanese industrial-policy model. They have targeted the same industries, using quite similar policy tools.[51]

Yet, it is easier for government policymakers to target for their economies the industries that have historically been shown to be critical to the development of the great industrial powers of the nineteenth and twentieth centuries (apparel, steel, automobiles, machine tools, consumer electronics, computers) than it is to forecast industries critical to continued economic growth in the twenty-first century. Furthermore, as Okimoto points out, Japanese industrial policy has had much less to do with the commercial success of Japan's new industries of the 1980s than it did in the 1940s through 1970s.[52] Japanese firms simply do not need government help, and they resist government intervention. Finally, the nature of contemporary commercial competition within global markets makes the nationalism of government targeting anachronistic. Firms must be free to research and develop, design, finance, produce, and market in multiple national markets. Corporate strategy and state strategy are not always congruent any more: it is not always true, to paraphrase, that "what's good for Mitsubishi is good for Japan and vice versa." An industrial policy of targeting probably is better suited to compressing economic development during the developmental stage of industrialization than accelerating economic growth during the maturity stage of postindustrialism. Nevertheless, whether or not an industrial policy of targeting does or does not[53] make economic or policy sense, states do it. Hence, the question: can the GATT regime accommodate an industrial policy of targeting?

A government industrial policy of targeting presumes a "smart" state, i.e., one with the bureaucratic structures and processes to pick the key industries that ought to be promoted. The mere intellectual exercise by government bureaucrats of selecting the critical industry they believe will maximize national development is not incompatible with the GATT regime. The publication of such government white papers might seem silly to the Anglo-American architects of the GATT, but ideas and words do not violate GATT rules. Indeed, the GATT regime must accept that it manages trade among more that 100 members now, not the few advanced industrialized societies of Europe and North America. The regime can and must tolerate different conceptions of the proper role of government in economy and society.

If words cannot endanger the GATT regime, however, deeds can. The policy actions of government industrial targeting can be incompatible with the GATT regime. The policy tools of targeting are import trade protection, export trade promotion, inward-investment protection, subsidization, and firm dumping. As we have seen, import trade protection as a policy tool has largely been taken away from East Asian policymakers by the GATT regime and by American unilateralism, and inward-investment protection as a policy tool has largely been taken away from East Asian policymakers. East Asian policymakers can continue to promote exports through institutions such as the Japan Export Trade Organization (JETRO), the Korea Export Promotion Corporation, and the China External Trade Development Council without running afoul of GATT rules. Thus, some important policy tools of targeting are not significant problems to the GATT regime.

Government subsidization and firm dumping, however, continue to be problems for the GATT principle of fair trade. Neither government subsidization nor firm dumping violates GATT rules under all circumstances, however. Indeed, government subsidization is a legitimate policy tool. Roads, harbors, and schools are all legitimate subsidies. But GATT rules specify some government subsidies as unfair advantages for recipient firms in market competition because they injure nonrecipient competitors. Unfortunately, GATT rules are inadequately developed regarding subsidies and their remedies, countervailing duties.[54] International rules on government subsidization are ambiguous and national policies and practices are contentious because states disagree about what government should and should not do to promote industry. The United States has long maintained a national countervailing-duty law, implemented that law most vigorously, and pressed for GATT regime rule creation because the American way of political economy has generally favored minimal government promotion of particular industries. National types of political economy clash in the subsidy/countervailing-duty policy area.

Some conclude that as a matter of both national and international policy, subsidy/countervailing-duty law should be excised. Some contend that subsidy/countervailing-duty policy is just protectionism and that the safeguards policy should be the only remedy available. Others suggest that, at any rate, writing effective subsidy/countervailing-duty law is impossible. To the contrary, government subsidies to specific industries or firms do distort markets.[55] Furthermore, such government subsidies injure competing firms and ought to be regulated. An effective international subsidy/countervailing-duty policy can solve the fundamental problem of interfacing different types of national political economies within the world economy. Within the GATT regime, the elimination of the anachronistic domestic subsidy and export subsidy distinction (meaningless in global markets), the addition of the specificity test, and rule refinement of investigation procedures can reduce trade conflict.

Firm dumping, too, is restricted, not prohibited, under GATT rules. Like subsidy policy, antidumping policy is highly contentious, with complaints that it does not make any sense to have such a policy and ought to be completely regrounded intellectually and/or that the manner in which states (especially the United States) administer it produces blatant protectionism.[56] By my count, of the 794 active AD and CVD cases investigated by the US Department of Commerce during the 1980s, 203 involved East Asian states (Japan 76, Korea 40, Taiwan 38, China 19, Macao 1, Malaysia 8, Singapore 11, Thailand 10).[57] Economists may be right that antidumping law as administered is blatant protectionism, but the market-distorted and still latently protectionist East Asian political economies invite these charges from American business. The political pressure of the business demand for remedy must have some outlet. The elimination of the antidumping law would seem to invite only worse trade policy problems. Continued refinement of GATT rules on antidumping and use of national antidumping laws, then, even if still imperfect, provide remedy to firms' dumping behavior.

In short, East Asian industrial policy need not be a great threat to the GATT regime principle of fair trade. Extant rules, new rule creation, and changes in the world economy largely solve the problems.

East Asian intellectual-rights policies have been the source of international trade problems for some time. Korean and Taiwanese IPR laws have, until recently, been seriously short of OECD state norms. American unilateralism and the demand of increasingly knowledge-intensive firms have, however, encouraged the writing of IPR laws in both countries. Enforcement of these laws is improving in both countries, more in Korea than in Taiwan.[58] Japanese IPR law, on the other hand, is highly developed and detailed. But American firms often complain about Japanese IPR law and enforcement. The complaints about the law result primarily from the lack of international consensus on IPR law. Japanese IPR differs from American law but in some ways is similar to European law. Japanese enforcement of IPR law, on the other hand, often makes de facto protection of intellectual-property rights less effective than de jure rules would suggest.[59] Nevertheless, the problems regarding IPR are solvable with new rule creation by the GATT members collectively and individually. The East Asian states have ample domestic motivation to provide effective protection of intellectual-property rights, for their firms are increasingly world leaders in the advancement and use of technology.

MULTILATERALISM, RECIPROCITY, AND ECONOMIC-DEVELOPMENT PRINCIPLES

The principles of multilateralism, reciprocity, and economic development are fundamental to the GATT regime. Multilateralism rests on two assumptions: (1) According to neoclassical economic theory, free trade in an economy maximizes resource-use efficiency and increases economic wealth. (2) State interdependence results in mutually dependent economic and political relationships among states. Multilateralism means that the state contracting parties commit themselves to act cooperatively in the management of the world economy. Unfortunately for the GATT regime, neither the Japanese nor the Koreans nor the Taiwanese have been committed to multilateralism. Each state has pursued the economic-development strategy of mercantilist import substitution and export promotion. This state strategy, brilliantly devised and implemented, has compressed into two generations the industrial development that took many decades in Europe and North America. The strategy has been devised and implemented with little regard, however, for either the multilateralism principle of the GATT regime or for the economic, social, and political impacts of their policies on other countries within the regime. In the world trading system, Japan, Korea, and Taiwan have been free riders. The judgment of Stephen Cohen that the Japanese state acted irresponsibly in the world economy in the 1970s and 1980s and indeed endangered the GATT regime by creating protectionist pressures all over the world is, I believe, correct.[60]

But East Asian commitment to multilateralism is growing. It is growing, however, not because of a newfound belief in the logic of comparative advantage but because of a realization about the logic of interdependence. The logic of interdependence operates at two levels of the world economy— firm and state. Firm interdependence, as Helen Milner has shown, leads firms to oppose protectionism.[61] Protectionism leads to state policy retaliation and to the raising of firm input costs. Interdependent firms lobby their governments against protectionism and for open markets. State interdependence, as Robert Axelrod and Robert Keohane have argued, lead states to cooperate.[62] We can expect that first the Japanese and then the Koreans and Taiwanese will become more multilateralist over time.

Reciprocity is a fundamental principle of the GATT regime. The meaning of "reciprocity" within the GATT regime, however, differs today from the original Havana Conference meaning. It then meant "substantially equivalent concessions of trade barrier reduction"; now it means "substantially equivalent competitive opportunities."[63] As we have seen, the East Asian states have not offered substantially equivalent competitive opportunities. Nevertheless, the direction of policy change in Japan, Korea, and Taiwan is toward such an outcome. By the end of the 1990s, the policy environments of Japan, Korea, and Taiwan will likely closely resemble the environments of North America and Europe. Residual differences will likely be more of firm strategy and industrial organization and will likely not challenge the GATT regime.

The principle of economic development also is fundamental to the GATT regime. Yet this notion, too, has evolved within the regime over time. The GATT architects believed strongly in the need for economic development. To them, it was the means toward rising standards of living, democracy, and international peace. The GATT architects believed that open markets resulted in economic development. Hence, the original rules did not extend preferences to the underdeveloped. After decolonization and through the political mechanism of less-developed-country unity in the 1970s (such as the Group of 77), the GATT regime added preferences, such as the Generalized System of Preferences, for less developed countries.

During the 1980s, however, the East Asian states challenged the neoclassical notion of economic development. Rapid industrial development, they showed, is the result of a high level of political development paired with government market intervention through a mercantilist import substitution and export promotion strategy. The success of this strategy has caused both scholars and policymakers of the neoclassical IMF—World Bank school and of the neo-Marxist *dependencia* school to rethink their premises, arguments, and conclusions.

CONCLUSION

This chapter shows that, contrary to much conventional wisdom, the East Asian political economies are not fundamentally incompatible with the GATT regime. The norms, rules, and procedures of the GATT regime are guided by six underlying principles: reduction of trade barriers, nondiscrimination, fair trade, multilateralism, reciprocity, and economic development. The fit between the East Asian political economies and the GATT regime is generally good under the principle of reduction of trade barriers, not good under the principle of nondiscrimination, manageable under the principle of fair trade, and getting better under the principles of multilateralism, reciprocity, and economic development. The East Asian political economies are different, but the differences are of degree, not kind, and are decreasing.

East Asian competitive advantage rests today more on firm strategy and industrial organization than on government policy, and since global interdependence is changing East Asian state trade policy preferences, the principles, norms, rules, and procedures are up to the task of managing trade relations. The challenges for rule-oriented trade diplomacy are great, however, for much additional rule creation is needed, as are improvements in both multilateral and minilateral Pacific regional-dispute settlement capabilities, without which the regime may increasingly become irrelevant. Otherwise, rule-oriented liberal trade diplomacy would be gradually supplanted by power-oriented managed trade diplomacy.

CHAPTER 8

Trade Dispute Diplomacy with China

China possesses the largest population in the world and one of the fastest growing economies in the world; it possesses impressive natural-resource stocks, enormous productive capacity, and astonishing consumption potential. China claims new significance in the Pacific economy because of deliberate policy choices that its leaders made in the 1980s. The shift Chinese leaders took in the 1980s away from an industrial-policy strategy of independence from the world economy and of planning resource allocation and toward a limited interdependence with the world economy and limited market allocation has shifted upward the growth trajectory of the country. China under communism has become China under reform, and by engaging in the world economy and allocating significant ranges of resources through markets, the government in Beijing has launched China on a heading that will fundamentally change its economy, polity, society, and culture and make a rapid pace of change a permanent aspect of Chinese affairs. The Chinese government has been implementing a socialist development strategy, an unprecedented new variant in the tradition of Japan, Korea, and Taiwan. As a result, and if present trends continue, Chinese producers are bringing new competition into the region, disrupting the contemporary trade and investment patterns, and in the twenty-first century, China may become an economic superpower and the greatest threat to the stability of the Pacific economy. As an economic superpower with a massive standing army and nuclear weapons, China may possess the capabilities in the next century to challenge existing rules, institutions, and norms of behavior in the Pacific economy and in the world economy. Yet, though China may upset the status quo, Chinese markets offer extraordinary opportunities for the world's producers. If adjustment to the economic change and disruption takes place and if Chinese consumers become a major market for the goods and services produced by the other countries in the Pacific, then the outcome for the Pacific economy will be economic growth, rationalization, and interdependence. Thus, trade disputes between China and the United States are inevitable, and for American trade dispute diplomacy, China is second only to Japan as the most important and challenging state in the 1990s. In this chapter, the analytic framework employed to study American trade dispute diplomacy with Japan, Korea, and Taiwan and the lessons learned from the experience are applied to trade diplomacy with China.

A detailed analysis of the US-China textile dispute—the only major trade dispute between the two countries in the 1980s—is offered here for the insights it brings to the likely nature and patterns of US-China trade dispute settlement in the 1990s. The textile case study shows a combative, confrontational China, denying the legitimacy of American allegations, refusing to respond to US government investigation questionnaires, threatening trade retaliation if the United States employed sanctions, and not complying with the settlement agreement (whether the noncompliance was willful or due to an inability to implement the changes within the bureaucracy is unclear). China's response strategy is called here combative counterpunch, a response strategy to US trade demands quite unlike the response strategies of Japan, Korea, and Taiwan. The GATT regime possesses the potential to mediate Sino-American trade conflict in the Pacific, preventing trade disputes from becoming trade wars.

In this chapter, the Chinese political-economy and industrial-policy strategy is reviewed and assessed, the textile and apparel trade dispute is studied, and the dynamics of Sino-American trade dispute diplomacy are presented.

STATIST, SOCIALIST DEVELOPMENTAL, POSTISOLATIONIST

The People's Republic of China has been organized as a single-party, hierarchically structured, bureaucratic polity with headquarters in Beijing. The original model was (roughly) the Stalinist Soviet Union, and for the economy that meant centralized planning, not free markets (though centralization never became as thorough as in the Soviet Union). The Chinese central government (administratively the State Planning Commission) set specific output targets for individual industries and matched supply and demand of production inputs and outputs. The central government in Beijing planned production in heavy industry; the regional and local government authorities planned production in light industry (and the centralization differences by sector have been important to the reform process). Carl Riskin explains that "output quantity, variety, and quality targets; equipment utilization, maintenance, and repair schedules; sources of supply and consumption rates of raw materials and working capital; distribution of the product; total work-force, working hours, wages; and much else as well" were specified.[1] The plans were vertically as well as horizontally coordinated.

Until 1978, China's economic strategy had been classic import substitution—import barriers, foreign-exchange controls, foreign direct-investment restrictions[2]—and thus American foreign economic policy had little interest in China. The industrial-policy strategy of "self-reliance" largely isolated China from the world economy and resulted in chronic poverty, poor infrastructure, a widening technological gap between world standards and Chinese capabilities, and a visible standard-of-living gap between China and its rapidly industrializing East Asian neighbors. The strategy, when combined with Maoist, Communist ideological politics, had resulted in a famine of 20–30 million deaths around 1960 and economic, political, and social chaos in the late 1960s and 1970s.[3] Advocates within China for change argued that "socialism" must not mean "egalitarianism on the basis of universal poverty."[4] After the reacquisition and consolidation of power by Deng Xiaoping, the Chinese government announced in December 1978 the new economic-policy strategy of the "Open Door." The Open Door policy aimed to stimulate China's modernization in science and technology. The logic of the policy, however, was not free markets and import liberalization but adoption of Western technology and export of manufactured goods.[5] Hence, import barriers would be removed and decentralization of the institutions of decision making on trade and investment would occur only when necessary for achieving the goals of technology acquisition and export promotion.

The market reforms indicated a shift from centralized planning to market socialism or, as enshrined in the Chinese Constitution in March 1993, a shift from a "planned economy under public ownership" to a "socialist market economy."[6] The nomenclature meant that markets would increasingly allocate resources, that profits would be incentives, that producers would compete for sales, and that managers would gain decision-making autonomy. But it did not mean (if the government maintained sufficient political capacity) that private ownership of production would become the rule nor that "unfair" income distributions would be tolerated. Deng Xiaoping's reform strategy (a smart strategy, argues Susan Shirk)[7] was to decollectivize agriculture first, thus offering profit incentives to several hundred million peasant farmers and avoiding the opposition of the entrenched interests of the powerful ministries that administered the heavy industries, then to establish "special economic zones" that would create new market-oriented enterprises, thus offering profit motives to entrepreneurs in the coastal cities and again avoiding the opposition of the entrenched heavy-industry ministries.

In 1980, four special economic zones (similar to export-processing zones in other parts of Asia) were established in coastal Shenzhen, Zhuhai, Shantou, and Xiamen, and in 1984, fourteen more coastal cities were opened to trade and investment. Guangzhou especially took off economically. The keys to its success were (1) its proximity to Hong Kong; (2) the special economic-zone policy changes; (3) the relative lack of big, state-run enterprises; (4) the liberal tax policies of the local government; (5) the billion-dollar capitalization provided by the Chinese government and the aggressiveness of the China International Trade and Investment Corporation (CITIC), headed by Beijing's favorite capitalist, Rong Yiren; and (6) the great geographic distance from Beijing.[8]

During the 1980s, many foreign companies made investments into China's special economic zones, attracted to the cheap labor and/or the huge market potential. Investment rose as investors entered China with optimism, but fell as word got around about problems in practice. The original 1979 Joint Venture Law had been ambiguous on some crucial issues—technology transfer, profit reparation, and foreign exchange—and Chinese commitment to investment seemed lukewarm at first. Hence, the Chinese government clarified JV law in 1983 with the "Joint Venture Implementing Regulations" and the "Foreign-Economic Contract Law" and again in 1986 with the "Provisions for the Encouragement of Foreign Investment".[9] By 1988, 16,000 FDI projects had been established in China. Forty-three percent were contractual JVs in which the foreign investor supplied materials and simple processing machinery and the Chinese supplied labor. Each side brought limited expectations (and the foreigners brought only a couple of million dollars for investment). Only 4% of investments were wholly owned by the foreigners. The balance of investments were mainly joint equity ventures, in which both sides committed money, the Chinese committed labor, equipment, and buildings, and the foreigners committed equipment, technology, and management practices. Investors from Hong Kong and Japan have made the most investments in China, but their investments tend to be small, contractual JVs without long-term commitment. The larger, more technology-intensive JVs tend to be American or European.[10] By 1991, US foreign direct investment in China totaled $350 million ($50 million more than in 1990); in 1992, US investment into China increased dramatically with 3265 signed contracts representing $3.1 billion. Indeed, total foreign direct investment into China showed extraordinary growth in 1992. By that year, a total of 90,782 contracts had been signed by foreign investors.[11]

Since 1985 and largely due to the foreign direct investment, Chinese exports in manufacturing have increased manifold, especially in apparel, toys, sporting goods, and telecommunications equipment.[12] By 1993, Chinese exports to the US exceeded $31 billion, a surplus of almost $23 billion.[13] The World Bank estimates that only about 9% of Chinese exports go to the United States directly from China and more than 25% pass through Hong Kong trading companies.[14] In contrast, only about 12% of Chinese exports go to Japan, but nearly 20% of Chinese exports go to the European Community. Thus, the export dependence of China upon the US market is as great as is the export dependence of Japan (35%), Korea (26%), and Taiwan (30%).

The trade growth was encouraged by decentralization by the Ministry of Foreign Trade and Economic Cooperation (MOFTEC, formerly MOFERT) of importing and exporting. By mid-1992, 5000 enterprises were authorized by MOFTEC to sign import and export contracts without Ministry approval.[15] MOFTEC has been giving up tight authority over Chinese trade volume and composition but continues to be responsible for the implementation of Chinese trade policy, including bilateral negotiations with the United States and multilateral negotiations in GATT, APEC, the World Intellectual Property Organization, the UN Commission on International Trade Law, and other fora.[16] It aims to promote the export of Chinese goods, administers China's new antidumping and countervailing-duty laws and FDI policy and treaty negotiation. Thus, MOFTEC is not like Japan's MITI or Korea's MTI but more like a combined Department of Commerce and USTR. An increasing number of its staff are young people educated in American law and graduate schools with experience working in foreign embassies and consulates and in law firms.

Chinese import patterns resemble those of Taiwan and Korea and are the result of deliberate policy choices by the Chinese government.[17] Liberalization of the import policies varies across markets considerably: High tariffs (43% average overall, with a 30–60% range) and foreign exchange restrictions limit imports in agricultural commodities, manufactured imports, and nonessential consumer goods, but special import duty exemptions offered to capital equipment have afforded huge, rapid import increases in these sectors.[18] Insulation from international competition and factor inputs results in hugely inflated prices for consumer goods such as computers and automobiles on Chinese markets, in grossly inefficient production by state-owned enterprises, and in low-quality products. Nevertheless, small coastal JV enterprises, aided by the government's China Council for the Promotion of International Trade and the small, specialized Hong Kong trading houses, have achieved spectacular export growth in labor-intensive, light-manufacturing sectors.

A substantial portion of the exports to the United States in the 1980s were in the textile and apparel sector. The Chinese exports brought new disruption and anguish to American apparel makers, who first had adjusted to Japanese competition, then to Korean and Taiwanese competition, through import protection under the Multifiber Arrangement and who were wholly unprepared to compete against a new major low-cost supplier. The textile and apparel trade dispute teaches much about trade dispute diplomacy between the United States and China.

TEXTILE AND APPAREL TRADE DISPUTE

The American Textile Manufacturers Institute, the Amalgamated Clothing and Textile Workers Union, and the International Ladies Garment Workers Union in September 1983 charged in a petition to the Commerce Department under the authority of the US countervailing-duty law that the government of China subsidized the production of apparel and textiles for export to the US market.[19] Under US law dating to 1897, the US executive should levy a countervailing duty (CVD)

> whenever any country, dependency, colony, province, or other political subdivision of government, person, partnership, association, cartel, or corporation, shall pay or bestow, directly or indirectly, any bounty or grant upon the manufacture or production or export of any article or merchandise manufactured or produced in such country, dependency, colony, province or other political subdivision of government, then upon the importation of such article or merchandise into the United States . . .

By US executive practice, a "bounty or grant" means a "subsidy," though the terms are not identical to the specialist. A subsidy is a direct or indirect grant for the production or export of goods, including tax credits, cash transfers, or low-interest-rate loans. A wide array of government economic and social policies may be found to confer a bounty or grant on a foreign business firm, but an actionable subsidy under US law is an unfair benefit provided to a specific firm or industry, not a generally available subsidy. That is, according to the so-called specificity test, government-funded training provided to workers in several industries would probably not be found to confer a bounty or grant.

In antidumping cases, the petitioner must always claim that it has been "materially injured" by the foreign trade practice and must file written statements to that effect with the International Trade Commission. Under US trade law, however, the material-injury test is not required in all CVD cases. GATT Article VI requires that injury to the industry occur before CVD duties may be levied. But because the American CVD law predated GATT, the GATT grandfather clause allows the US to continue its policy of not offering an injury test to all countries. The US, pursuing a policy known as "code conditionality," offers an injury test only to states that become contracting parties to the Tokyo Round Subsidies Code. (At this writing, twenty four states are signatories to the Code, but not China.)

Countervailing-duty cases are typically investigated by relatively junior trade analysts in DoC's Import Administration Office of Investigation, and compliance is ensured by analysts in the Office of Compliance. These same offices administer US antidumping law. But since a subsidy, unlike dumping, is typically an act of government, a petition filed with DoC under the countervailing-duty law leads Import Administration to deal not only with private foreign firms (the recipients of the subsidy) but with governments. As a result, a CVD case may lead to a negotiated settlement, as it did in the China textile and apparel case. The usual outcome in CVD cases nevertheless is the imposition of a duty to offset or countervail the amount of the subsidy.

Since China would not receive an injury test, attorneys for the Textile Manufacturers filed the petition only with DoC, and the International Trade Administration announced in October 1983 that it would investigate the case.[20] Never before had the countervailing-duty statute been applied to a nonmarket economy; hence, the policy implications of the case extended beyond China and apparel to all nonmarket economies and many other markets, for an affirmative finding against China would invite CVD petitions against other nonmarket economies and their goods.[21]

The Textile Manufacturers argued that the Chinese government subsidized its textile and apparel exporters by granting a more favorable currency rate of exchange (Rmb 2.8:$10.00 rather than the official Rmb 1.99:$1.00) to enterprises engaged in foreign trade.[22] The petition also cited preferential access to raw materials, foreign-exchange loans, transportation, and tax policies as additional subsidies. The petitioners pointed out that countervailing duties had been applied in the past by the United States against other governments for dual exchange rate preferences. Chinese textile and apparel imports, it followed, should be countervailed. The Textile Manufacturers presumed that the government of a country with a nonmarket economy could subsidize its producers both in theory and in practice. DoC, however, questioned this presumption and in November 1983 held a public hearing to consider various points of view. Attorneys representing the American Association of Exporters and Importers, who represented the major retailers relying on inexpensive apparel imports from China, argued that (1) no clear consideration was given in the language of the legislative history of the CVD statute to its application to nonmarket economies; (2) the statute assumes a dividing line between government decision making and private-market decision making, and in an NME no dividing line exists; (3) other trade actions such as antidumping have specific provisions for application to NMEs; and (4) conceptual and measurement problems of application would lead to "arbitrary," "even bizarre" results. The Importers concluded that application of CVD law to NMEs would be neither "sensible" nor "realistic."[23]

Several scores of business associations, companies, and politicians, including the National Retail Merchants Association, Federated Department Stores, Kmart Corporation, the US Wheat Associates, the National Council for US-China Trade, North Carolina Governor Hunt, and Senators Strom Thurmond and Daniel Patrick Moynihan submitted briefs and letters to DoC's public hearing. Each aligned itself either with the position of the Textile Manufacturers Institute or the position of the Exporters and Importers Association.

DoC, too, questioned the validity of the conclusion that the Chinese dual exchange rate system should be found countervailable because other states' dual exchange rate systems had been found countervailable in the past. The Importers contended that (1) many states employ multiple exchange rates (as many as one-third of IMF member states); (2) the legislative history of the CVD statute does not indicate that Congress considered whether multiple exchange rates could be a bounty or grant; (3) the case history of CVD application to multiple exchange rate systems is ambiguous; and (4) the Chinese system neither treats certain industries preferentially nor applies to exports only, i.e., it is a generally available subsidy that fails the specificity test.

Commerce Department representatives and the Deputy Assistant Secretary for East Asia and the Pacific met with Chinese Embassy staff members, including the Ambassador, to notify them about the petition and explain how the investigation would be conducted.[24] The Chinese Embassy responded that (1) the petition was not supported by facts; (2) since the two economic systems were fundamentally different, it is irrational to compare them; and

(3) as a matter of Chinese economic policy, prices do not fluctuate as they do in the United States. The Chinese government rejected the Textiles Manufacturers' petition, calling it "groundless."[25] The Ministry of Foreign Economic Relations and Trade (MOFERT, which made and implemented Chinese foreign economic policy during this period) stated, "The same settlement prices apply to both import and export, to all import and export commodities, to the import and export trade with all countries, and to all enterprises and corporations in the country."[26] The MOFERT tack, then, was to argue, like the Importers Association brief to ITA, that the Chinese dual exchange rate policy was a generally available subsidy and hence not countervailable under US law.

American textile and apparel makers since the early 1960s had pressured the US government into negotiating a series of bilateral and multilateral treaties restricting access to the US market, including the Multifiber Arrangement and its renewals.[27] Chinese textile exports to the US, then, upset a delicate balance. Textile trade volume between the United States and China increased markedly, just as US textile interests predicted, after Jimmy Carter and Bo Yibo in September 1980 signed a bilateral textile and apparel treaty.[28] American apparel makers immediately criticized the agreement and some observers at the time believed that US negotiators had underestimated China's export capacity.[29] The quotas led as well to market imbalances, such as the entire quota of shirts being filled on 1 June, the same day the new quota year begins.[30] The growing volume of Chinese imports of textiles and apparel goods into the US market encouraged trade conflict.

In August 1982, DoC and the ITC received two petitions alleging textile and apparel dumping in the US market by Chinese enterprises: the Textile Manufacturers complained about Chinese polyester-cotton print cloth,[31] and Milliken and Company complained about Chinese cotton shop towels.[32] In both cases, DoC determined that China had dumped, the ITC determined that firms had been materially injured, and China denied that it had dumped.

In October 1982, the Acting Deputy Assistant Secretary of Commerce for Textiles and Apparel told a meeting of the American Association of Exporters and Importers that the United States had demanded that China reduce its apparel export growth and reported that China had responded by reducing its purchases of US cotton and raw materials.[33] By the end of 1982, Sino-American negotiations to write a new textile and apparel trade agreement to replace the 1980 treaty (to expire 31 December 1982) had stalled, and American chief negotiator Peter Murphy had threatened to impose quotas unilaterally.[34]

The American Association of Exporters and Importers, which represented large retailers such as Sears, Kmart, and J. C. Penney, had long opposed textile and apparel quotas because the restrictions disrupted merchandise delivery schedules and raised merchandise costs. In November 1982, the Importers challenged the US government's textile and apparel quota system in the US Court of International Trade.[35] They argued that the government failed to comply with US law when it negotiated import limits without regard to statutory requirements that quotas only follow a "reasoned finding of actual or threatened market disruption based upon current data." The US quota system on textiles and apparel, the Importers charged, was based on poor, out-of-date data. Hence, domestic pressures on textile quotas were contradictory.

US-China trade relations were frayed throughout 1983 as negotiations toward a new textile and apparel agreement failed. The CVD action and subsidy dispute late in the year resulted from these troubled negotiations. On 13 January the US announced that negotiations had been suspended and the US had imposed quotas unilaterally retroactive to the first of the year. *People's Daily*, China's official party newspaper, warned that trade relations with the United States would suffer if quotas were not lifted,[36] and MOFERT announced a few days later that it had ordered the suspension of Chinese purchases of US cotton, synthetic fibers, and soybeans until the US lifted the quotas.[37] Throughout the spring and summer, the Chinese purchased neither these goods from US sellers nor US wheat or corn. American agricultural producers suffered heavy losses, and offshore oil drillers claimed to have lost contracts to Japanese and British competitors. These groups pressed the Reagan administration, directly and through Congress, to reach agreement with China on new quota levels.[38]

The US and China agreed in mid-August, retroactive to 1 January 1983, to new quotas. The new levels allowed 3% annual growth throughout 1987 on Chinese textile imports into the US.[39] The 3% growth figure was a compromise between the Chinese call for a 6% per annum increase and the US proposal for a 1.5% per annum increase. Soon after the agreement was signed, MOFERT lifted its ban on American agricultural and fiber imports.[40] Though US agricultural producers were jubilant, US textile and apparel producers denounced the new quotas. Industry groups, such as the American Fiber, Textile, and Apparel Coalition and the Federation of Apparel Manufacturers, especially objected to the cumulative increase that 3% per annum growth would permit by 1987.[41] The American Textile Manufacturers Institute, the Amalgamated Clothing and Textile Workers Union, and the International Ladies Garment Workers Union reacted swiftly to the new treaty: they charged in a CVD petition that the Chinese subsidized textile and apparel exports to the US. The CVD petition against China blasted the quota agreement. The dispute resumed only months before Chinese Premier Zhao Ziyang's January 1984 visit to Washington and President Reagan's April 1984 visit to Beijing. The Chinese, for their part, were beginning to employ multilateral strategies in their economic and foreign policy: in December 1984, the GATT Committee on Textiles announced that it would welcome the application of China into the MFA.[42]

The Office of Investigations of DoC's International Trade Administration presented a CVD questionnaire to Chinese government representatives at their Washington embassy on 20 October 1983.[43] The Chinese government, however, refused to complete the questionnaire, claiming that the case was illegitimate.[44] Counsel for the Textile Manufacturers criticized the DoC questionnaire, charging that "the scope of the questionnaire [had been] limited in the course of senior level review within the Department" and that key questions on the multiple exchange rate system had been dropped.[45] Their letter prompted DoC officials to discuss the questionnaire with the Textile Manufacturers' lawyers and to send a supplementary questionnaire to the Chinese Embassy.[46] This time the Chinese government responded, but only by repeating formally its earlier positions.[47] The Chinese government's response revealed that on 27 September 1983, Chinese government officials "held negotiations with the United States, hoping that it would take measures to prevent the case from being accepted so as not to affect the development of the economic and trade relations between the two countries." Attorneys for the Textile Manufacturers chastised DoC that "countervailing duty cases are *legal* proceedings—not exercises in diplomatic 'persuasion' backed by the threat of reprisals by a foreign government."[48] A negotiated settlement, however, was clearly the Commerce Department's objective: The DoC determination was due on 6 December 1983, but the DoC postponed the announcement until 16 December, although they had initially ruled out a delay because China had refused to cooperate in the investigation.[49] Commerce Department officials requested and received from the Textile Manufacturers' attorneys a letter notifying Commerce that the American Textile Manufacturers Institute was withdrawing its CVD petition against China. The Textile Manufacturers extracted the concession that it could refile the petition for any reason within ten days and that ITA would issue a preliminary determination in the case within two days after refiling.[50] The agreement between the Textile Manufacturers and DoC occurred on 6 December, thus buying ten more days to find a negotiated solution.

Ten days of wrangling among US policymakers—from USTR, the State Department, the White House staff, and the Commerce Department—the Textile Manufacturers Institute, the agricultural products associations, and everybody's attorneys ensued.[51] The Commerce Department decision in the case faced the following dilemma: a negative determination would anger the textile interests, while an affirmative determination would anger agricultural interests. Neither course of action appeared inviting. On 13 December, Senator Strom Thurmond of South Carolina, Senator Jesse Helms of North Carolina, and other members of the Congressional textile caucus met with President Reagan to press him to impose further quotas on Chinese textile and apparel imports.[52] Senator Robert Dole of Kansas warned the President on 14 December that further textile quotas would damage US trading interests, i.e., agricultural trading interests.[53] A final two days of Trade Policy Committee and other Cabinet-level meetings led to the Reagan announcement on 16 December 1983 that by executive order, controls on textile and apparel imports would be tightened.[54] Hence, Secretary of Commerce Baldrige and White House advisors Edwin Meese and James Baker (though motivated by different goals, the DITI reorganization for Baldrige and the elections for Meese and Baker) won the day over Secretary of State George Schultz, who contended that Sino-American relations would be injured, and US Trade Representative Bill Brock, who opposed injuring American export interests in order to support a fading domestic industry. Reagan ordered the interagency Committee for the Implementation of Textile Agreements (CITA) to implement the new restrictions. He ordered CITA to initiate bilateral consultations immediately on China textiles and apparel. CITA would issue a "call" whenever imports in a particular import category rose by more than 30% from the previous year or whenever imports amounted to 20% or more of US production.[55] Calls, all concerned knew, generally led to restrictions. The new policy applied this procedure not only to imports from China but from all other sources as well.

Two weeks after the Presidential executive order, CITA requested consultations with the Chinese government to restrict further many categories of Chinese textile and apparel exports to the US market.[56] Consultations between CITA and Chinese government officials occurred continuously on one category or another of textile and apparel goods. Nevertheless, Congressman Ed Jenkins of Georgia claimed in 1987 that the December 1983 executive order limiting Chinese textile and apparel imports was never implemented and that imports continued to rise rapidly.[57] He asserted that China received special treatment "in order to fulfill some foreign policy objective." Broader foreign-policy considerations notwithstanding, CITA's implementation efforts have been hampered significantly by Chinese noncompliance with the bilateral agreements. Noncompliance has taken two forms—counterfeit export visas and country-of-origin evasions. The US Customs Service reported that millions of dollars of Chinese textile exports have entered the US covered by counterfeit export visas,[58] thereby allowing Chinese enterprises to evade quotas. Customs responded to this problem by holding all Chinese textile imports at the dock for a week until the visas could be verified with the Chinese Embassy.[59] In addition, Customs publicized in trade publications, such as the *Journal of Commerce*, descriptions of genuine and counterfeit visas.[60] CITA responded to this problem by negotiating a commitment from the Chinese to improve their export visa system.[61]

Chinese producers also sought to evade quotas by transshipping goods through third countries, such as New Zealand and Hong Kong, where only minor finishing processing occurred. In particular, sweaters of Chinese fabric that received final processing in New Zealand concerned customs.[62] Customs responded by changing country-of-origin rules so that fabric cut in China and sewn together in third countries would be charged against China's quotas.[63] The Chinese threatened to retaliate against the United States (i.e., reduce agriculture purchases) over the changed country-of-origin rules.[64] The Chinese found American supporters in their efforts: US agriculture groups and Congressional representatives such as Senator Dole pressured the administration to rescind the charges. US retailers filed a petition before the US Court of International Trade aimed at invalidating the new rules. The dispute also prompted the Chinese to challenge before the GATT Textile Surveillance Board the December 1983 quotas imposed by the United States. The low level of Chinese compliance with the quota agreements is explained by the ample incentives for Chinese noncompliance (either voluntary by decision of the central government or nonvoluntary by decision of local officials) and the difficulties with agreement compliance verification.

Complaints of Chinese textile and apparel quota noncompliance persisted into the 1990s. American apparel makers claimed that 1993 Chinese transshipments in violation of country-of-origin and quota rules amounted to $2 billion in excess of China's $4.5 billion total quota.[65]

DISPUTE SETTLEMENT DYNAMICS AND 301

The noncompliance claims are difficult to verify, but Chinese interests are easier to verify: access to the American market is an important means to full domestic employment and hard currency. Nevertheless, the Chinese negotiation strategy was combative counterpunch, demonstrating a willingness not only to deny the legitimacy of US demands (a common reaction by the Japanese, Korean, and Taiwanese governments) but to complain about US behavior to the GATT Textile Surveillance Board and retaliate by refusing to purchase American goods. By targeting US businesses that wanted either export access to China or cheap imports from China, the Chinese government demonstrated savviness about how to exploit its own market power. The result was that their best allies in trade dispute diplomacy were the well-financed, politically powerful US agriculture and apparel retail interests. It is a tactic that neither the Japanese nor the Koreans nor the Taiwanese have been able to use with alacrity because they have not taken in sufficient US imports, and it offers the lesson that interdependence can cut both ways. American business export and investment interests in China make the bargaining-power dynamics of US-Chinese trade dispute diplomacy quite different from the patterns established with the Japanese, Koreans, and Taiwanese.

Chinese policymakers appear intent on taking policy steps to enhance further their bargaining leverage in international trade diplomacy. During summer 1993, MOFTEC lawyers completed the drafting of Chinese safeguards with antidumping and countervailing-duty laws. The laws, said by Chinese policymakers to be modeled after European Community practices (because US procedures are considered too administratively complicated) and compliant with GATT rules, are motivated by the Chinese belief that they must have the trade policy instruments to retaliate against American, Japanese, and European trade policy practices and to discourage foreign-firm dumping.[66] As one interviewee remarked, "Since other governments have it, China should have it."[67]

The writing of antidumping and countervailing-duty laws demonstrates also that the Chinese government is moving toward legalization of its foreign-trade policy to world standards as established by the GATT regime and other international economic regimes. Studies have found that Chinese behavior in the international economic organizations such as the IMF, the World Bank, UNCTAD, UNESCO, and the International Labor Organization has been responsible and supportive of the missions of the institutions.[68] It is good news to GATT regime participants considering the merits of a Chinese accession to the World Trade Organization. On the other hand, the GATT/WTO regimes demand much more rule compliance than these other organizations, China is neither in compliance with the original GATT treaty nor the

Tokyo Round Codes nor the new WTO Codes despite Chinese economic reforms, and American businesses and policymakers have many complaints about Chinese import policies.

Despite considerable liberalization, China maintains extensive import barriers. As described above, the World Bank states that high tariffs and targeted foreign-exchange restriction are policy tools of an industrial policy that favors the import of capital equipment but almost nothing else. American businesspeople opine that many other import barriers exist in China and that as a matter of corporate strategy, export entry mode is unavailable to them, thus prompting direct-investment entry strategies. Under 301 policy authority, USTR priorities in bilateral negotiations with the Chinese government in recent years have been import quotas, restrictions, and controls, intellectual-property protection, standards and certification requirements, and the absence of regulatory transparency.[69] Bilateral agreements were signed in 1992 on intellectual property and market access, with policy implementation proceeding in terms of administrative rule writing but falling short in terms of enforcement throughout China.

USTR multilateral priorities in negotiations on China's GATT/WTO accession have been similar, emphasizing the lack of regulatory transparency, national treatment problems of discrimination against foreign firms, and the lack of uniformity in the administration of Chinese trade policies throughout the country. All of these problems, however, are matters that the GATT regime has not been able to deal with effectively in the past because of ambiguous GATT rules and extensive noncompliance. Hence, these problems may persist regardless of whether China is offered accession to GATT/WTO or not.

CONCLUSION

Evidence from the only trade dispute settled by China and the United States in the 1980s shows that the Chinese response strategy to US unilateral trade policy change demands may be called combative counterpunch and differs significantly from the response strategies of Japan, Korea, and Taiwan. Though the Chinese are as export dependent upon the US as their East Asian neighbors, they are willing to exploit their import and investment power to threaten counterretaliation against the United States. Thus, multilateral and minilateral regime rules and dispute settlement procedures may be useful means to encourage Chinese settlement agreement in compliance with international norms.

Countries such as Korea, Taiwan, Singapore, Indonesia, Malaysia, Thailand, the Philippines, and Vietnam have the most to lose from massive Chinese exports without counterbalancing Chinese imports. The rest of the region will greatly benefit from improved access to the Chinese market (admittedly Japan more than anyone) and minilateral legitimacy, pressure, and bargaining strategies can replace the bilateral acrimony of US unilateral demand. Thus, one policy option will be to regionalize pressure on China to open its import markets through minilateral institutions in the Pacific. Second, the members of GATT/WTO should demand extensive Chinese policy change as a condition for full GATT membership. Regime members recall that comparatively easy terms of entry offered for political reasons with Japan in the 1950s and with Korea in the 1960s led to years of acrimony in international trade diplomacy. Nevertheless, regime dispute settlement procedures aim to encourage compliance with rules of the regime, and these procedures can be important to changing Chinese policy through the normative pressure of GATT/WTO legitimacy rather than the coercive pressure of American trade power. The Chinese government has made impressive strides toward marketization, and additional Chinese policy change may be more likely obtained inside the regime than outside it. Thus, liberal political economy recommends that China's accession to GATT/WTO along the Yugoslav phased-accession model will get results.[70] American 301 policy can continue to be usefully deployed by taking rule-noncompliant Chinese trade barriers before WTO dispute settlement panels. Panel findings can offer political cover to the Chinese government, as they have for other East Asian states. Use of 301 policy in this way will offer the United States not only market openings but also domestic political payoffs from demonstrating that tough action is being taken against China. Economic sanctions (after legitimized by WTO dispute settlement procedures) can be threatened or even deployed against China as part of an aggressive 301 strategy to achieve specific economic-policy changes. Section 301 has been used with finesse against Japan, Korea, and Taiwan to create more open markets in East Asia, encourage more compliance with international trade regime rules, and promote commercial competition in the Pacific. It can do the same with China, but it should supplement multilateralism and minilateral regionalism in American trade diplomacy, not supplant them.

CHAPTER 9

Institutions of Trade Diplomacy in the Pacific

USTR carried out American 301 unilateralism in the Pacific during the 1970s and 1980s with considerable success, as measured by the increases in commercial competition and in GATT compliance that trade dispute diplomacy engendered. Still, 301 unilateralism fomented acrimony and calls for rebellion throughout East Asia, where governments resented being bullied by the US government into changing their trade policies. According to liberal political economy, the problem was one of multilateral institutional weakness: neither dispute settlement procedures nor the rules of GATT were adequate for trade dispute settlement diplomacy in the Pacific. According to liberal political economy, the policy solution lies in improving both the dispute settlement procedures and the rules of the GATT regime. The Uruguay Round agreements do just that. As important as these multilateral institutional improvements are, however, they likely are inadequate for effective trade dispute settlement diplomacy in the Pacific in the years to come. In this chapter, liberal political-economy theory on regional institutions and integration is drawn from in order to explore institution-building potential in the Pacific region.

Recent analysis by economists takes a dim view of the prospects for a regional integration in the form of a free-trade area in the Pacific. An Asian free-trade area "lacks a compelling economic rationale," in the judgment of Linda Lim.[1] Liberal political-economy theory from political science, however, shows that regional integration and institution building is a political process that is often motivated more by political goals than by economic goals. Liberal political economy shows that regional cooperation is best predicted by the analysis of three variables—structural conditions (state political-economy structures), process conditions (transactions), and perceptual conditions (cost benefit and salience). Using this analytic framework, this chapter concludes that prospects for regional institution building through APEC and the

Asian Development Bank are favorable but that American leadership is crucial. It is also concluded here that regional institutions can supplement WTO multilateralism by leaving dispute settlement to WTO dispute settlement procedures in cases where WTO rules apply and by promoting minilateral cooperation through (1) information gathering and dissemination, especially on state trade policies, (2) the establishment of an appeals body (on the model of the NAFTA body) for antidumping/countervailing-duty decisions that pertain to regional trade, and (3) ongoing consultations on commercial-standards harmonization.

This chapter begins with an analysis of the limitations of 301 unilateralism and GATT multilateralism for trade dispute diplomacy in the Pacific, followed by a review of liberal political-economy theory on minilateral cooperation. Liberal political-economy theory on regional institution building is applied to the contemporary setting in the Pacific, with conclusions for theory and policy.

LIMITATIONS OF UNILATERALISM AND MULTILATERALISM

For the United States, the Uruguay Round dispute settlement negotiations were about improving procedures, but for the rest of the GATT membership—and especially for the East Asian countries who found themselves so often on the wrong end of the 301 gun barrel—the negotiations were about ridding the world trade community of 301, Super 301, and Special 301. Section 301 trade policy has reached some limits as a tool of American trade dispute diplomacy. Commercial conflict between the United States and Japan, Korea, and Taiwan in the late 1980s raced ahead of GATT rules: construction, satellite, and supercomputer procurement with Japan, product standards with Japan, intellectual-property rights with Korea and Taiwan, services with all three countries. The root of an increasing number of Pacific trade disputes (e.g., semiconductors and supercomputers) is industrial organization: *keiretsu* in Japan and *chaebol* in Korea. USTR was less often able to take its complaint before a GATT dispute settlement panel, for when GATT rules are ambiguous or nonexistent, legalistic GATT dispute settlement procedures cannot function,[2] and rule-oriented trade diplomacy is left behind for power-oriented trade diplomacy. At the end of the 1980s, GATT rules were ambiguous in important issues of trade dispute diplomacy, such as national treatment and health, safety, product, and environmental standards, or nonexistent in issues such as services, intellectual-property rights, and antitrust. As a result, domestic critics of GATT multilateralism in the United

States contend that GATT is dead or irrelevant, and foreign and domestic critics of American 301 unilateralism contend that US trade dispute diplomacy is the product of an arrogant, but declining hegemon. The GATT critics call for more unilateralism and managed-trade diplomacy; the 301 critics call for more multilateral diplomacy.[3]

The Uruguay Round resulted in unprecedented institution building: substantial progress in market sectors with a long history of institutionalized protectionism (textiles and agriculture); new rule creation in services and intellectual-property rights; refined international trade law regarding subsidies, antidumping, and government procurement; reformed dispute settlement procedures; and the establishment of the World Trade Organization. The WTO will be the institutional successor to the GATT beginning in July 1995, but only for countries that agree to sign all Uruguay Round agreements. Formal accession by all GATT members may not be achievable. The "Understanding on Rules and Procedures Governing the Settlement of Disputes" formalizes dispute settlement procedures for greater legal adjudicatory settlements rather than negotiated compromise settlements. The important innovations of the new procedures are that the establishment of a dispute settlement panel can no longer be blocked by one member (typically the respondent), the panel works under strict time guidelines, adoption of the final panel decision cannot be blocked by one member (again, typically the respondent), and compensation from the respondent is authorized in the event the initiator prevails. A respondent who believes the panel finding in error may appeal the decision to the new Appellate Body. The WTO offers new rules and refined rules for adjudication of disputes about government procurement, services, and intellectual property. The WTO Dispute Settlement Body should be quite busy for some years settling the disputes that have backed up during the Uruguay Round. These agreements are extraordinary achievements of international trade diplomacy.

Yet WTO multilateralism can bring only partial relief to the problems of trade dispute diplomacy in the Pacific. Though ultimately successful after seven years of negotiation, achieving cooperation in these difficult areas of economic relations among more than 100 countries and without a dominant US hegemon proved to be exceedingly difficult. The tortuous process toward "success" suggests that substantial change is called for in international trade diplomacy. Some critics of GATT diplomacy conclude that the problem is rule-oriented diplomacy itself (whether it is naive in an anarchic world or simply impractical in a world with so many differing national political economies) and that some kind of managed-trade regime should be implemented.

Still, the world economy already has managed trade in some markets (e.g., apparel, agriculture, steel), and nobody thinks that the industries in these sectors are as efficient as they could be or that consumers are getting a good deal. Peter Cowhey and Jonathan Aronson offer useful prescriptions for improvement, rather than abandonment, of rule-oriented trade diplomacy.[4] They recommend a "Market Access Regime" with more reliance on bilateral and minilateral (i.e., regional) negotiating fora and on sector-specific codes, but within the GATT-based multilateral framework. This international policy strategy possesses the considerable merit of being congruent with some trends already present in the world economy. Sectorism, though always present in the form of protectionist orderly marketing arrangements and voluntary export restraints, has found new proponents in market-opening attempts such as the GATS service talks in the Uruguay Round, with its framework General Agreement on Trade in Services and a number of service-sector-specific codes. Minilateral regionalism has found many advocates in the past few years, beginning with the EC92 initiative and including the North American Free Trade Area, the ASEAN free trade agreement, and regional integration initiatives in Central and South America. Minilateral regionalism is considered as a matter of liberal political-economy theory in the next section.

LIBERAL POLITICAL ECONOMY ON REGIONALISM

The extant minilateral institutions that aim to promote cooperation in various regions of the world political economy are not equally ready to meet the demands of the task. The European Community, despite its present troubles with monetary-policy cooperation, is the world's most impressive minilateral regime for the promotion of economic cooperation. Extrapolating from the US-Canada Free Trade Agreement, the North American Free Trade Agreement creates model institutions of regional cooperation and aims to harmonize trade-related policies. That NAFTA integrates an industrializing political economy with advanced industrialized political economies is all the more significant. But the institutions for cooperation in the Pacific region, the third leg of the so-called triad in the world economy, are not at all as impressive as the EC or NAFTA. Why?

In a recent article, Donald Crone draws from 1980s realist and liberal political-economy theory on international interdependence and regimes to argue that Pacific minilateral cooperation has been poorly developed because of American hegemony in the region.[5] He contends that the United States encouraged minilateralism in Europe but discouraged it in the Pacific and that the decline of American hegemony has allowed the minimal institutionalization that has occurred. Crone's thesis is largely right, for analysis of power structures is always the best starting point and US power has been crucial to the organization of the Pacific. The problem is a good deal more complicated, however, than a reduction to changes in regional power structures. Crone and most everyone else who has written on this topic have ignored the regional-integration scholarship initiated in 1958 by Ernst Haas with *The Uniting of Europe* and closed in 1975 by Haas with *The Obsolescence of Regional Integration Theory*.[6] Ignoring this liberal political-economy scholarship has been justified by the contention that political events regarding regional integration better explained the rise and fall of regional-integration theory than the other way around, but this scholarship nevertheless made useful, if tentative, contributions to understanding these issues.[7]

Countries integrate, despite the loss of sovereignty it entails, in order to market opportunities for their domestic business firms, create economies of scale, promote resource use efficiencies, and enhance competitiveness. Integration increases economic growth, leading not only to further-expanding market opportunities but also engendering greater political stability and, in the long term, more democratic polities. It heightens interdependence, i.e., mutual dependence among the partners, reducing the likelihood of war (though bringing more low-level conflict). The policies of the partners tend to be more stable and predictable, for they have been bound internationally with their regional partners. With their bigger markets and more efficient industries, countries also augment their bargaining power in multilateral trade and economic relations when they integrate.

How regional integration happens or whether regional integration happens at all depends upon three sets of variables—structural conditions, process conditions, and perceptual conditions.[8] Structural conditions mean the structures of the actors and their circumstances, including the size and composition of the economic units of member states, their cultural values, and their adaptability. Process conditions mean the type and number of interactions and transactions among the actors, including trade, investment, and technology flows, coalitions and alliances, and external-actor participation in the region (IGOs, NGOs, other states). Perceptual conditions mean the actors' perceived assessments of the utility of pursuing regional integration, including the distribution of benefits and costs, and the salience of integration to them. The research of the era, based upon empirical study of regional-integration regimes such as the European Community, the European Free

Trade Association, the Latin American Free Trade Association, and COME-CON, tentatively concluded that nonhegemonic cooperation is facilitated by more equal distribution within the structural conditions, that a perceived equity in distribution of benefits at relatively low cost facilitates cooperation, and that increasing transactions and technical linkages spill over to encourage continuing integration. Hegemonic power, though a possible catalyst (e.g., the EEC) is not necessary, these scholars found. Every case study of regional integration, however, indicated that leadership was important.

The evidence that the United States at the end of World War II choked off regional integration is quite strong. The United Nations established the Economic Commission for Asia and the Far East (ECAFE) in 1946, but with a mission limited to data collection and dissemination. Many of the members wanted ECAFE to focus on promoting development, and India and China wanted it to implement a Marshall Plan for Asia, but the United States, the Western powers, and the UN Secretariat leadership opposed this broader mission. ECAFE nevertheless extended its data collection mandate to get all the members to standardize trade statistics with the GATT members (SITCS) and worked to harmonize customs regulations. ECAFE, later renamed the Economic and Social Commission for Asia and the Pacific (ESCAP), toiled in relative obscurity, responsible to the UN Secretariat (as the UN insisted) and not to its membership (as ESCAP leaders wanted).[9] The next major institutional initiative in the Pacific region did not occur until the mid-1960s, with the establishment of the Asian Development Bank (ADB). ADB was the creation of President Lyndon Johnson, an achievement made possible by the crisis atmosphere of the hot war with Vietnam, the Cold War with the Soviet Union, and the Cultural Revolution in China and despite the opposition of the World Bank and the US Department of the Treasury.[10] These same conditions led to the creation of the Association of Southeast Asian Nations (ASEAN) in 1967.

By the late 1960s and during the 1970s, however, a number of the states of the region had established their national development strategies around trade relations with the United States (not with each other), US foreign-policy makers were playing the strategic triangle game in the "high politics" of the region and cutting bilateral trade deals in the "low politics" of the region, and the ASEAN members were split between allegiance (in a manner of speaking) to free trade and alliance with the US and allegiance to the New International Economic Order and alliance with UNCTAD, the Group of 77, and the nonaligned movement. Since the 1980s, Pacific minilateralism has received much discussion but has so far been only talk, and businesspeople, academics, and journalists have been doing most of the talking. Thus, American power encouraged limited institutionalization (ESCAP, ADB, ASEAN) and discouraged deeper institutionalization, but it was not the only factor. The structural conditions—size and composition of economic units, cultural values, and member state adaptability—may have been positive in the 1950s, but process conditions—type and number of transactions, technical linkages, regional coalitions, and external actors (the UN)—worked against ESCAP becoming a major minilateral institution. Furthermore, US opposition implied that the minilateralism's perceived benefits were lower and its costs higher than bilateralism. During the 1960s and 1970s, neither structural nor process nor perceptual conditions favored cooperation. What are prospects for the growth of minilateral regimes in the Pacific region in the 1990s?

THE PACIFIC REGIONAL OPPORTUNITY

Conditions changed in the 1980s and are favorable for cooperation in the 1990s.

Structural conditions: The economies of the region are the fastest growing in the world. GDP growth per year in the 1980s was about 7% in Taiwan and Hong Kong and about 10% in South Korea and China and ranged from 5–8% in the ASEAN countries (except for the troubled Philippines).[11] The populations in the region are large: ASEAN 317 million, Japan 123 million, Taiwan and South Korea 63 million, Vietnam 70 million, and, of course, China 1.2 billion. Japan, Korea, and Taiwan have lowered trade barriers, largely as a result of US pressure. ASEAN has pledged to lower its trade barriers within the group. China and Vietnam have reentered the world economy and are lowering their trade and economic barriers. Cultural values still vary widely in the region, but the NIEO (New International Economic Order) and Marxism are dead; there is broad agreement favoring liberal economics (if still of a neomercantilistic brand). Despite recent political liberalization in Japan, Korea, and Taiwan, the governments of the region largely remain capable of taking the political actions needed for minilateral cooperation.

Process conditions: The number of transactions within the region are increasing dramatically, as are the technical linkages across money and finance, trade, and investment (portfolio and direct). Though trade relations in the region continue to be more bilateral with the US, the patterns of trade are gradually changing as investment (especially Japanese) has spread, leading to greater intrafirm trade. Trade in the region exceeds $700 billion. About 70% of non-Japanese exports of Pacific countries are exported within the region; only 26% of the East Asian Newly Industrializing Countries exports and only about 19% of ASEAN exports go to the United States. Previously impossible regional coalitions may be put together, for a new, possibly bolder Japanese leadership has taken over that seems intent on improving its standing in the region, China's relations with South Korea and ASEAN are cordial (with Singapore quite close) and with Taiwan and Japan manageable. Relations within ASEAN recently produced a free-trade agreement.

Perceptual conditions: The US market is saturated, and regional businesses are searching for new market opportunities. The European Community markets are also saturated. Region members fear rising protectionism in both the United States and the EC. Continuing to focus on the US market will sow more seeds of trouble with the economically, politically, and militarily most important single actor in the region. The business and political leaders see great market opportunities in Asia. Thus, benefits of minilateralism seem great, the costs of not acting seem high, and the salience of minilateralism has never been higher.

Yet American leadership remains decisive to cooperation in the region, for neither China nor Japan nor ASEAN possesses the capability to lead in the region. It is in US interests to pursue a major initiative aimed at creating institutions of minilateral cooperation in the region. East Asian markets are already the fastest growing in the world, though much of the growth is owed to access to the relatively open US market. Greater regional market integration can open new markets for US business interests. It can regionalize pressure on the East Asian states to open their markets to international competition, thus reducing the bilateral tensions between the US and the East Asian states. This is salient to US-Japan relations now and will become ever more salient to US-China relations in the years ahead. Greater economic growth can contribute to empowering business and labor groups, thus pluralizing the political economies in a region given to authoritarianism. Greater pluralism and greater regional economic interdependence can reduce the threat of war (though they will increase the need for better minilateral dispute settlement procedures for low-level conflict).

The minilateral organization must be governmental in membership, so the forum should not be the nongovernmental Pacific Economic Cooperation Conference (PECC). The UN-ESCAP, ADB, and Asia Pacific Economic Conference (APEC) are thus possible governmental institutions to encourage cooperation in the region. ESCAP is not likely to be able to do much because it is a UN agency and thus does not have the confidence of the major powers in the region and because it has long been eclipsed by the United Nations.

ADB and APEC, however, are good candidates for minilateral institutions to promote regional cooperation, if the compatibility problems with the World Bank and GATT can be solved.

WHAT REGIONAL INSTITUTIONS CAN DO

Implementing this strategy in the world economy will be easier said than done, of course. Some observers assert that minilateral regionalism is a movement toward regional blocs and away from a liberal world economy. Minerva Etzioni wrote in 1970 that policymakers who think that the world's problems are global and therefore demand only multilateral solutions are too doctrinaire and too ambitious and fail to consider the heterogeneity of the world. Circumstances in the world economy in the 1990s make this more true, not less true. The dilemma, however, is how to find the right fit between regionalism and multilateralism.

Etzioni argued that compatibility rests mainly on the type of problem and is most likely when the exercise of a particular function devolves primarily to one level or the other or when a regional organization asserts its jurisdiction only over problems whose consequences remain within the region. The regional institutions must be designed carefully to be compatible with extant international organizations and regimes. The compatibility problem is manageable in the trade areas (including services, national-treatment and standards harmonization, and intellectual-property rights) because the GATT regime members recognize that it needs minilateral help to achieve its multilateral purposes and because regional cooperation (the EC and NAFTA) is already legitimate.

The compatibility problem is manageable in the direct-investment area because international regimes in this area are weak. Thus, policymakers in the world economy are today presented with a historic opportunity to establish new regimes for direct investment under the auspices of the World Bank and the Asian Development Bank and to establish new regimes for trade-related areas under GATT and APEC auspices. Direct investment has become a matter of GATT negotiation, with some observers calling for a GATT for investment. Direct investment was also addressed in the November 1993 Seattle APEC framework agreement. (The World Bank and the Asian Development Bank, however, may be better suited as the institutions with the expertise to promote cooperation in direct investment.) Though international regimes for currency and finance are generally recognized to be in need of major overhaul and because regional cooperation (e.g., the European

Monetary System) is already legitimate, thus offering Pacific regional policy-makers opportunity to take action, cooperation in these matters has proven to be exceedingly difficult to achieve; hence, they are probably best left out of it in the near term.

The nongovernmental PECC and similar business, labor, journalistic, and academic fora can play important supplementary roles in promoting Pacific cooperation. The PECC forum is especially useful because it includes participation of business leaders in the Pacific. The exchange of information and the promotion of cooperation among business enterprises in the region promote the reduction of commercial conflicts that lead to interstate commercial disputes (and sometimes the use of American 301 policy). The PECC forum will allow business and labor leaders of the region a means to recommend policy initiatives to the governmental regional fora. USTR and Commerce department policymakers thus ought to encourage American business enterprises with significant interests in the Pacific economy to attend meetings of the PECC.

The Pacific minilateral institution(s) of cooperation can do much to promote regional cooperation through augmented information-gathering activities. A secretariat or commission of APEC can gather information on the economic policies of the states of the Pacific economy: tariffs, quotas, customs procedures, and other import policies, standards for product safety and performance, regulations on production (labor, health, and safety and the environment), and policies on competition (antitrust, intellectual-property rights, direct investment, joint venture, and licensing). The secretariat can institutionalize the organizational capabilities to create study groups on anything of concern within the Pacific economy. It can also institutionalize a commitment to publishing and disseminating these study findings. Knowledge about the policies of the countries in the region is important to business and government policymakers, since it is information necessary for the gradual harmonization of these policies.

A Pacific institution can also create an appeals body for antidumping and countervailing-duty actions. Antidumping and countervailing-duty disputes have become a major issue in trade dispute diplomacy in the Pacific in the 1980s. East Asian governments and businesspeople, as well as many American economists, contend that the Commerce Department is implementing protectionism with these policies. The NAFTA treaty (as had the US-Canada FTA before it) addressed this problem of trade diplomacy by establishing an appeals panel in order to give business firms that believe they are the victims of a wrongful AD/CVD decision an opportunity to get their case reheard. The establishment of a similar appeals body for the Pacific could be an institutional innovation that might legitimize antidumping and countervailing-duty procedures and remove a contentious issue from Pacific trade diplomacy.

A Pacific institution can also create a forum for ongoing consultations on commercial-standards harmonization. The harmonization of standards is one of the most important tasks of international trade diplomacy in the contemporary world. Standards are an important policy means of national governments to ensure that their consumers receive quality products and services. But differing national standards for goods and services are expensive for international business. Harmonization can provide the rationalization of international production. Standards harmonization in the 1990s will require a massive effort through multilateral, minilateral, bilateral, and unilateral strategies. The major European Community initiatives at standards harmonization under way through directives and mutual recognition show that minilateral institutions can serve an important role and do so in a way that is compatible with multilateral efforts.

CONCLUSION

Unilateralism through 301 policy and multilateralism through GATT face limitations, even as they promote dispute settlement diplomacy in the Pacific. In this chapter, theory from liberal political economy has been applied to the contemporary setting in the Pacific and contrasted with the history of institution building in the region, with the conclusion that structural conditions, process conditions, and perceptual conditions favor minilateral, regional cooperation, though the diplomacy of the United States will likely be needed. Pacific institutions such as APEC and/or the Asian Development Bank make an important contribution to trade dispute diplomacy in the Pacific by gathering and disseminating information on trade and economic policies and practices in the region, by establishing an appeals body for antidumping and countervailing-duty disputes, and by providing a forum for consultations on standards harmonization. Trade diplomacy in the world economy demands full exploitation of the institutions of international cooperation, and American 301 trade unilateralism, Pacific regionalism, and GATT multilateralism can complement each other.

CHAPTER 10

Rules, Power, and the Pacific Economy

Both realist political economy and liberal political economy significantly contribute to our understanding of the 301 initiation decisions by USTR and of the trade dispute settlement processes and outcomes between the United States and Japan, Korea, and Taiwan. As philosopher of science Larry Laudan explains, a research tradition that is making progress in the solution of interesting problems has reason to persist, and as the liberals might say, the competition is healthy for the field.

In *Rules, Norms, and Decisions*, Friedrich Kratochwil argues deductively that power and rules influence decision makers by offering reasons for action. That power influences decision making in world politics is not news, but the hypothesis that rules influence decision making in ways logically similar to power is a contribution of the liberal research tradition. Although liberal political economy has often asserted that regimes and their rules influence state behavior in world politics, it has not supported this with much evidence. This study has empirically shown that in bilateral trade dispute settlement, power and rules do indeed influence state decision makers in initiation decisions, processes, and settlement outcomes.

In this concluding chapter, the implications of this study are drawn out for government policymakers in the Pacific countries, for business enterprise managers in the Pacific economy, and for researchers in international relations and political economy.

IMPLICATIONS FOR GOVERNMENT POLICYMAKERS

Impressed by the logic of the tit-for-tat strategy in game theory accounts of the evolution of cooperation,[1] several political scientists have recommended the tit-for-tat strategy to American trade policymakers. Judith Goldstein and Stephen Krasner urge that

---

179

American interests lie with the continuation of a liberal trading regime. The United States can best insure international cooperation by responding in kind to foreign practices. If states are willing to cooperate, so should the United States; if states defect from accepted GATT rules and norms, the United States should retaliate. If the practice is halted, American sanctions should be stopped.[2]

Similarly, Carolyn Rhodes argues that her "case research confirms that coercive tactics, whether part of a reciprocal strategy or not, have the effect of inducing a cooperative response from a trading partner" and that "the best strategy against being a victim [of a noncooperative action] is to pursue a reciprocal strategy oneself."[3] The implications of the present study are broadly congruent with the tit-for-tat strategy. This study shows that as a matter of state strategy, trade policy can encourage more compliance with trade regimes and thereby promote the interests of domestic industries. An implication of this study, however, is that a negotiate first, then sanction strategy of rule-oriented trade diplomacy will achieve more cooperative outcomes—settlement agreements with political cover and more examples of substantial compliance—than will a tit for tat of power-oriented trade diplomacy. Rule-oriented diplomacy should be the policy response to regime-noncompliant trade behavior. Negotiation under the regime offers the opportunity to change trade behavior before economic sanctions are threatened or used. Rule-oriented diplomacy offers the opportunity to build an American consensus around the successful resolution of the dispute and around the threat or actual use of national power in support of goal achievement. Rule-oriented diplomacy also offers the opportunity to acquire international legitimacy for any use of American power, especially through the use of GATT dispute settlement procedures. In this way, unilateral action can contribute to the maintenance of trade regimes.

Tit for tat assumes a purely bilateral relationship; trade relations are inherently multilateral. Hence, even bilateral dispute settlement must be carried out with multilateral considerations in mind. This study shows that the dispute often can be resolved without the actual deployment of American retaliation, without the American "tat." The US (and all states) should use its "tat" as a tactic to move the recalcitrant negotiator the last mile, not the first mile. Nevertheless, as long as the world political economy is decentralized and the regime lacks enforcement capability, states need the option to use national power in support of their policy goals.

This study lends support to the arguments made by Robert Hudec that some unilateral action brought under the 301 policy may be "justified disobedience" and with Alan Sykes that a "limited case for Section 301"[4] can be made. The empirical evidence presented in this study of 301 trade dispute settlement in the Pacific shows that American negotiators implement Section 301 policy with great attention to the maintenance and growth of the GATT regime. American unilateral enforcement of multilateral and bilateral economic treaties with the East Asian states has not only contributed to achieving the goal of increasing American wealth by promoting domestic business interests abroad but also, in the process, furthered the US goal of promoting the maintenance of the liberal, rule-oriented GATT regime in Pacific commercial relations. The US has been acting as an agent for the membership of the GATT regime and has contributed an international public good.

As a matter of national policy, state trade policy can protect domestic industries when threatened with injury from foreign competition, and it can open foreign markets for domestic industries that confront barriers. These capabilities of state strategy are especially important in the contemporary world economy, when commercial competition is so intense. As Helen Milner and David Yoffie point out, modern high-technology industries face sizable R&D demands and steep learning curves; they need large economies of scale. Hence, they need global markets and demand that their government provide them.[5] Although trade dispute diplomacy has achieved considerable success, it has been carried out to the near exclusion of export promotion diplomacy. Erland Heginbotham's *Asia's Rising Economic Tide: Unique Opportunities for the US* offers a primer for international marketing diplomacy in the Pacific.[6]

Nevertheless, the rule-oriented diplomacy that the US has been pursuing in the Pacific economy, especially toward Japan, has been criticized as softheaded and naive. Trade policy is now seen as a vital aspect of national-security policy, and for some observers this suggests that traditional Cold War American national-security strategy ought to guide trade policy toward Japan. The national-security strategy of the United States that has guided American national policy in the Cold War era has been, in the words of George Kennan, a "long-term, patient but firm and vigilant containment of Russian expansive tendencies."[7] The strategy of containment (as articulated by NSC-68) aimed to meet the Soviet Union with counterforce at all points along its perimeter in order to safeguard the ideals of free society in the world outside the Soviet bloc. The strategy of containment, some suggest,[8] should be reformulated, so that US policy aims to contain not the Soviet Union but

Japan. Some commentators contend that Japan, Inc., threatens American wealth, prosperity, and power and therefore must be contained.

The "contain Japan" policy strategy, however, is based on misunderstanding about the Japanese political-economy and industrial structure, which no longer depends upon the administered guidance of MITI planners for its success (see Chapter 7). Though it is true that the Japanese state promotes firm competitiveness through prudent domestic policy (if tilted toward producers and away from consumers) and through enlightened foreign policy (Japanese foreign-policy makers from the Ministries of Foreign Affairs, Finance, International Trade and Industry, and others, look out for the international interests of Japanese firms), in the main, Japan's wealth and prosperity today rest on the competitiveness of its firms.

Contain Japan is based on a misunderstanding about the implications of the present world economy for world politics. In the past, states sought territory; today states seek the ability to create wealth.[9] More than ever before, the main locus for the creation of wealth is the multinational business enterprise. Multinational business enterprises possess the intellectual, organizational, and capital capacities to create technology- and information-intensive products and services for a twenty-first-century world economy. The technologies and information are globally diffused; hence, the business enterprises must be globally dispersed. The most sophisticated demand conditions, the most intense firm rivalries, and the ablest suppliers tend to cluster in different parts of the world economy. Business enterprises, therefore, seek the demanding, sophisticated consumers and the knowledgeable and skilled employees wherever they can be found. Japanese consumers and producers ought to be made more interdependent with the world economy and cannot be contained.

At present, most internationally competitive industries are located in Europe, North America, and Japan. But the rapid diffusion of knowledge and technology ensures that competition in the world economy will continue to diversify geographically. If American wealth, prosperity, and power are threatened, it is due to the failure of American business leaders to manage global competition effectively, and of American policymakers to create through strategy and policy the conditions for firm competitive advantage in the world economy. American policymakers have placed trade policy at the center of their global economic strategy. State trade policy can open foreign markets and countervail foreign government subsidies. (State trade policy can also close markets through many policy tools.) Yet, as a matter of state strategy, trade policy is now reaching its limits and can no longer do much in support of the key goals that state policymakers and their citizens now demand. State trade policy of the advanced industrialized states can do little more to increase the vital goals of national wealth, prosperity, and power. Wealth today primarily rests on the commercial competitiveness of firms, and the commercial competitiveness of firms in the advanced industrialized states does not rest much on state trade policy.

Analysis of the semiconductor dispute between the United States and Japan underscores the point. The dispute was superficially about trade, and the US government sought to solve the problem through trade policy, but the dispute was really (as the Japanese explained) about the differing industrial organizations of the two industries: large, vertically integrated producers and users of semiconductors in Japan and small, specialized producers in the United States. The semiconductor industry, like many emergent technology-intensive industries, demands massive commitments of capital for R&D and for production, huge economies of scale, world-class technological capabilities, and organizational flexibility—in short, global strategy with global capabilities. The Japanese producers—Toshiba, NEC, Fujitsu, etc.—possessed global strategy and capabilities. The American survivors—Intel, Motorola, Texas Instruments, IBM—also possess global strategies and capabilities. The managed-trade solution to the semiconductor dispute—the 20% market share targets—was perhaps the best available solution in politically difficult circumstances but was fundamentally flawed. It reinforced MITI power in the Japanese economy (by demanding that it administer the chip prices and import shares with the companies) when MITI power had been eroding as a consequence of change in the Japanese political economy. It contradicted USTR's strategy to "attack the Japanese system." The solution did nothing about the cross-subsidization within the integrated Japanese firms, made possible by their cartel control of the distribution of consumer electronics in the Japanese marketplace. And it did little to help American companies become more competitive in global markets. Admirers of the target share solution offer the evidence that the American share eventually hit 20% (after six years of minimal gains), but I submit that the achievement had more to do with the products being produced by the American companies, especially the microprocessors of Intel, than the governmental agreement. In short, the semiconductor case should have been quietly forgotten as an aberrant 301 case; it should not have become the precedent for the Clinton administration's "results-oriented," managed-trade strategy toward Japan. USTR had articulated an excellent strategy toward Japan with its rule-oriented strategy to "attack the Japanese political economy." Rule-oriented diplomacy notched real successes and is consistent with the direction of change in the Japanese economy, the Pacific economy, and the world economy.

Politicians who respond to quarterly trade balance figures with bombastic talk about what can be done with trade policy crowbars do little to create conditions for change. The goal of state strategy must be to improve the commercial competitiveness of firms, which rests primarily on what firms do, though state governments can help. Michael Porter's *Competitive Advantage of Nations*, Michael Dertouzos and colleagues' *Made in America: Regaining the Productive Edge*, and Gunnar Sletmo and Gavin Boyd's *Pacific Industrial Policies*[10] offer useful starting places for policy discussion.

As a matter of multilateral trade diplomacy, the Uruguay Round of multilateral trade negotiations, initiated in 1986 and completed in December 1993, was an extraordinary achievement of international trade diplomacy. The Uruguay Round extended GATT rules to trade in services and made progress toward free trade in apparel and agriculture. But, the demand now is for the creation of new international economic—albeit trade-related—regimes: the international harmonization of policy on competition/antitrust, intellectual property, investment, environmental regulations, labor, health, safety, and product standards. In the Uruguay Round, substantial progress in these issue areas was only achieved on intellectual property. The "wise men" (as they are sometimes called) who created the network of international regimes and organizations at the end of the Second World War provided the institutional means for state cooperation in these functional areas. Competition in the world economy now demands their full exploitation.

Thus, I recommend that the US return to its rule-oriented strategy of attacking the Japanese political economy but move it forward. I offer the following recommendations for solving the US-Japan economic problem, a twelve-point plan:

(1) Publicize in the world economy all Japanese GATT-noncompliant trade barriers.

(2) Encourage other Pacific states to publicize all Japanese GATT-noncompliant trade barriers.

(3) Pursue aggressive 301 unilateralism against Japanese GATT-violating trade barriers, especially Uruguay Round agreement violations in government procurement and telecommunications. Be sure to seek the legitimacy of GATT dispute settlement procedures.

(4) Encourage other Pacific states to pursue GATT dispute settlement procedures against Japanese noncompliant trade barriers.

(5) Improve the export capabilities of American firms.

(6) Pressure the Japanese government to rationalize the distribution system, especially at the consumer retail level.

(7) Promote the entry of major American retailers into the Japanese market.

(8) Pressure the Japanese government to enforce vigorously its antitrust policies.

(9) Write new rules regarding competition and antitrust under GATT/WTO auspices.

(10) Encourage through merger and strategic alliance the establishment of firms with global capabilities and strategies in emerging high-technology sectors.

(11) Write new framework agreements on standards and regulations harmonization under GATT/WTO auspices.

(12) Write agreements specifying definitive rules regarding the harmonization of specific product standards and safety, health, and environmental regulations under APEC auspices.

The American commitment to a rule-oriented trade policy strategy ought to include US compliance with GATT rules. The Japanese government now publishes its own annual "Report on Unfair Trade Policies by Major Trading Partners," which purports (along with the European Community Commission's annual "Trade Barriers and Unfair Trade Practices") to respond to USTR's annual "National Trade Estimates Report on Foreign Trade Barriers." The Japanese government cites US-demanded orderly marketing agreements in steel, machine tools, textiles and apparel, and (disingenuously) automobiles.[11] They also cite extensive abuse by the US government of its antidumping procedures. Scholars in the United States have similarly found examples of US noncompliance with GATT panel findings against it.[12] The existence of the Japanese report is a positive step toward more rule-oriented trade diplomacy in the Pacific.

IMPLICATIONS FOR BUSINESS ENTERPRISE MANAGERS

American 301 trade policy can be a useful means through which American business enterprise managers can get the US government to help them change competitive opportunities in their environment. But global managers must get USTR to act, so it is important to be aware of USTR's initiation tendencies (see Chapter 2). Industries that are commercially competitive and can demonstrate high GATT regime utility are most likely to move USTR to action. Industries that are commercially competitive but cannot offer high GATT regime utility probably will get action. Industries that possess low commercial competitiveness but can offer high GATT regime utility possibly will get USTR action. And industries that offer neither high commercial competitiveness nor GATT regime utility are unlikely to get 301 action on their behalf.

The Uruguay Round agreements, including the "Dispute Settlement Understanding," will not bring much change to USTR's implementation of 301 policy. The variables that have explained the initiation decision will likely continue to do so, and the investigation and negotiation processes will likely change marginally. Henceforth, all, rather than most, cases alleging GATT noncompliance will go before a GATT panel. Despite the rhetoric that GATT panel procedures slow down bilateral dispute settlement, there is no evidence in the Pacific experience that they did so (if anything, the evidence points in the other direction), and the new expedited procedures will speed the process a bit. The regime rule growth in services, intellectual property, investment, agricultural subsidies, import licensing, customs valuation, rule of origin, and government procurement suggests that disputes that have lingered without resolution for some time can and will now be raised and settled.

USTR will, however, continue to take up the cases that involve disputes not covered by extant GATT rules. USTR might look especially favorably over the next few years on cases involving issues that promote its overall strategy, such as standards and regulations harmonization, services, and competition policy, and those involving emerging major markets, such as China, India, and Southeast Asia. Cases involving Central and South America must overcome USTR's reluctance to revisit the squandered effort on Brazil informatics but will become increasingly viable as more exports from these countries are sent to the US and as talks progress on enlargement of NAFTA southward. Those involving eastern Europe and Russia risk entanglement with security and diplomatic-policy considerations, so they may be more difficult to get initiated.

With this in mind, here are a few recommendations for global managers on the use of 301:

(1) When confronting a trade policy problem in a foreign country, always try first to solve the problem yourself through techniques

of marketing. Initiating 301 may cause friction on the other side, so avoid it if you can.

(2) If your efforts fail with the foreign government, hire a trade lawyer who knows the 301 players, the arguments that will move them to action, and the wheels that need greasing.

(3) Announce to the businesspeople and government officials of the other country that you intend to file a 301 petition. The threat of 301 and the hope of keeping it from being formally initiated may encourage them to change their position.

(4) Throughout the 301 investigation and negotiations, be prepared to devote considerable executive and staff time to the problem. You always want the USTR negotiators to know exactly what the problems are and what your goals are. USTR will put only a couple of very busy people on your case, so you and your lawyers must offer a lot of help.

(5) Throughout the 301 investigation and negotiations, keep your eyes open for hints that the other side is ready to cut a deal that will terminate the 301 process.

(6) After an agreement is signed, expect to devote staff time and more legal fees to ensure compliance by the foreign country with the settlement agreement. The staff at USTR will move on to new trade problems and will not devote much attention to monitoring compliance in old cases. It's your business; it's up to you to provide surveillance.

(7) The whole process will likely take a year. If the survival of your firm is threatened by that timetable, then find a non-trade policy solution to your problem.

IMPLICATIONS FOR RESEARCHERS

The present research encourages further study into the strategic choices of firms. All the trade disputes investigated here were the result of business enterprise decisions to pursue political strategies to achieve goals. Systematic research is needed on the costs and benefits of political strategies. These findings must be weighed against the pros and cons of standard techniques of marketing, management, and organization. Rule-oriented diplomacy may be the better means to resolve interstate conflict when the alternative is power-oriented diplomacy, but for business enterprises, political strategies of any kind may represent a solution only second-best when compared to those provided by global capabilities and strategies.

As a matter of international relations theory, this study has not fully explained the contingent ways in which power and rules influence bargaining strategies of states in international economic dispute diplomacy. Additional research can offer a better understanding of these processes not only in international trade relations but in other issues of the world political economy, such as direct investment and intellectual-property rights. The major limitation of research design in the present study is its confinement to US-initiated disputes. More comprehensive study of dispute settlement in the world economy must vary the poles of state power in the disputes, so that playing by the rules is not studied only as the demand by the stronger on the weaker in international trade diplomacy.

Notes

NOTES TO CHAPTER 1

1. David Halberstam, *The Reckoning* (New York: William Morrow, 1986); Stephen S. Cohen and John Zysman, *Manufacturing Matters: The Myth of the Post-Industrial Economy* (New York: Basic Books, 1987); Michael L. Dertouzos et al., *Made in America: Regaining the Productive Edge* (Cambridge: MIT Press, 1989). For industry-by-industry analysis, see Gary C. Hufbauer, Diane T. Berliner, and Kimberly Ann Elliott, *Trade Protection in the United States: 31 Case Studies* (Washington: IIE, 1986); John Zysman and Laura Tyson, eds., *American Industry in International Competition: Government Policies and Corporate Strategies* (Ithaca: Cornell University Press, 1983). For analyses of the broader economic problems of the region and of the world, see C. Fred Bergsten and William R. Cline, *The United States-Japan Economic Problem* (Washington: IIE, 1987); C. Fred Bergsten, ed., *Global Economic Imbalances* (Washington: IIE, 1985); Bela Balassa and John Williamson, *Adjusting to Success: Balance of Payments Policy in the East Asian NICs* (Washington: IIE, 1987); Thomas O. Bayard and Soo-Gil Young, eds., *Economic Relations between the United States and Korea: Conflict or Cooperation?* (Washington: IIE, 1988).

2. David B. Yoffie, *Power and Protectionism: Strategies of the Newly Industrialized Countries* (New York: Columbia University Press, 1983).

3. I. M. Destler, *Making Foreign Economic Policy* (Washington: Brookings Institution, 1980); Robert A. Pastor, *Congress and the Politics of US Foreign Economic Policy* (Berkeley: University of California Press, 1980); Robert E. Baldwin, *The Political Economy of US Import Policy* (Cambridge: MIT Press, 1985); G. John Ikenberry, David A. Lake, and Michael Mastanduno, eds., *The State and American Foreign Economic Policy*, special issue of *International Organization* 42 (winter 1988).

4. John A. C. Conybeare, "Tariff Protection in Developed and Developing Countries: A Cross-Sectional and Longitudinal Analysis," *International Organization* 37 (summer 1983), 441–468; Timothy J. McKeown, "Firms and Tariff Regime Change: Explaining the Demand for Protection," *World Politics* 36 (1984), 215–233; Judith Goldstein, "The Political Economy of Trade: Institutions of Protection," *American Political Science Review* 80 (March 1986), 162–184; Stefanie Ann Lenway, *The Politics of US International Trade: Protection, Expansion, and Escape* (Marshfield, Mass.: Pit-

man, 1985); H. Richard Friman, *Patchwork Protectionism: Textile Trade Policy in the United States, Japan, and West Germany* (Ithaca: Cornell University Press, 1990).

5. I. M. Destler, *American Trade Politics: System under Stress* (Washington: IIE, 1986).

6. I. M. Destler and John S. Odell, *Anti-Protectionism: Changing Forces in United States Trade Politics* (Washington: IIE, 1987); Helen V. Milner, *Resisting Protectionism: Global Industries and the Politics of International Trade* (Princeton: Princeton University Press, 1988).

7. Judith Goldstein and Stefanie Ann Lenway, "Interests or Institutions: An Inquiry into Congressional-ITC Relations," *International Studies Quarterly* 33 (September 1989), 303–328.

8. Interview by author, #9018 (27 April 1990).

9. Interview by author, #9016 (15 December 1989).

10. Interview by author, #9009 (26 April 1990).

11. Interview by author, #9113 (4 October 1991).

12. Interview by author, #9006 (26 April 1990).

13. John H. Jackson, "The Crumbling Institutions of the Liberal Trade System," *Journal of World Trade Law* 12 (March-April 1978), 93.

14. General Agreement on Tariffs and Trade, opened for signature 30 October 1947, 61 Stat. A3, T.I.A.S. No. 1700, 55 U.N.T.S. 187. See Robert E. Hudec, *The GATT Legal System and World Trade Diplomacy*, 2d ed. (Salem, N.H.: Butterworth, 1990), 78–88.

15. William J. Diebold, *The End of the ITO* (Princeton: Princeton University Press, 1952); John H. Jackson, *World Trade and the Law of GATT: An Analysis of the General Agreements on Tariffs and Trade* (Indianapolis: Bobbs-Merrill, 1969); Kenneth W. Dam, *The GATT: Law and International Economic Organization* (Chicago: University of Chicago Press, 1970).

16. Jock A. Finlayson and Mark W. Zacher, "The GATT and the Regulation of Trade Barriers," in Stephen D. Krasner, ed., *International Regimes* (Ithaca: Cornell University Press, 1983), 274.

17. Vinod K. Aggarwal, *Liberal Protectionism: The International Politics of Organized Textile Trade* (Berkeley: University of California Press, 1985).

18. R. Michael Gadbaw, "Reciprocity and Its Implications for US Trade Policy," *Law and Policy in International Business* 14 (1982), 691–746.

19. Hudec, *GATT Legal System and World Trade Diplomacy*, 85–95.

20. Pierre Pescatore, William J. Davey, and Andreas F. Lowenfeld, *Handbook of GATT Dispute Settlement* (Ardsley-on-Hudson, N.Y.: Transnational Juris Publications, 1992).

21. Hudec, *GATT Legal System and World Trade Diplomacy*, 85–95.

22. John H. Jackson, "Dispute Settlement Techniques between Nations concerning Economic Relations—With Special Emphasis on GATT," in Thomas E. Carbonneau, ed., *Resolving Transnational Disputes Through International Arbitration* (Charlottesville: University Press of Virginia, 1984), 39–72.

23. "Testimony to the House Ways and Means Committee of Ambassador Michael Kantor," USTR, Washington, D.C., 26 January 1994.

24. W. Christopher Lenhardt and Michael P. Ryan, "Rules, Power, and Outcomes in GATT Dispute Settlement," paper presented at the American Political Science Association annual meeting, Washington, D.C., 2–5 September 1993.

25. Larry Laudan, *Progress and Its Problems: Towards a Theory of Scientific Growth* (Berkeley: University of California Press, 1977), 55.

26. Ibid., 57.

27. Robert O. Keohane and Joseph S. Nye, *Power and Interdependence: World Politics in Transition* (Boston: Little, Brown, 1977), 37.

28. Robert Gilpin, *The Political Economy of International Relations* (Princeton: Princeton University Press, 1987); Stephen D. Krasner, *Structural Conflict: The Third World against Global Liberalism* (Berkeley: University of California Press, 1985); David A. Lake, *Power, Protection, and Free Trade: International Sources of US Commercial Strategy, 1887-1939*; Joseph M. Grieco, *Cooperation among Nations: Europe, America, and Non-Tariff Barriers to Trade* (Ithaca: Cornell University Press, 1990).

29. Keohane and Nye, *Power and Interdependence*, 37.

30. I. M. Destler, *American Trade Politics* (Washington: IIE, 1992); Harold K. Jacobson, *Networks of Interdependence: International Organizations and the Global Political System* (New York: Alfred A. Knopf, 1984); Robert O. Keohane, *After Hegemony: Cooperation and Discord in the World Political Economy* (Princeton: Princeton University Press, 1984); Oran R. Young, *International Cooperation: Building Regimes for Natural Resources and the Environment* (Ithaca: Cornell University Press, 1989).

31. I. M. Destler, *Making Foreign Economic Policy*; Pastor, *Congress and the Politics of US Foreign Economic Policy*; Joanne Gowa, *Closing the Gold Window: Domestic Politics and the End of Bretton Woods* (Ithaca: Cornell University Press, 1983); Benjamin J. Cohen, *In Whose Interest? International Banking and American Foreign Policy* (New Haven: Yale University Press, 1986); Milner, *Resisting Protectionism*.

32. Timothy J. McKeown, "The Limitations of 'Structural' Theories of Commercial Policies," *International Organization* 40 (winter 1986), 43–64.

33. E. E. Schattschneider, *Politics, Pressures, and the Tariff* (New York: Prentice-Hall, 1935); McKeown, "Firms and Tariff Regime Change"; James Cassing, Timothy J. McKeown, and Jack Ochs, "The Political Economy of the Tariff Cycle," *American Political Science Review* 80 (September 1986), 843–862; Vinod K. Aggarwal, Robert O. Keohane, David B. Yoffie, "The Dynamics of Negotiated Protectionism," *American Political Science Review* 81 (June 1987), 345–366.

34. Pastor, *Congress and the Politics of US Foreign Economic Policy*.

35. Lenway, *The Politics of US International Trade*; Baldwin, *The Political Economy of US Import Policy*; I. M. Destler, *American Trade Politics* (Washington: IIE, 1986/1992); Goldstein, "The Political Economy of Trade"; Judith Goldstein, "Ideas, Institutions, and American Trade Policy," *International Organization* 43 (winter 1988), 31–72; Edwin J. Ray, "Changing Patterns of Protectionism: The Fall in Tariffs and the Rise in Nontariff Barriers," *Northwestern Journal of International Law and Business* 8 (1987), 285–327; Goldstein and Lenway, "Interests or Institutions."

36. International Organization 42 (winter 1988).

37. Graham T. Allison, *Essence of Decision: Explaining the Cuban Missile Crisis* (Boston: Little, Brown, 1971); Morton A. Halperin, *Bureaucratic Politics and Foreign Policy* (Washington: Brookings Institution, 1974).

38. Alexander George, "Case Studies and Theory Development: The Method of Structured, Focused Comparison," in Paul Gordon Lauren, ed., *Diplomacy: New Approaches in History, Theory, and Policy* (New York: Free Press, 1979), 43–68; Alexander George and Timothy J. McKeown, "Case Studies and Theories of Organizational Decision Making," in Robert J. Coulam and Richard A. Smith, eds., *Advances in Information Processing in Organizations* (Greenwich, Conn.: JAI Press, 1985). See also Christopher Achen and Duncan Snidal, "Rational Deterrence Theory and Comparative Case Studies," *World Politics* 41 (January 1989), 143–169; Lawrence B. Mohr, "The Reliability of the Case Study As a Source of Information," in Coulam and Smith, *Advances in Information Processing in Organizations*, 65–93; Jack Snyder, "Richness, Rigor, and Relevance in the Study of Soviet Foreign Policy," *International Security* 9 (1984–85), 89–108.

39. Thomas F. Shannon et al., "Petition for Relief under Section 301 of the Trade Act As Amended on Behalf of Footwear Industries of America, Inc., Amalgamated Clothing and Textile Workers Union, AFL-CIO, and the United Food Commercial Workers Union, AFL-CIO," Collier, Shannon, Rill & Scott, Washington, D.C., October 1982.

40. USTR, *Federal Register* 50–37609.

41. Ibid.

42. Alan Wolff et al., "Petition of the Semiconductor Industry Association before the Section 301 Committee, Office of the United States Trade Representative," Dewey, Ballantine, Washington, D.C., June 1985.

43. USTR, *Federal Register* 50–37609.

44. Richard Rivers et al., "Comments Regarding the Investigation into Korean Restrictions on Insurance Services," Akin, Gump, Strauss, Hauer & Feld, Washington, D.C., October 1985.

45. USTR, *Federal Register* 50–37609.

46. Paul Rosenthal et al., "Petition for Relief under Section 301 of the Trade Act of 1974, As Amended, on Behalf of the American Meat Institute," Collier, Shannon, Rill & Scott, Washington, D.C., February 1988.

47. Bart S. Fisher and Steven M. Schneebaum, "Section 301 Petition of the Rice Millers' Association," Patton, Boggs & Blow, Washington, D.C., July 1983; *International Trade Reporter* (20 July 1983).

48. Michael Mastanduno, "Setting Market Access Priorities: The Use of Super 301 in US Trade with Japan," *World Economy* 15 (November 1992), 765–788; Ellis S. Krauss and Simon Reich, "Ideology, Interests, and the American Executive: Towards a Theory of Foreign Competition and Manufacturing Trade Policy," *International Organization* 46 (autumn 1992), 857–899.

49. Peter B. Evans, "Declining Hegemony and Assertive Industrialization: US-Brazil Conflicts in the Computer Industry," International Organization 43 (spring 1989) 207–238; Jagdish N. Bhagwati and Hugh Patrick, eds., *Aggressive Unilateralism: America's 301 Trade Policy and the World Trading System* (Ann Arbor: University of Michigan Press, 1990).

50. David A. Lake, *Power, Protection, and Free Trade: International Sources of Commercial Strategy 1887–1939* (Ithaca, NY: Cornell University Press, 1988).

51. Thomas O. Bayard and Kimberly Elliott, "'Aggressive Unilateralism' and Section 301: Market Opening or Market Closing?" *World Economy* 15 (1992), 685–706; Alan O. Sykes, "Constructive Unilateral Threats in International Commercial Relations: The Limited Case for Section 301," *Law and Policy in International Business* 23 (spring 1992), 263–330; Robert E. Hudec, "Thinking about the New Section 301: Beyond Good and Evil," in eds., Bhagwati and Patrick, *Aggressive Unilateralism* 113–162.

52. Yoffie, *Power and Protectionism.*

53. Linda Lim, "Engines of Regional Integration in Asia," in *AFTA after NAFTA* (Washington: Korea Economic Institute of America, 1993), 145–159.

NOTES TO CHAPTER 2

1. Raymond A. Bauer, Ithiel de Sola Pool, and Lewis Anthony Dexter, *American Business and Public Policy: The Politics of Foreign Trade* (New York: Aldine-Atherton, 1972); Zysman and Tyson, eds., *American Industry in International Competition*; Milner, *Resisting Protectionism*; Helen V. Milner and David B. Yoffie, "Between Free Trade and Protectionism: Strategic Trade Policy and a Theory of Corporate Trade Demands," *International Organization* 43 (spring 1989), 239–273.

2. John S. Odell, "The Outcomes of International Trade Conflicts: The US and South Korea, 1960–1981," *International Studies Quarterly* 29 (September 1985), 263–286.

3. Yoffie, *Power and Protectionism.*

4. Interview by author, #9027 (12 December 1989).

5. Paul A. Anderson, "Foreign Policy As a Goal-Directed Activity," *Philosophy of Social Science* 14 (1984), 159–181.

6. Alfred K. Kahn, *The Economics of Regulation: Principles and Institutions* (Cambridge: MIT Press, 1988).

7. Theodore J. Lowi, *The End of Liberalism: The Second Republic of the United States* (New York: W. W. Norton, 1979), 125.

8. Martin Sklar, *The Corporate Reconstruction of American Capitalism, 1890-1916* (New York: Cambridge University Press, 1988), 88.

9. Lowi, *End of Liberalism.*

10. James W. Wilson, ed., *The Politics of Regulation* (New York: Basic Books, 1980).

11. David Vogel, *National Styles of Regulation: Environmental Policy in Great Britain and the United States* (Ithaca: Cornell University Press, 1986).

12. Stephen D. Krasner, "State Power and the Structure of Foreign Trade," *World Politics* 28 (April 1976), 317–347; David Lake, *Power, Protection, and Free Trade.*

13. Stephanie Ann Lenway, *The Politics of US International Trade.*

14. DoC-ITA, US Foreign Trade Highlights, various years.

15. For the year 1991, see International Monetary Fund, *Direction of Trade Statistics Yearbook 1992.*

16. DoC-ITA, *US Foreign Trade Highlights* (1988).

17. Useful legal analyses of the statute can be found in Fisher and Steinhardt, "Section 301 of the Trade Act of 1974"; Bello and Holmer, "Section 301 of the Trade Act of 1974"; Judith H. Bello and Alan F. Holmer, "The Heart of the 1988 Trade Act: A Legislative History of the Amendments to Section 301," in Bhagwati and Patrick, eds., *Aggressive Unilateralism*, 49–90.

18. "Office of the US Trade Representative," Washington, D.C., circa 1989.

19. Organizational chart of USTR, Washington, D.C., January 1990.

20. "USTR Announces Staff Changes," press release, Washington, D.C., 20 March 1990.

21. Albert Bandura, *Social Foundations of Thought and Action: A Social Cognitive Theory* (Englewood Cliffs, N.J.: Prentice-Hall, 1986).

22. Biographical documents, Office of Public Affairs, USTR, Washington, D.C. Coded by highest degree earned.

23. Interview by author, #9007 (24 April 1990).

24. Interviews by author, #9021 (14 December 1990), #9022 (18 January 1990), #9033 (26 April 1990).

25. *Journal of Commerce* (21 March 1985), A4.

26. Daniel Patrick Moynihan, "US Should Centralize Trade Responsibility," *Journal of Commerce* (23 December 1982).

27. Press release, Office of the Press Secretary, White House, Washington, D.C., 11 April 1985; *New York Times* (12 April 1985), 1.

28. *Journal of Commerce* (21 March 1985), A4.

29. Clyde V. Prestowitz, Jr., *Trading Places: How We Allowed Japan to Take the Lead* (New York: Basic Books, 1988), 57.

30. *National Journal* (4 December 1985), 2865–2866.

31. John H. Jackson, "Perspectives on the Jurisprudence of International Trade: Costs and Benefits of Legal Procedures in the United States," *Michigan Law Review* 82 (April-May 1984), 1570–1587.

32. Interviews by author, #9006 (26 April 1990), #9011 (24 April 1990), #9027 (12 December 1989). A useful outline of procedures appears in Bello and Holmer, "Section 301 of the Trade Act of 1974."

33. Interviews by author, #9008 (27 April 1990), #9030 (24 April 1990).

34. John Sullivan Wilson, "The US Performance in Advanced Technology Trade, 1982–93 (est.): Measurement Issues and Policy Relevance," working paper, National Academy of Sciences, Washington, D.C., 1993.

35. The high-technology industries according to the DoC-ITA methodology are (1) biotechnology, (2) life science, (3)optoelectronics, (4) computers, (5) telecommunications, (6) computer-integrated manufacturing, (7) electronics, (8) advanced materials, (9) aerospace, (10) weapons, and (11) nuclear technology.

36. Paul Smith, "Taiwan Gambles on a Dicey Export Equation," *Far Eastern Economic Review* (5 April 1984).

37. Michael Mastanduno, "Do Relative Gains Matter? America's Response to Japanese Industrial Policy," *International Security* 16 (summer 1991), pp. 73–113.

38. Interview by author, #9002 (12 December 1989).

39. Interview by author, #9033 (26 April 1990).

40. Interview by author, #9014 (15 December 1989).

41. Interviews by author, #9033 (26 April 1990), #9027 (16 January 1990).

42. Interview by author, #9033 (26 April 1990).

43. Interview by author, #9007 (24 April 1990).

44. Edward J. Lincoln, *Japan's Unequal Trade* (Washington: Brookings Institution, 1990), 80.

NOTES TO CHAPTER 3

1. Dennis J. Encarnation, *Rivals beyond Trade: America versus Japan in Global Competition* (Ithaca: Cornell University Press, 1992); Lincoln, *Japan's Unequal Trade*; for a differing view, see any of the numerous papers by Gary Saxonhouse, including "What Does Japanese Trade Structure Tell Us about Japanese Trade Policy?" *Journal of Economic Perspectives* 7 (summer 1993), 21–44.

2. Chalmers A. Johnson, *MITI and the Japanese Miracle* (Stanford: Stanford University Press, 1982); Marie Anchordoguy, "A Challenge to Free Trade? Japanese Industrial Targeting in the Computer and Semiconductor Industries," in Kozo Yamamura, ed., *Japan's Economic Structure* (Seattle: Society for Japanese Studies, 1990); Daniel I. Okimoto, *Between MITI and the Market: Japanese Industrial Policy for High Technology* (Stanford: Stanford University Press, 1989).

3. David Friedman, *The Misunderstood Miracle: Industrial Development and Political Change in Japan* (Ithaca: Cornell University Press, 1988); Okimota, *Between MITI and the Market*.

4. Alice H. Amsden, *Asia's Next Giant: South Korea and Late Industrialization* (New York: Oxford University Press, 1989); Robert Wade, *Governing the Market: Economic Theory and the Role of Government in East Asian Industrialization* (Princeton: Princeton University Press, 1990).

5. Stephen Haggard, *Pathways from the Periphery: The Politics of Growth in the Newly Industrializing Countries* (Ithaca: Cornell University Press, 1990); Tun-jen Cheng, "Political Regimes and Development Strategies: South Korea and Taiwan," in Gary Gereffi and Donald Wyman, eds., *Manufacturing Miracles: Paths of Industrialization in Latin America and East Asia* (Princeton: Princeton University Press, 1990), 139–178.

6. Wade, *Governing the Market*.

7. Amsden, *Asia's Next Giant*.

8. Warren Hunsberger, *Japan and the United States in World Trade* (New York: Harper & Row, 1964), 12.

9. Ibid., 12–13.

10. Friedrich Victor Meyer, *International Trade Policy* (New York: St. Martin's Press, 1978), 193.

11. Gary R. Saxonhouse and Robert M. Stern, "An Analytical Survey of Formal and Informal Barriers to International Trade and Investment in the United States, Canada, and Japan," *IPPS Discussion Paper* (Ann Arbor: Institute of Public Policy Studies, 1988), 8.

12. Paul W. Kuznets, *Economic Growth and Structure in the Republic of Korea* (New Haven: Yale University Press, 1977), 153.

13. Okyu Kwon, "An Assessment of Korean Trade Policies," in *US-Korea Economic Relations* (Bloomington, Ind.: Korea Economic Institute of America, 1992), 144.

14. Kuznets, *Economic Growth in Korea*, 153.

15. USTR, *1992 National Trade Estimate Report on Foreign Trade Barriers* (Washington: GPO, 1992), 158.

16. Wade, *Governing the Market*, 123.

17. USTR, *1992 Foreign Trade Barriers*, 123.

18. Bunroku Yoshino, "Japan and the Uruguay Round," in Henry Nau, ed., *Domestic Trade Politics and the Uruguay Round* (New York: Columbia University Press, 1989), 115–116.

19. Okimoto, *Between MITI and the Market*, 9.

20. Interview by author, #9115 (4 October 1991).

21. Okimoto, *Between MITI and the Market*, 9.

22. Johnson, *MITI and the Japanese Miracle*, 265–274.

23. Ibid., 265.

24. Ibid.; Daniel I. Okimoto, "Political Inclusivity: The Domestic Structure of Trade," in Takashi Inoguchi and Daniel I. Okimoto, eds., *The Political Economy of Japan: The Changing International Context* (Stanford: Stanford University Press, 1988).

25. B. C. Koh, *Japan's Administrative Elite* (Berkeley: University of California Press, 1989), 29.

26. Interviews by author, #9112 (4 October 1991), #9113 (5 October 1991).

27. Interview by author, #9112 (4 October 1991).

28. Interview by author, #9014 (15 December 1989); Okimoto makes the same point in "Political Inclusivity," 335.

29. Interviews by author, #9033 (26 April 1990), #9110 (3 October 1991), #9112 (5 October 1991), #9115 (4 October 1991).

30. Aurelia George, *The Politics of Liberalization in Japan: The Case of Rice* (Canberra: Research School of Pacific Studies, Australian National University, 1990).

31. Interviews by author, #9110 (3 October 1991), #9112 (4 October 1991), #9113 (5 October 1991), #9115 (4 October 1991).

32. Chalmers A. Johnson, "MITI, MPT, and the Telecom Wars," in *Politics and Productivity: The Real Story of How Japan Works* (New York: Ballinger, 1989).

33. Interview by author, #9001 (27 April 1990).

34. Interviews by author, #9129 (11 October 1991), #9130 (10 October 1991), #9132 (11 October 1991).

35. Interview by author, #9130 (10 October 1991).

36. J. W. Wheeler and Perry L. Wood, *Trade Policy Formation in Selected Developing Countries* (Indianapolis: Hudson Institute, 1986).

37. Ibid., 120.

38. Kim Kihwan and Chung Hwa Soo, "Korea's Domestic Trade Politics and the Uruguay Round," in Nau, ed., *Domestic Trade Politics and the Uruguay Round*, 137.

39. Amsden, *Asia's Next Giant*, 169.

40. Kim and Chung, "Korea's Domestic Trade Politics," 137.

41. Ibid., 138.

42. Hung-mao Tien, *Politics of Social Change in the Republic of China.*

43. Wheeler and Wood, *Trade Policy Formation*, 109.

44. Interview by author, #9112 (4 October 1991).

45. Wade, *Governing the Market*, 220.

46. Wheeler and Wood, *Trade Policy Formation*, 110.

47. Interviews by author, #9120 (24 August 1991), #9122 (7 October 1991), #9128 (7 October 1991).

48. Interviews by author, #9122 (7 October 1991), #9120 (24 September 1991).

49. Interviews by author, #9127 (7 October 1991), #9132 (11 October 1991).

50. *National Journal* (9 October 1989), 1712.

51. *New York Times* (10 December 1989), F1.

52. Yoffie, *Power and Protectionism.*

NOTES TO CHAPTER 4

1. David B. Yoffie, "Adjustment in the Footwear Industry," in Zysman and Tyson, *American Industry in International Competition*, 324.

2. Milner, *Resisting Protectionism*, 104.

3. Ibid., 106.

4. Letter to Ambassador Bill Brock from members of Congress dated 29 September 1982, public file #301–36, USTR, Washington, D.C.

5. Ibid.

6. Shannon et al., "Footwear Petition," 161.

7. Ibid., "Footwear Petition," 2, 134. Taiwan is bound bilaterally with the United States to observe the GATT and the Tokyo Round codes.

8. Ibid., "Footwear Petition," 138.

9. Dennis James, "Memorandum on Behalf of the Taiwan Footwear Manufacturers Association Regarding the Footwear Section 301 Petition," Kaplan, Russin & Veechi, Washington, D.C., November 1982.

10. Ibid., 10.

11. "Response of the Government of the Republic of Korea Concerning the Section 301 Investigation Involving Nonrubber Footwear Products from the Republic of Korea," no author, December 1982, public file #301–37, USTR, Washington, D.C.

12. Ibid., 2.

13. Shannon et al., "Footwear Petition," 146.

14. Letter to Jeanne S. Archibald, USTR, from Michael R. Kershow of Collier, Shannon, Rill & Scott, Washington, D.C., page 12, public file #301–37, USTR, Washington, D.C.

15. USTR, *Federal Register* 47–56428.

16. "Statement of NIKE, Inc.," public file #301–36, USTR, Washington, D.C.

17. Letter to Ambassador Michael Smith, USTR, from Ambassador Sang Yong Park, Republic of Korea, dated 1 February 1983, public file #301–37, USTR, Washington, D.C.

18. *Footwear News* (31 January 1983), 2.

19. Thomas F. Shannon et al., "Petition under Section 301of the Trade Act of 1974, As Amended, Filed on Behalf of Footwear Industries of America, Inc., Amalgamated Clothing and Textile Workers Union, AFL-CIO, and United Food and Commercial Workers International Union, AFL-CIO," Collier, Shannon, Rill & Scott, Washington, D.C., June 1983.

20. *International Trade Reporter* (17 August 1983).

21. USTR, *Federal Register* 48–36729.

22. Statement of Fawn Evenson, Vice President for Government Relations, Footwear Industries Association, quoted in *Footwear News* (8 August 1983), 1.

23. Ibid.

24. Memorandum from USTR to Lauren R. Howard, of Collier, Shannon, Rill & Scott, Washington, D.C., 19 October 1983, public file #301–37, USTR, Washington, D.C.

25. USTR, *Federal Register* 48–56561.

26. Interview by author, #9115 (4 October 1991).

27. "Termination of Investigation Against Brazil and the Republic of Korea," USTR, Washington, D.C., 31 March 1984.

28. *International Trade Reporter* (25 January 1984).

29. Interviews by author, #9027 (12 December 1989), #9033 (27 April 1990).

30. "Japanese Position Paper on the Import Restrictions on Leather," no author or date, public file #301–13, USTR, Washington, D.C.

31. Interview by author, #9033 (26 April 1990).

32. Interview by author, #9007 (24 April 1990).

33. Interview by author, #9033 (26 April 1990).

34. *GATT Activities in 1983*, doc. #GATT/1984–2, June 1984.

35. Interview by author, #9027 (12 December 1989).

36. "GATT Panel Report on Japanese Leather Import Quotas," *US Export Weekly* 20 (19 June 1984), 1082–1089.

37. *New York Times* (6 December 1985), 1.

38. *International Trade Reporter* (1 January 1986); USTR, *Federal Register* 51–9437.

39. *Journal of Commerce* (8 August 1985), 3A.

40. *Footwear News* (15 December 1986), 2.

41. USTR, *Federal Register* 51–21036.

42. DoC, *US Foreign Trade Highlights 1988* (Washington: GPO, 1988), 187, 299.

43. *Journal of Commerce* (21 May 1987), A2.

44. *New York Times* (5 April 1990), C14.

45. Fisher and Schneebaum, "Section 301 Petition of the Rice Millers' Association" *International Trade Reporter* (20 July 1983).

46. *International Trade Reporter* (20 July 1983); *Far Eastern Economic Review* (20 October 1983), 78–79.

47. *Far Eastern Economic Review* (20 October 1983), 78–79.

48. Exchange of letters between Bart S. Fisher and Steven M. Schneebaum of Patton, Boggs & Blow, Washington, D.C., and Jeanne Archibald of USTR dated 26 and 19 August 1983, public file #301–43, USTR, Washington, D.C.

49. Thomas H. McGowan, "Memorandum in Opposition to Acceptance of Section 301 Petition Regarding Rice," Kaplan, Russin & Veechi, Washington, D.C., August 1983.

50. Ibid., 4.

51. Ibid., 9.

52. Interview by author, #9006 (26 April 1990).

53. *Far Eastern Economic Review* (20 October 1983), 78–79.

54. *Far Eastern Economic Review* (19 November 1982), 74–77; Joseph A. Yager, *Transforming Agriculture in Taiwan: The Experience of the Joint Commission on Rural Reconstruction* (Ithaca: Cornell University Press, 1988).

55. Letter from Bart S. Fisher and Steven M. Schneebaum of Patton, Bogg & Blow, Washington, D.C., to Jeanne Archibald of USTR dated 29 September 1983, public file #301–43, USTR, Washington, D.C.

56. Letter from John Baize of the American Soybean Association to Jeanne Archibald of USTR circa December 1983; letter from Darwin E. Stolte of US Feed Grains Council to Chairman, Section 301 Committee, USTR, dated 10 January 1984; letter from Winston Wilson of the US Wheat Associates to Jeanne Archibald of USTR dated 12 January 1984; public file #301–43, USTR, Washington, D.C.

57. Letter from John Breuz et al. to Ambassador Bill Brock dated 23 January 1984, public file #301–43, USTR, Washington, D.C.

58. Letter from Senator David Pryor to Ambassador William Brock dated 27 January 1984, public file #301–43, USTR, Washington, D.C.

59. Letters dated 1 March 1984 between David Dean, Chairman of the Board and Managing Director, American Institute in Taiwan and Frederick F. Chien, Representative, Coordination Council for North American Affairs; letter dated 9 March 1984 from Bart S. Fisher and Steven M. Schneebaum of Patton, Boggs & Blow (Washington, DC) to Jeanne Archibald, USTR, public file #301–43, USTR, Washington, DC; USTR, *Federal Register* 84–7636.

60. Interviews by author, #9006 (26 April 1990), #9120 (24 September 1991), #9122 (7 October 1991).

61. USTR, *1990 National Trade Estimate Report on Foreign Trade Barriers* (Washington, DC: Government Printing Office, 1990), 187.

62. *New York Times* (27 August 1985), 27; *New York Times* (8 September 1985), 1.

63. "Section 301 Table of Cases," USTR, Washington, D.C., December 1989.

64. United States Cigarette Export Association, "Response of the United States Export Association to the Investigation Pursuant to Section 301 of the Trade Act of 1974 with Respect to the Manufacture, Importation, and Sale of Tobacco Products in Japan," USCEA, Washington, D.C., October 1985.

65. *International Trade Reporter* (18 January 1983); *Forbes* (21 February 1983), 99–104.

66. *Forbes* (21 February 1983), 99–104.

67. *Journal of Commerce* (21 April 1982), 36.

68. *Journal of Commerce* (17 September 1982), 36.

69. *International Trade Reporter* (17 August 1982).

70. *International Trade Reporter* (18 January 1983); *Forbes* (21 February 1983), 99–104.

71. *International Trade Reporter* (18 January 1983); *Far Eastern Economic Review* (3 February 1983), 10–12.

72. *International Trade Reporter* (19 July 1983).

73. *Far Eastern Economic Review* (27 December–3 January 1985), 74–75.

74. Ibid.

75. Carl J. Green et al., "Comments of Japan Tobacco Inc.," Wander, Murase & White, Washington, D.C., October 1985.

76. Ibid., 4.

77. USCEA, "Response."

78. Carl J. Green et al., "Reply of Japan Tobacco Inc."; United States Cigarette Export Association, "Supplemental Response," Washington, D.C., October 1985.

79. Green et al., "Reply of Japan Tobacco," 2.

80. Ibid., 17.

81. USCEA, "Response," 4.

82. Ibid., 8.

83. Ibid., 4.

84. Ibid., 10.

85. Letter to J. Christine Bliss, USTR, from Shigeo Kuroki, President, Japan Tobacco Growers Association, dated 22 November 1985, public file #301–50, USTR, Washington, D.C.

86. Letter from Ambassador Clayton Yeutter, US Trade Representative, to Senator Jesse Helms dated 11 February 1986, public file #301–50, USTR, Washington, D.C.

87. Letter from Senator Mitch McConnell dated 22 January 1986 and letter from Senator Jesse Helms dated 4 February 1986 to Ambassador Clayton Yeutter, US Trade Representative, public file #301–50, USTR, Washington, D.C.

88. Letter to Christopher Parlin, USTR, from Carl J. Green, Milbank, Tweed, Hadley & McCloy, Washington, D.C., dated 25 August 1986, public file #301–50, USTR, Washington, D.C.

89. *Journal of Commerce* (20 August 1986), 4A.

90. USTR, *Federal Register* 51–35995; *International Trade Reporter* (8 October 1986); *Wall Street Journal* (6 October 1986), 28.

91. *Wall Street Journal* (6 October 1986), 28.

92. *International Trade Reporter* (8 October 1986).

93. DoC, *US Foreign Trade Highlights, 1988* (Washington: GPO, 1988), 192.

94. Ibid.

95. Interview by author, #9024 (25 April 1990).

96. Paul C. Rosenthal, Laurence J. Lasoff, and Robin H. Beeckman, "Petition for Relief under Section 301 of the Trade Act of 1974, As Amended, on Behalf of the American Meat Institute," Collier, Shannon, Rill & Scott, Washington, D.C., February 1988.

97. USTR, *Federal Register* 53–10995; *New York Times* (29 March 1988), 41.

98. Rosenthal, Lasoff, and Beeckman, "Petition for Relief," 16.

99. "Comments of the Government of the Republic of Korea on the Issues Raised by the Petition filed by the American Meat Institute before the Office of the US Trade Representative," Embassy of the Republic of Korea, Washington, D.C., 22 April 1988, 23–26.

100. *Legal Times* (11 April 1989), 4.

101. *New York Times* (9 April 1989), 3; Press release, USTR, Washington, D.C., 18 May 1989.

102. *New York Times* (25 October 1988), 1; Balassa and Williamson, *Adjusting to Success.*

103. *New York Times* (26 October 1988), 34.

104. *Far Eastern Economic Review* (17 November 1988), 12; *New York Times* (29 December 1988), 30.

105. *Journal of Commerce* (10 April 1989), A1.

106. *Journal of Commerce* (15 August 1989), A1.

107. Korean Embassy, "Beef Petition Comments," 9.

108. Korean Embassy, "Beef Petition Comments."

109. Korean Embassy, Ibid., 17.

110. *Journal of Commerce* (16 May 1988), A9.

111. *Journal of Commerce* (4 October 1988), A1.

112. Interview by author, #9001 (27 April 1990).

113. *GATT Focus* (April-May 1988), 3.

114. *Journal of Commerce* (16 May 1988), A9.

115. *Journal of Commerce* (4 October 1988), A1.

116. USTR, *Federal Register* 54–35422.

117. USTR, *Federal Register* 54–35442.

118. *New York Times* (13 June 1989), 31; *Far Eastern Economic Review* (29 June 1989).

119. Paul Rosenthal and Robin H. Gilbert, "Comments of the American Meat Institute," Collier, Shannon & Scott, Washington, D.C., 22 September 1989.

120. *New York Times* (18 October 1989), 29.

121. USTR, *Federal Register* 90–11383.

122. Odell, "The Outcomes of International Trade Conflicts"; John A. C. Conybeare, *Trade Wars: The Theory and Practice of International Commercial Rivalry* (New York: Columbia University Press, 1987).

123. Yoffie, *Power and Protectionism.*

124. See also Odell, "The Outcomes of International Trade Conflicts"; Conybeare, *Trade Wars.*

125. William Mark Habeeb, *Power and Tactics in International Negotiation: How Weak Nations Bargain with Strong Nations* (Baltimore: Johns Hopkins University Press, 1988).

126. Interview by author, #9033 (26 April 1990).

127. Interview by author, #9027 (29 December 1989).

128. I. William Zartman and Maureen Berman, *The Practical Negotiator* (New Haven: Yale University Press, 1982).

NOTES TO CHAPTER 5

1. Wolf et al., "Petition of the Semiconductor Industry Association," 4.
2. Borrus, Millstein, and Zysman, "Trade and Development."
3. Prestowitz, *Trading Places*, 36.

4. Ibid., 36.

5. Ibid., 52.

6. Clyde V. Prestowitz, Jr., speech at SIA seminar, Kellogg Business School, Northwestern University, Evanston, Ill., 25 April 1989.

7. Ibid., 8.

8. Wolff, "Petition of the Semiconductor Association," 1–2.

9. Michael Borrus, James E. Millstein, and John Zysman, "Trade and Development in the Semiconductor Industry: Japanese Challenge and American Response," in Zysman and Tyson, *American Industry in International Competition*, 143–248.

10. Alan W. Wolff, "A New Round of GATT Negotiations for High Technology Products," speech before the Computer and Business Equipment Manufacturers Association International Trade Conference, Annapolis, Md., 5 March 1985, 4.

11. *Journal of Commerce* (27 June 1985), 1; *New York Times* (27 June 1985), 31.

12. *Electronic News* (17 June 1985), 1, cited in Ross L. Denton, "The Semiconductor Arrangement and Its Implementation," S.J.D. thesis, University of Michigan Law School.

13. *Electronic News* (22 July 1985), 1, cited in Denton, "Semiconductor Arrangement." See the Denton thesis for a review of reactions to the SIA petition.

14. Prestowitz, *Trading Places*, 56.

15. *Journal of Commerce* (15 July 1985), 5.

16. *Business Week* (15 September 1985), 126, cited in Denton, "Semiconductor Arrangement"; Prestowitz, *Trading Places*, 37.

17. H. William Tanaka, et al., "Brief of the Electronics Industries Association of Japan," Tanaka, Walders & Ritger, Washington, D.C.; Anderson, Hibeg, Nauheim & Blair, Washington, D.C.; Mudge, Rose, Guthrie, Alexander & Ferdon, New York, N.Y., August 1985.

18. Ibid., 32–36.

19. Ibid., 111.

20. *New York Times* (1 August 1985), 18.

21. Denton, "Semiconductor Arrangement."

22. *Electronic News* (7 October 1985), 1.

23. Thomas R. Howell et al., "Brief of the Semiconductor Industry Association," Dewey, Ballantine, Bushby, Palmer & Wood, Washington, D.C., October 1985.

24. Ibid., 5.

25. H. William Tanaka et al., "Reply of the Electronics Industries Association of Japan," Tanaka, Walders & Ritger, Washington, D.C., November, 1985.

26. Tanaka, "Brief of the Electronics Industry Association," 7.

27. Interviews by author, #9008 (27 April 1990), #9033 (26 April 1990); see Prestowitz, *Trading Places*, 64; for a detailed chronology, see Denton, "Semiconductor Arrangement."

28. Prestowitz, *Trading Places*, 60.

29. *United States News Service* (9 December 1985), cited in Denton, "Semiconductor Arrangement."

30. DoC, *Federal Register* 51–9087; DoC, *Federal Register* 51–9475.

31. H.R. 4800, *Congressional Record* (21 May 1986).

32. Prestowitz, *Trading Places*, 64.

33. Ibid., 50.

34. DoC suspended the pending semiconductor investigations on 6 August 1986. See *Federal Register* 51–28253. ITC suspended the pending semiconductor investigations on 7 August 1986. See *Federal Register* 51–28452.

35. Interview by author, #9033 (26 April 1990).

36. Interviews by author, #9008 (27 April 1990), #9027 (12 December 1989), #9033 (26 April 1990).

37. "Arrangement between the Government of Japan and the Government of the United States of America Concerning Trade in Semiconductor Products," 2 September 1986.

38. Letter to Ambassador Clayton Yeutter from Ambassador Matsunaga, quoted in Wolff et al., "Identification of Japan's Failure to Abide by the Semiconductor Agreement, Submission before the United States Trade Representative," Dewey, Ballantine, March 1989, 8.

39. *New York Times* (5 July 1986), 21.

40. *New York Times* (2 August 1986), 17 *Far Eastern Economic Review* (17 July 1986), 52.

41. *New York Times* (8 October 1986), 32.

42. Amelia Porges, "GATT Dispute Settlement Panel: Japan-Trade in Semiconductors, No.L6309," *American Journal of International Law* 83 (April 1989), 388–394.

43. *Wall Street Journal* (6 October 1986), 28.

44. *Far Eastern Economic Review* (25 September 1986).

45. *Far Eastern Economic Review* (9 October 1986), 70–71.

46. *Wall Street Journal* (30 January 1987), 20.

47. *Wall Street Journal* (27 February 1987), 44.

48. USTR, *Federal Register* 52–13419; *New York Times* (27 March 1987), 1; *New York Times* (28 March 1987), 1; *Wall Street Journal* (30 March 1987), 1.

49. USTR, *1990 National Trade Estimate Report*, 120.

50. Ibid.

51. *International Trade Reporter* (12 June 1991), 888.

52. *New York Times* (6 April 1990), C5.

53. *Wall Street Journal* (17 June 1991), B4.

54. *International Trade Reporter* (5 June 1991), 845; *New York Times* (5 June 1991), C11; *Wall Street Journal* (5 June 1991), A3.

55. USTR, *Federal Register* 50–37609.

56. Richard Rivers, Claude G. B. Fontheim, and Susan M. Frank, "Comments Regarding the Investigation into Korean Restrictions on Insurance Services," Akin, Gump, Strauss, Hauer & Feld, Washington, D.C., October 1985, 1.

57. "Treaty of Friendship, Commerce, and Navigation between the United States of America and the Republic of Korea," TIAS 3947,8 UST 2218–2237.

58. Exchange of letters between Melvin H. Levine, Counsellor of Embassy of Economic Affairs, Embassy of the United States, Seoul, Korea, and Lee Kyu-Sung, Assistant Minister of Finance, Ministry of Finance, Republic of Korea, dated 5–15 January 1981.

59. Rivers, Fontheim, and Frank, "Comments," 19.

60. Interview by author, #9029 (26 April 1990).

61. *International Trade Reporter* (2 October 1985).

62. *Far Eastern Economic Review* (16 September 1985), 12.

63. Memorandum from Henry G. Parker II, Chairman, International Insurance Advisory Council, dated 17 October 1985, public file #301–43, USTR.

64. Sukhan Kim et al., "Comments of Korean Insurance Associations Regarding the Section 301 Investigation of the Korean Insurance Market," Arnold & Porter, Washington, D.C., October 1985.

65. Ibid., 6.

66. *International Trade Reporter* (26 March 1986).

67. *Far Eastern Economic Review* (6 April 1989), 78–79; *Korea Business World* (October 1991), 51.

68. *Trade Losses Due to Piracy and Other Market Access Barriers Affecting the US Copyright Industries* (Washington: International Intellectual Property Alliance, August 1985).

69. Interview by author, #9028 (25 April 1990).

70. Statements by Pfizer Inc., New York, N.Y., dated 14 June 1985, and by the Pharmaceutical Manufacturers Association, Washington, D.C., dated 2 December 1985, public file #301–52, USTR, Washington, D.C.

71. Ibid., 2.

72. Ibid., 6.

73. Ibid., 2.

74. Statement by the International Intellectual Property Alliance, Washington, D.C., dated 2 December 1985, public file #501–52, USTR, Washington, D.C.

75. R. Michael Gadbaw, "Republic of Korea," in R. Michael Gadbaw and Timothy J. Richards, eds., *Intellectual Property Rights: Global Consensus, Global Conflict?* (Boulder, Colo.: Westview Press, 1988), 276.

76. International Intellectual Property Alliance, *Trade Losses Due to Piracy* (1985).

77. Ibid.

78. Interviews by author, #9028 (25 April 1990), #9031 (25 April 1990).

79. Interview by author, #9031 (25 April 1990).

80. *International Trade Reporter* (23 July 1986); USTR, *Federal Register* 51–29445; "Record of Understanding on Intellectual Property Rights," signed by Ambassador Kyung-Won Kim and Ambassador Clayton Yeutter, 28 August 1986.

81. Interviews by author, #9130 (10 October 1991), #9132 (11 October 1991).

82. USTR, *Federal Register* 52–3369.

83. Interview by author, #9031 (25 April 1990).

84. *Far Eastern Economic Review* (30 June 1988), 48.

85. USTR, *Federal Register* 53–22758.

86. *Far Eastern Economic Review* (30 June 1988), 48–49; *New York Times* (19 June 1988), 3A.

87. *Trade Losses Due to Piracy and Other Market Access Barriers Affecting the US Copyright Industries* (Washington: International Intellectual Property Alliance, April 1989).

88. USTR, *1990 Trade Estimate Report on Foreign Trade Barriers* (Washington: GPO, 1990), 133.

89. *New York Times* (2 November 1989), 23.

90. Interviews by author, #9001 (27 April 1990), #9031 (25 April 1990).

91. Ibid.

92. David T. Methe, *Technological Competition in Global Industries: Marketing and Planning Strategies for American Industry* (New York: Quorum Books, 1991), 75.

93. Interview by author, #9001 (27 April 1990).

94. USTR, *Federal Register* 51–29443; *Journal of Commerce* (22 July 1986), A1; *International Trade Reporter* (23 July 1986).

95. Interviews by author, #9036 (8 September 1990), #9130 (24 April 1990).

96. Interview by author, #9027 (12 December 1989).

97. Interview by author, #9001 (27 April 1990).

98. *International Trade Reporter* (23 July 1986).

99. *Far Eastern Economic Review* (29 July 1986), 86.

100. Interviews by author, #9132 (11 October 1991), #9129 (11 October 1991).

NOTES TO CHAPTER 6

1. Louis Henkin, *How Nations Behave: Law and Foreign Policy* (New York: Columbia University Press, 1979).

2. Keohane, *After Hegemony*, 98–107.

3. Robert O. Keohane, "Reciprocity, Reputation, and Compliance with International Commitments," paper presented at the American Political Science Association annual meeting, Washington, D.C., 1–4 September 1988, 9.

4. Roger Fisher, *Improving Compliance with International Law* (Charlottesville: University Press of Virginia, 1981).

5. Robert Axelrod, *The Evolution of Cooperation* (New York: Basic Books, 1984).

6. Robert Axelrod and Robert O. Keohane, "Achieving Cooperation under Anarchy: Strategies and Institutions," *World Politics* 38 (October 1985), 226–254.

7. Harold K. Jacobson, *Networks of Interdependence.*

8. Friedrich V. Kratochwil, *Rules, Norms, and Decisions: On the Conditions of Practical and Legal Reasoning in International Relations and Domestic Affairs* (New York: Cambridge University Press, 1989).

9. Thomas C. Schelling and Morton H. Halperin, *Strategy and Arms Control* (Washington: Pergamon-Brassey, 1985).

10. Interview by author, #9031 (25 April 1990).

11. "Record of Understanding on Intellectual Property Rights," public file #301–52, USTR, Washington, D.C.; emphasis added.

12. Keohane, "Reciprocity, Reputation, and Compliance with International Commitments."

13. See Johnson, *MITI and the Japanese Miracle*; Chalmers A. Johnson, "Political Institutions and Economic Performance: The Government-Business Relationship in Japan, South Korea, and Taiwan," in Frederic C. Deyo, ed., *The Political Economy of Asian Industrialism* (Ithaca: Cornell University Press, 1987), 136, 151–156; Hung-mao

Tien, *The Great Transition: Political and Social Change in the Republic of China* (Stanford: Stanford University Press, 1989), 12–125.

NOTES TO CHAPTER 7

1. Lincoln, *Japan's Unequal Trade*, 146.
2. Omnibus Trade and Competitiveness Act of 1988, Public Law 100–418, 102 Stat. 1107.
3. USTR, *1992 Foreign Trade Barriers*, 231.
4. USTR, *1990 Foreign Trade Barriers*, 108–109.
5. David P. Houlihan and J. Christine Bliss, "Statement of the Japan Lumber Importers' Association," Mudge, Rose, Guthrie, Alexander & Ferdon, Washington, D.C., July 1989.
6. USTR, *Federal Register* 90–14544.
7. USTR, *1992 Foreign Trade Barriers*, 160.
8. USTR, *1990 Foreign Trade Barriers*, 114.
9. Letter from Takuma Yamamoto, Japan Electronic Industry Development Association, to USTR dated 14 July 1989, public file #301–76, USTR, Washington, D.C.
10. Ibid.
11. Press release, USTR, Washington, D.C., 23 March 1990; *New York Times* (24 March 1990), 1.
12. USTR, *1990 Foreign Trade Barriers*, 114.
13. *Legal Times* (22 May 1989), 10–13.
14. *New York Times* (29 June 1989), 1.
15. USTR, press release, 3 April 1990; *New York Times* (4 April 1990), C1.
16. Christopher Sheehey, "Japan's New Foreign Lawyer Law," *Law and Policy in International Business* 19 (1987)2, 361–384; *Far Eastern Economic Review* (20 February 1992), 49.
17. Omnibus Trade and Competitiveness Act.
18. USTR, *1990 Foreign Trade Barriers*, 118.
19. Ibid., 117.
20. Ibid., 118.
21. *New York Times* (18 September 199), C19; *Wall Street Journal* (23 November 1990), A4.
22. *Wall Street Journal* (23 November 1990), A4.
23. *Journal of Commerce* (31 January 1991), 8A.
24. USTR, *1992 Foreign Trade Barriers*, 162.
25. Ibid., 234.
26. Ibid., 107.
27. "Interim Report and Assessment of the US-Japan Working Group on the Structural Impediments Initiative," (USTR, Washington, D.C., April 1990), 1.
28. "Testimony of Deputy US Trade Representative S. Linn Williams before the Senate Finance Committee Subcommittee on International Trade," press release, USTR, Washington, D.C., 5 March 1990.

29. Mitsuo Matsushita and Thomas J. Schoenbaum, *Japanese International Trade and Investment Law* (Tokyo: University of Tokyo Press, 1989), 116.

30. Cited in *New York Times* (22 March 1990), A1.

31. Ibid.

32. Johnson, *MITI and the Japanese Miracle*, 41.

33. Michael L. Gerlach, "Twilight of the Keiretsu? A Critical Assessment," *Journal of Japanese Studies* 18 (winter 1992), 85.

34. Ibid., 84.

35. Ibid., 84.

36. *Wall Street Journal* (16 May 1991), A17.

37. Kozo Yamamura, "Will Japan's Economic Structure Change?" in Yamamura, *Japan's Economic Structure* (Seattle: University of Washington Press, 1991), 29.

38. Matsushita and Schoenbaum, *Japanese International Trade and Investment Law*, 139.

39. Lincoln, *Japan's Unequal Trade*, 80.

40. Yamamura, "Will Japan's Economic Structure Change?" 36.

41. Matsushita and Schoenbaum, *Japanese International Trade and Investment Law*, 159.

42. Ken-Ichii Imai, "Japanese Business Groups and the Structural Impediments Initiative," in Yamamura, ed., *Japan's Economic Structure*, 167–202; Masahiko Aoki, *Information, Incentives and Bargaining in the Japanese Economy* (New York: Cambridge University Press, 1988).

43. USTR, *1992 Foreign Trade Barriers*, 165.

44. Ibid.

45. Ibid., 237.

46. Amsden, *Asia's Next Giant*, 133.

47. Aristotle, *Nicomachean Ethics*, in Richard McKeon, ed., *Introduction to Aristotle* (New York: Random House, 1947), 420.

48. Anchordoguy, "A Challenge to Free Trade?" 302.

49. Johnson, *MITI and the Japanese Miracle*; Anchorduguy, "A Challenge to Free Trade?"; Okimoto, *Between MITI and the Market*.

50. Friedman, *Misunderstood Miracle*.

51. Wade, *Governing the Market*; Amsden, *Asia's Next Giant*.

52. Okimoto, *Between MITI and the Market*.

53. Paul R. Krugman, "Strategic Sectors and International Competition," in Robert M. Stern, ed., *US Trade Policies in a Changing World Economy* (Cambridge: MIT Press, 1987), 207–244; Paul R. Krugman, ed., *Strategic Trade Policy and the New International Economics* (Cambridge: MIT Press, 1986).

54. Jacques H. J. Bourgeois, ed., *Subsidies and International Trade: A European Lawyers' Perspective* (Boston: Kluwer Law and Taxation Publishers, 1991).

55. Gary Clyde Hufbauer and Joanna Shelton Erb, *Subsidies in International Trade* (Cambridge: MIT Press, 1984).

56. J. Michael Finger, H. Keith Hall, and Douglas R. Nelson, "The Political Economy of Administered Protection," *American Economic Review* 72 (June 1982), 452–466; J. Michael Finger and Tracey Murray, "Policing Unfair Imports: The United States Example," *Journal of World Trade Law* (October 1989).

57. DoC Import Administration Office, "Antidumping and Countervailing Duty Cases," (Washington, D.C.: ITA, April 1990).

58. USTR, *1992 Foreign Trade Barriers Report*, 163, 235.

59. Ibid., 145; Masaaki Kotabe, "A Comparative Study of US and Japanese Patent Systems," *Journal of International Business Studies* 23 (1992)1, 147–168; Gadbaw and Richards, eds., *Intellectual Property Rights*.

60. Stephen D. Cohen, *Uneasy Partnership: Competition and Conflict in US-Japanese Trade Relations* (Cambridge Mass.: Ballinger, 1985), 191.

61. Milner, *Resisting Protectionism*.

62. Axelrod and Keohane, "Achieving Cooperation under Anarchy."

63. Gadbaw, "Reciprocity and Its Implications for US Trade Policy."

NOTES TO CHAPTER 8

1. Carl Riskin, *China's Political Economy: The Quest for Development since 1949* (New York: Oxford University Press, 1987), 101.

2. Nicholas Lardy, *Foreign Trade and Economic Reform in China, 1978-1990* (New York: Cambridge University Press, 1992), 37–63.

3. Edward Friedman, Paul G. Pickowicz, and Mark Selden, *Chinese Village, Socialist State* (New Haven: Yale University Press, 1991).

4. Margaret M. Pearson, *Joint Ventures in the People's Republic of China* (Princeton: Princeton University Press, 1991).

5. Samuel P. S. Ho and Ralph W. Huenemann, *China's Open Door Policy: The Quest for Foreign Technology and Capital* (Vancouver: University of British Columbia Press, 1992).

6. Peter Harrold and Rajiv Lall, *China Reform and Development in 1992-93* (Washington, D.C.: IBRD, 1993), 30.

7. Susan Shirk, *The Political Logic of Economic Reform in China* (Berkeley: University of California Press, 1993), 12–15.

8. Ezra F. Vogel, *One Step Ahead in China: Guangdong under Reform* (Cambridge: Harvard University Press, 1989), 102; Lardy, *Foreign Trade and Economic Reform in China*, 135.

9. Pearson, *Joint Ventures in China*, 70.

10. Ibid., 76.

11. "China Briefing," US-China Business Council, Washington, D.C., October 1993.

12. World Bank, *China: Foreign Trade Reform* (Washington, D.C.: IBRD, 1994), 6–12.

13. USTR, *1994 National Trade Estimate's Report*, 43.

14. World Bank, *China: Foreign Trade Reform*, 13.

15. Interview by author, #9301 (1 June 1993).

16. Interviews by author, #9301 (1 June 1993), #9306 (1 June 1993), #9307 (1 June 1993).

17. World Bank, *China: Foreign Trade Reform*, 17.

18. Ibid., 40–62.
19. USIW 8 (1983)23, 878.
20. DoC, *Federal Register* 48–46600.
21. *Wall Street Journal* (5 November 1983), 28; *Far Eastern Economic Review* (23 November 1983), 74–75; *Journal of Commerce* (22 December 1983), 4A.
22. Alan W. Wolfe et al., "Countervailing Duty Petition of the American Textile Manufacturers Institute et al. before the Department of Commerce Regarding Textiles, Apparel, and Related Products from the People's Republic of China," Verner, Liipfert, Bernhard & McPherson, Washington, D.C., September 1983; "Textiles, Apparel and Related Products from the People's Republic of China, Memorandum of Additional Information Concerning Subsidy Practices," Verner, Liipfert, Bernhard & McPherson, Washington, D.C., October 1983.
23. Robert E. Herzstein et al., "Statement on Behalf of American Association of Exporters and Importers in Connection with Special Conference on November 3, 1983, before the ITA of the US Department of Commerce," Arnold & Porter, Washington, D.C., 1983.
24. Memoranda from Roland McDonald, DoC-ITA Office of Investigations, dated 6 October 1983 and 7 October 1983, file #C–570–005, DoC-ITA, Washington, D.C.
25. *Beijing Review* 26 (7 November 1983)45, 8.
26. *Far Eastern Economic Review* (24 November 1983), 74–75; on MOFERT's decisive role in Chinese foreign economic policy-making during this period, see A. Doak Barnett, *The Making of Foreign Policy in China: Structure and Process* (Boulder, Colo.: Westview Press, 1985).
27. See Vinod K. Aggarwal with Stephan Haggard, "The Politics of Protection in the US Textile and Apparel Industries," in Zysman and Tyson, eds., *American Industry in International Competition*, 249–312; Aggarwal, *Liberal Protectionism*; Craig R. Giesse and Martin J. Lewin, "The Multifiber Arrangement: 'Temporary' Protection Run Amuck," *Law and Policy in International Business* 19 (1987)1, 51–170.
28. "Agreement Relating to Trade in Cotton, Wool, and Man-Made Fiber Textiles and Textile Products between the Government of the United States of America and the Government of the People's Republic of China," TIAS 9820, 32 UST 2071–2082.
29. *New York Times* (19 September 1980), 24; *Citibank* (June 1980), 4.
30. *New York Times* (14 April 1980), D2.
31. DoC, *Federal Register* 47–3565; *Wall Street Journal* (6 August 1982).
32. Petition filing: DoC, *Federal Register* 47–46777; antidumping order: DoC, *Federal Register* 48–45277; Chinese denial: *New York Times* (28 October 1983), 39.
33. *Journal of Commerce* (26 October 1982), 3A.
34. USIW 7 (8 December 1982), 333.
35. *New York Times* (30 November 1982), 35.
36. *New York Times* (17 January 1983), D5.
37. *Wall Street Journal* (20 January 1983), 29.
38. *Journal of Commerce* (27 July 1983), 3A; *Journal of Commerce* (2 August 1983), 4A; *Journal of Commerce* (24 June 1983), 3A.

39. *Beijing Review* (29 August 1983), 8; *Far Eastern Economic Review* (11 August 1983), 72–73.

40. *Wall Street Journal* (7 September 1983), 3.

41. *Journal of Commerce* (1 August 1983), 5A.

42. GATT/1352 (15 December 1983); *Beijing Review* (2 January 1984), 11.

43. "Questionnaire: Textiles, Apparel, and Related Products," DoC-ITA, Washington, D.C., 20 October 1983.

44. *National Journal* (3 December 1983), 2526–2528.

45. Letter from John D. Greenwald of Verner, Liipfert, Bernhard & McPherson, Washington, D.C., to Alan Holmer, Deputy Assistant Secretary for Import Administration, DoC, dated 8 November 1983, file #C–570–005, DoC-ITA, Washington, D.C.

46. Memorandum from Judith Hippler Bello, DoC-ITA, dated 10 November 1983, file #C–570–005, DoC-ITA, Washington, D.C.; "Supplemental Countervailing Duty Questionnaires: Textiles, Apparel, and Related Products from the People's Republic of China," DoC-ITA, Washington, D.C., 23 November 1983.

47. "Statement by Spokesman of the Ministry of Foreign Economic Relations and Trade," dated 30 November 1983, file #C–570–005, DoC-ITA, Washington, D.C.

48. Letter from John D. Greenwald and Ann K. H. Simon of Verner, Liipfert, Bernhard and McPherson, Washington, D.C., to Alan Holmer, Deputy Assistant Secretary for Import Administration, dated 2 December 1983, file #C–570–005, DoC-ITA, Washington, D.C.

49. *National Journal* (3 December 1983), 2526–2528; DoC, *Federal Register* 48–55492.

50. Memorandum from Judith Hippler Bello, DoC-ITA, dated 7 December 1983, file #C–570–005, DoC-ITA, Washington, D.C.; letter from Alan Holmer, Deputy Assistant Secretary of Commerce for Import Administration, to John D. Greenwald of Verner, Liipfert, Bernhard & McPherson, Washington, D.C., dated 6 December 1983, file #C–570–005, DoC-ITA, Washington, D.C.; *New York Times* (6 December 1983), 30.; *Wall Street Journal* (7 December 1983), 8; *Journal of Commerce* (8 December 1983), 5A.

51. DoC-ITA public file #C–570–005 offers only an incomplete record of these meetings, conversations, letters, and memos. Documents on exchanges among USTR Bill Brock, Secretary of Commerce Malcolm Baldrige, Deputy Assistant Secretary of Commerce for Textiles and Apparel Walter Lenahan, and President Reagan exist, but they remain out off the public record. The record suggests that a number of exchanges occurred but were not recorded.

52. *New York Times* (12 December 1983), 30.

53. *New York Times* (15 December 1983), 47.

54. *New York Times* (17 December 1983), 1; *Journal of Commerce* (22 December 1983), 4A; *Far Eastern Economic Review* (22 December 1983), 10.

55. *Journal of Commerce* (21 December 1983), 1A.

56. DoC, *Federal Register* 49–927.

57. Ed Jenkins, "The Multilateral Fiber Arrangement: Its Shortcomings and Remedies," *Law and Policy in International Business* 19 (1987)1, 205–212.

58. *Journal of Commerce* (30 April 1987), 3A.

59. DoC, *Federal Register* 53–463.

60. *Journal of Commerce* (14 May 1987), 1A.

61. Ibid.

62. DoC, *Federal Register* 49–3671.

63. *New York Times* (8 August 1984), 29.

64. Ibid.; *Journal of Commerce* (28 August 1984); *Far Eastern Economic Review* (30 August 1984); *Wall Street Journal* (10 September 1984), 30; *New York Times* (30 October 1984), 42.

65. *Wall Street Journal* (4 January 1994), A5B.

66. Interview by author, #9307 (1 June 1993).

67. Ibid.

68. Harold K. Jacobson and Michel Oksenberg, *China's Participation in the IMF, the World Bank, and GATT: Toward a Global Economic Order* (Ann Arbor: University of Michigan Press, 1993); Michael P. Ryan, "Chinese Diplomacy in Specialized Economic and Social IGOs: UNESCO, UNCTAD, and ILO, 1978–1987," A.M. thesis, University of Michigan, May 1987.

69. USTR, *1994 National Trade Estimate's Report*, 44–57.

70. Robert E. Herzstein, "China and the GATT: Legal and Policy Issues Raised by China's Participation in the General Agreement on Tariffs and Trade," *Law and Policy in International Business* 18 (1986), 371–416.

NOTES TO CHAPTER 9

1. Lim, "Engines of Regional Integration in Asia."

2. W. Christopher Lenhardt and Michael P. Ryan, "Rules, Power, and Outcomes."

3. Twentieth Century Fund Task Force on the Future of American Trade Policy, *The Free Trade Debate* (New York: Priority Press, 1989).

4. Peter Cowhey and Jonathan Aronson, *Managing the World Economy: The Consequences of Corporate Alliances* (New York: Council on Foreign Relations, 1993).

5. Donald Crone, "Does Hegemony Matter? The Reorganization of the Pacific Political Economy," *World Politics* 45 (July 1993), 501–525.

6. Ernst Haas, *The Uniting of Europe: Political, Social, and Economic Forces, 1950–57* (Stanford: Stanford University Press, 1958); Bela Balassa, *The Theory of Economic Integration* (Homewood, Ill.: Richard D. Irwin, 1961); Ernst Haas and Philippe Schmitter, "Economics and Differential Patterns of Political Integration: Projections about Unity in Latin America," *International Organization* 18 (autumn 1964), 705–37; Richard N. Cooper, *The Economics of Interdependence: Economic Policy in the Atlantic Community* (New York: McGraw-Hill, 1968); Minerva M. Etzioni, *The Majority of One: Towards a Theory of Regional Compatibility* (Beverly Hills, Calif.: Sage, 1970); Joseph S. Nye, *Peace in Parts: Integration and Conflict in Regional Organization* (Boston: Little, Brown, 1971); Victoria Curzon, *The Essentials of Economic Integration: Lessons of EFTA Experience* (New York: St. Martin's Press, 1974); Ernst Haas, *The Obsolescence of Regional Integration Theory* (Berkeley: Institute of International Studies, University of California, 1975).

7. Beth V. Yarbrough and Robert M. Yarbrough, *Cooperation and Governance in International Trade: The Strategic Organizational Approach* (Princeton: Princeton University Press, 1992), 87.

8. Haas and Schmitter, "Differential Patterns of Political Integration"; Nye, *Peace in Parts.*

9. David Wightman, *Toward Economic Cooperation in Asia: The United Nations Economic Commission for Asia and the Far East* (New Haven: Yale University Press, 1963).

10. W. W. Rostow, *The United States and the Regional Organization of Asia and the Pacific, 1965–1985* (Austin: University of Texas Press, 1986).

11. Linda Y. C. Lim, "Toward an Asian Economic Bloc? AFTA, APEC, and All That," Michigan Business School Teaching Note, October 1992.

NOTES TO CHAPTER 10

1. Axelrod, *The Evolution of Cooperation.*

2. Judith Goldstein and Stephen D. Krasner, "Unfair Trade Practices: The Case for a Differential Response," *American Economic Review* 74 (1984)2, 282–287.

3. Carolyn Rhodes, "Reciprocity in Trade: The Utility of a Bargaining Strategy," *International Organization* 43 (spring 1989), 273–300.

4. Sykes, "Constructive Unilateral Threats in International Commercial Relations."

5. Milner and Yoffie, "Between Free Trade and Protectionism."

6. Erland Heginbotham, *Asia's Rising Economic Tide: Unique Opportunities for the US* (Washington: National Planning Association, 1993).

7. John Lewis Gaddis, *Strategies of Containment: A Critical Appraisal of Postwar American National Security Policy* (New York: Oxford University Press, 1982), 4.

8. James Fallows, "Containing Japan," *Atlantic Monthly* (May 1989), 40–54.

9. John Stopford and Susan Strange, *Rival States, Rival Firms: Competition for World Market Shares* (New York: Cambridge University Press, 1991), 1.

10. Michael E. Porter, *The Competitive Advantage of Nations* (New York: Free Press, 1990); Dertouzos et al., *Made in America;* Gunnar K. Sletmo and Gavin Boyd, eds., *Pacific Industrial Policies* (Boulder, Colo.: Westview Press, 1994).

11. "Report on Unfair Trade Policies by Major Trade Partners," Subcommittee on Unfair Trade Policies and Measures, Uruguay Round Committee Industrial Structure Council.

12. Robert E. Hudec, Daniel L. M. Kennedy, and Mark Sgarbossa, "A Statistical Profile of GATT Dispute Settlement Cases: 1948–1989," *Minnesota Journal of World Trade* 2 (1993)1, 1–113.

Bibliography

Abbott, Kenneth and Conrad D. Totman. "'Black Ships' and Balance Sheets: The Japanese Market and US-Japan Relations." *Northwestern Journal of International Law and Business* 3 (1981): 103–154.

Achen, Christopher and Duncan Snidal. "Rational Deterrence Theory and Comparative Case Studies." *World Politics* 41 (January 1989): 143–169.

Aggarwal, Vinod K. *Liberal Protectionism: The International Politics of Organized Textile Trade.* Berkeley: University of California Press, 1985.

Aggarwal, Vinod K., Robert O. Keohane, and David B. Yoffie. "The Dynamics of Negotiated Protectionism." *American Political Science Review* 81 (June 1987): 345–366.

Aho, C. Michael and Jonathan David Aronson. *Trade Talks: America Better Listen.* New York: Council on Foreign Relations, 1985.

Allen, Deborah. "Tariff Games." In *Applied Game Theory* edited by S. J. Brams, A. Schotter, and G. Schwoediauer, 270–284. Würzburg: Physica-Verlag, 1979.

Allison, Graham T. *Essence of Decision: Explaining the Cuban Missile Crisis.* Boston: Little, Brown, 1971.

American Enterprise Institute. *Proposals to Establish a Department of Trade.* Washington: American Enterprise Institute for Public Policy Research, 1984.

Amsden, Alice H. *Asia's Next Giant: South Korea and Late Industrialization.* New York: Oxford University Press, 1989.

Anchordoguy, Marie. "Mastering the Market: Japanese Government Targeting of the Computer Industry." *International Organization* 42 (summer 1988): 509–544.

Anderson, Paul A. "Foreign Policy as a Goal Directed Activity." *Philosophy of Social Science* 14 (1984): 159–181.

Aoki, Masahiko. *Information, Incentives, and Bargaining in the Japanese Economy.* New York: Cambridge University Press, 1988.

Arndt, Sven W. and Lawrence Bouton. *Competitiveness: The United States in World Trade.* Washington: American Enterprise Institute for Public Policy Research, 1987.

Axelrod, Robert. *The Evolution of Cooperation.* New York: Basic Books, 1984.

Axelrod, Robert and Robert O. Keohane. "Achieving Cooperation under Anarchy: Strategies and Institutions." *World Politics* 38 (October 1985): 226–254.

Balassa, Bela. *The Theory of Economic Integration.* Homewood, Ill.: Richard D. Irwin, 1961.

Balassa, Bela and John Williamson. *Adjusting to Success: Balance of Payments Policy in the East Asian NICs.* Washington: Institute for International Economics, 1987.

Baldwin, David A. *Economic Statecraft.* Princeton: Princeton University Press, 1985.

Baldwin, Robert E. *The Political Economy of US Import Policy.* Cambridge: MIT Press, 1985.

Bandura, Albert. *Social Foundations of Thought and Action: A Social Cognitive Theory.* Englewood Cliffs, N.J.: Prentice-Hall, 1986.

Bauer, Raymond A., Ithiel de Sola Pool, and Lewis Anthony Dexter. *American Business and Public Policy: The Politics of Foreign Trade.* 2d ed. New York: Aldine-Atherton, 1972.

Bayard, Thomas O. and Kimberly Elliott. "'Aggressive Unilateralism' and Section 301: Market Opening or Market Closing?" *World Economy* 15 (1992): 685–706.

Bayard, Thomas O. and Soo-Gil Young, eds. *Economic Relations between the United States and Korea: Conflict or Cooperation?* Washington: Institute for International Economics, 1988.

Bello, Judith Hippler and Alan F. Holmer. "Section 301 of the Trade Act of 1974: Requirements, Procedures, and Developments." *Northwestern Journal of International Law and Business* 7 (fall-winter 1986): 633–669.

Benko, Robert P. *Protecting Intellectual Property Rights.* Washington: American Enterprise Institute for Public Policy Research, 1987.

Bergsten, C. Fred. *Global Economic Imbalances.* Washington: Institute for International Economics, 1985.

Bergsten, C. Fred and William R. Cline. *The United States-Japan Economic Problem.* Washington: Institute for International Economics, 1987.

Berman, Harold J. "The Law of International Commercial Transactions." *Emory Journal of International Dispute Resolution* 2 (spring 1988): 235–310.

Bhagwati, Jagdish N. *Protectionism.* Cambridge: MIT Press, 1988.

———. *The World Trading System at Risk.* Princeton: Princeton University Press, 1991.

Bhagwati, Jagdish N. and Hugh Patrick, eds. *Aggressive Unilateralism: America's 301 Trade Policy and the World Trading System.* Ann Arbor: University of Michigan Press, 1990.

Bilder, Richard B. "International Dispute Settlement and the Role of International Adjudication." *Emory Journal of International Dispute Resolution* 1 (spring 1987): 131–174.

———. "An Overview of International Dispute Settlement." *Emory Journal of International Dispute Resolution* 1 (fall 1986): 1–32.

Bliss, J. Christine. "GATT Dispute Settlement Reform in the Uruguay Round: Problems and Prospects." *Stanford Journal of International Law* 23 (spring 1987): 31–55.

Booz-Allen & Hamilton, Inc. *The Effects of Foreign Targeting on the US Automobile Industry.* Washington: Booz-Allen & Hamilton, 1985.

Borrus, Michael. *Competing for Control.* Cambridge, Mass.: Ballinger, 1988.

Bourgeois, Jacques H. J., ed. *Subsidies and International Trade: A European Lawyers' Perspective*. Boston: Kluwer Law and Taxation Publishers, 1991.

Bueno de Mesquita, Bruce, David Newman, and Alvin Rabushka, *Forecasting Political Events: The Future of Hong Kong*. New Haven: Yale University Press, 1985.

Butler, Alison. "Trade Imbalances and Economic Theory: The Case for a US-Japan Trade Deficit." *Federal Reserve Bank of St. Louis* 73 (March-April 1991): 19–31.

Caine, Wesley K. "A Case for Repealing the Antidumping Provisions of the Tariff Act of 1930." *Law and Policy in International Business* 13 (1981): 681–726.

Calder, Kent E. *Crisis and Compensation: Public Policy and Political Stability in Japan*. Princeton: Princeton University Press, 1988.

———. "The Emerging Politics of the Trans-Pacific Economy." *World Policy Journal* 2 (fall 1985): 593–623.

———. "Japanese Foreign Economic Policy Formation: Explaining the Reactive State." *World Politics* 60 (July 1988): 517–541.

Caporaso, James A. "Dependence, Dependency, and Power in the Global System: A Structural Analysis." *International Organization* 32 (winter 1978)1: 13–43.

Cassing, James, Timothy J. McKeown, and Jack Ochs. "The Political Economy of the Tariff Cycle." *American Political Science Review* 80 (September 1986): 843–862.

Chan, Kenneth. "The International Negotiation Game: Some Evidence from the Tokyo Round." *Review of Economics and Statistics* 67 (spring 1985): 456–464.

Cho, Lee-Jay and Yoon Hung Kim. *Economic Development in the Republic of Korea: A Policy Perspective*. Honolulu: East-West Center, 1991.

Clark, Cal. "The Taiwan Exception: Implications for Contending Political Economy Paradigms." *International Studies Quarterly* 31 (September 1987): 327–356.

Cline, William R. "'Reciprocity': A New Approach to World Trade Policy?" Washington: Institute for International Economics, 1982.

Cline, William R., ed. *Trade Policy in the 1980s*. Washington: Institute for International Economics, 1983.

———. et al. *Trade Negotiations in Tokyo Round: A Quantitative Assessment*. Washington: Brookings, 1978.

Coffield, Shirley A. "Using Section 301 of the Trade Act of 1974 As a Response to Foreign Trade Actions: When, Why, How." *North Carolina Journal of International Law and Commercial Regulation* 6 (1981): 386.

Cohen, Benjamin J. *In Whose Interest? International Banking and American Foreign Policy*. New Haven: Yale University Press, 1986.

Cohen, Stephen D. *Uneasy Partnership: Competition and Conflict in US-Japan Trade Relations*. Cambridge, Mass.: Ballinger 1985.

Cohen, Stephen S. and John Zysman. *Manufacturing Matters: The Myth of the Post–Industrial Economy*. New York: Basic Books, 1987.

Committee for Economic Development. *Breaking New Ground in US Trade Policy*. Boulder, Colo.: Westview Press, 1991.

Conybeare, John A. C. "Tariff Protection in Developed and Developing Countries: A Cross-Sectional and Longitudal Analysis." *International Organization* 37 (summer 1983): 441–468.

———. *Trade Wars: The Theory and Practice of International Commercial Rivalry*. New York: Columbia University Press, 1987.

Cooper, Richard N. *The Economics of Interdependence: Economic Policy in the Atlantic Community.* New York: McGraw-Hill, 1968.

Cornell International Law Journal. *The US-Japanese Trade Relationship: An Intradisciplinary Approach for the 1990s.* 22 (1989)3.

Coughlin, Cletus C. "US Trade-Remedy Laws: Do They Facilitate or Hinder Free Trade?" *Federal Reserve Bank of St. Louis* (July-August 1991): 3–18.

Council on Foreign Relations and the Asia Society. *Korea at the Crossroads: Implications for American Policy.* New York: Council on Foreign Relations and the Asia Society, 1987.

Cowhey, Peter and Jonathan Aronson. *Managing the World Economy: The Consequences of Corporate Alliances.* New York: Council on Foreign Relations, 1993.

Crone, Donald. "Does Hegemony Matter? The Reorganization of the Pacific Political Economy." *World Politics* 45 (July 1993)4: 501–525.

Cumings, Bruce. "The Origins and Development of the Northeast Asian Political Economy: Industrial Sectors, Product Cycles, and Political Consequences." *International Organization* 38 (winter 1984): 1–40.

Curzon, Victoria. *The Essentials of Economic Integration: Lessons of EFTA Experience.* New York: St. Martin's Press, 1974.

Cyert, Richard and James G. March. *A Behavioral Theory of the Firm.* Englewood Cliffs, N.J.: Prentice-Hall, 1963.

Dale, Richard. *Anti-Dumping Law in a Liberal Trade Order.* New York: St. Martin's Press, 1980.

Dam, Kenneth W. *The GATT: Law and International Economic Organization.* Chicago: University of Chicago Press, 1970.

Davey, William J. "Dispute Settlement in GATT." *Fordham International Law Journal* 11 (fall 1987): 51–109.

Dertouzos, Michael L., Richard K. Lester, Robert M. Solow, and the MIT Commission on Industrial Productivity. *Made in America: Regaining the Productive Edge.* Cambridge: MIT Press, 1989.

Destler, I. M. *American Trade Politics: System under Stress.* Washington: Institute for International Economics, 1986/1992.

———. *Making Foreign Economic Policy.* Washington, DC: Brookings Institution, 1980.

Destler, I. M., Haruhiro Fukui, and Hideo Sato. *The Textile Wrangle: Conflict in Japanese-American Trade Relations, 1969–1971.* Ithaca: Cornell University Press, 1979.

Destler, I. M. and Hideo Sato, eds. *Coping with US-Japan Economic Relations.* Lexington, Mass.: Lexington Books, 1982.

Destler, I. M. and John S. Odell. *Anti-Protection: Changing Forces in United States Trade Politics.* Washington: Institute for International Economics, 1987.

Deyo, Frederic C., ed. *The Political Economy of the New Asian Industrialism.* Ithaca: Cornell University Press, 1987.

Dickson, Bruce and Harry Harding, eds. *Economic Relations in the Asian Pacific Region.* Washington: Brookings Institution,1987.

Diebold, William J. *The End of the ITO.* Princeton: Princeton University Press, 1952.

Doyle, Michael W. "Liberalism and World Politics." *American Political Science Review* 80 (December 1986): 1115–1171.

El-Agraa, Ali M. *Japan's Trade Frictions: Realities or Misconceptions?* New York: St. Martin's Press, 1988.

Encarnation, Dennis J. *Rivals beyond Trade: America versus Japan in Global Competition.* Ithaca: Cornell University Press, 1992.

Etzioni, Minerva M. *The Majority of One: Towards a Theory of Regional Compatibility.* Beverly Hills, Calif.: Sage, 1970.

Evans, Peter B. "Declining Hegemony and Assertive Industrialization: US-Brazil Conflicts in the Computer Industry." *International Organization* 43 (spring 1989): 207–238.

Fallows, James. "Containing Japan." *Atlantic Monthly* (May 1989): 40–54.

Feng, Yushu. "Taiwan and GATT: The Political, Legal, and Economic Issues Raised by the Possibility of Taiwan Joining the GATT." *World Economy* 13 (March 1990): 129–144.

Finan, William F. and Chris B. Amundsen. *An Analysis of the Effects of Targeting on the Competitiveness of the US Semiconductor Industry.* Washington: USTR, 1985.

Finger, J. Michael, H. Keith Hall, and Douglas R. Nelson. "The Political Economy of Administered Protection." *American Economic Review* 72 (June 1982): 452–466.

Finger, J. Michael and Tracey Murray. "Policing Unfair Imports: The United States Example." *Journal of World Trade Law* (October 1989).

Finlayson, Jock A. and Mark W. Zacher. *Managing International Markets: Developing Countries and the Commodity Trade Regime.* New York: Columbia University Press, 1988.

Fisher, Bart S. and Ralph G. Steihardt, III. "Section 301 of the Trade Act of 1974: Protection for US Exporters of Goods, Services, and Capital." *Law and Policy in International Business* 14 (1982).

Fisher, Roger. *Improving Compliance with International Law.* Charlottesville: University Press of Virginia, 1981.

Fried, Robert C. *Performance in American Bureaucracy.* Boston: Little, Brown, 1976.

Friedman, David. *The Misunderstood Miracle: Industrial Development and Political Change in Japan.* Ithaca: Cornell University Press, 1988.

Friedman, Edward, Paul G. Pickowicz, and Mark Selden. *Chinese Village, Socialist State.* New Haven: Yale University Press, 1991.

Gadbaw, R. Michael. "Reciprocity and Its Implications for US Trade Policy." *Law and Policy in International Business* 14 (1982): 691–746.

Gadbaw, R. Michael and Timothy J. Richards, eds. *Intellectual Property Rights: Global Consensus, Global Conflict?* Boulder, Colo.: Westview Press, 1988.

George, Alexander. "Case Studies and Theory Development: The Method of Structured, Focused Comparison." In *Diplomacy: New Approaches in History, Theory, and Policy*, edited by Paul Gordon Lauren, 43–68. New York: Free Press, 1979.

George, Alexander and Timothy J. McKeown. "Case Studies and Theories of Organizational Decision Making." In *Advances in Information Processing in Organizations*, edited by Robert Coulam and Richard Smith. Greenwich, Conn.: JAI Press, 1985.

George, Aurelia. *The Politics of Liberalization in Japan: The Case of Rice.* Canberra: Research School of Pacific Studies, Australian National University, 1990.

Gereffi, Gary and Donald Wyman, eds. *Manufacturing Miracles: Paths of Industrialization in Latin America and East Asia.* Princeton: Princeton University Press, 1990.

Gerlach, Michael L. "Twilight of the Keiretsu? A Critical Assessment." *Journal of Japanese Studies* 18 (winter 1992): 79–118.

Gilpin, Robert. *The Political Economy of International Relations.* Princeton: Princeton University Press, 1987.

Goldstein, Judith. "Ideas, Institutions, and American Trade Policy." *International Organization* 42 (winter 1988): 179–217.

———. *Ideas, Interests, and American Trade Policy.* Ithaca: Cornell University Press, 1993.

———. "The Impact of Ideas on Trade Policy: The Origins of US Agricultural and Manufacturing Policies." *International Organization* 43 (winter 1989): 31–72.

———. "The Political Economy of Trade: Institutions of Protection." *American Political Science Review* 80 (March 1986): 162–184.

Goldstein, Judith and Stephen D. Krasner. "Unfair Trade Practices: The Case for a Differential Response." *American Economic Review* 74 (1984): 282–287.

Goldstein, Judith and Stefanie Ann Lenway. "Interests or Institutions: An Inquiry into Congressional-ITC Relations." *International Studies Quarterly* 33 (September 1989): 303–328.

Gowa, Joanne. *Closing the Gold Window: Domestic Politics and the End of Bretton Woods.* Ithaca: Cornell University Press, 1983.

Grieco, Joseph M. "Anarchy and the Limits of Cooperation: A Realist Critique of the New Liberal Institutionalism." *International Organization* 42 (summer 1988): 485–508.

———. *Cooperation among Nations: Europe, America, and Non-Tariff Barriers to Trade.* Ithaca: Cornell University Press, 1990.

Haas, Ernst. *The Obsolescence of Regional Integration Theory.* Berkeley: Institute of International Studies, University of California, 1975.

———. *The Uniting of Europe: Political, Social, and Economic Forces, 1950–57.* Stanford: Stanford University Press, 1958.

Haas, Ernst and Philippe Schmitter. "Economics and Differential Patterns of Political Integration: Projections about Unity in Latin America." *International Organization* 18 (autumn 1964): 705–737.

Habeeb, William Mark. *Power and Tactics in International Negotiation: How Weak Nations Bargain with Strong Nations.* Baltimore: Johns Hopkins University Press, 1988.

Haggard, Stephen. *Pathways from the Periphery: The Politics of Growth in the Newly Industrializing Countries.* Ithaca: Cornell University Press, 1990.

Haggard, Stephen and Beth A. Simmons. "Theories of International Regimes." *International Organization* 41 (summer 1987): 491–517.

Halberstam, David. *The Reckoning.* New York: William Morrow, 1986.

Haley, John Owen. *Authority without Power: Law and Japanese Paradox.* New York: Oxford University Press, 1991.

Halperin, Morton A. *Bureaucratic Politics and Foreign Policy.* Washington: Brookings Institution, 1974.

Hartland-Thunberg, Penelope. *China, Hong Kong, Taiwan, and the World Trading System.* New York: St. Martin's Press, 1990.

Hay, Keith A. J. and Andrei Sulzenko. "US Trade Policy and 'Reciprocity.'" *Journal of World Trade Law* 6 (November-December 1982).

Hazard, Heather A. "Resolving Disputes in International Trade." Ph.D. thesis, Harvard Kennedy School of Government, 1988.

Heginbotham, Erland. *Asia's Rising Economic Tide: Unique Opportunities for the U.S.* Washington, D.C.: National Planning Association, 1993.

Henkin, Louis. *How Nations Behave: Law and Foreign Policy.* New York: Columbia University Press, 1979.

Henkin, Louis et al. *International Law: Cases and Materials.* St. Paul, Minn.: West Publishing, 1980.

Herzstein, Robert E. "China and the GATT: Legal and Policy Issues Raised by China's Participation in the General Agreement on Tariffs and Trade." *Law and Policy in International Business* 18 (1986): 371–416.

Ho, Samuel P. S. *The Economic Development of Taiwan, 1960–1970.* New Haven: Yale University Press, 1978.

———. "Economics, Economic Bureaucracy, and Taiwan's Economic Development." *Pacific Affairs* 60 (summer 1987): 226–247.

Ho, Samuel P. S. and Ralph W. Huenemann. *China's Open Door Policy: The Quest for Foreign Technology and Capital.* Vancouver: University of British Columbia Press, 1992.

Howell, Thomas R., William A. Noellert, Janet H. McLaughlin, and Alan W. Wolff. *The Microelectronics Race: The Impact of Government Policy on International Competition.* Boulder, Colo.: Westview Press, 1988.

Hsiao, Gene T. "The Legal Status of Taiwan in the Normalization of Sino-American Relations." *Rutgers Law Journal* 14 (summer 1983): 839–913.

Hudec, Robert E. *Developing Countries in the GATT Legal System.* Brookfield, Vt.: Gower, 1987.

———. "GATT Dispute Settlement after the Tokyo Round an Unfinished Business." *Cornell University International Law Journal* 13 (1980): 145–203.

———. *The GATT Legal System and World Trade Diplomacy.* Salem, N.H.: Butterworth, 1975/1990.

Hudec, Robert E., Daniel L. M. Kennedy, and Mark Sgarbossa. "A Statistical Profile of GATT Dispute Settlement Cases, 1948–1989." *Minnesota Journal of World Trade* 2 (1993): 1–113.

Hufbauer, Gary Clyde and Joanna Shelton Erb. *Subsidies in International Trade.* Cambridge, Mass.: MIT Press, 1984.

Hufbauer, Gary Clyde. Joanna Shelton Erb, and H. P. Starr. "The GATT Codes and the Unconditional Most-Favored-Nation Principle." *Law and Policy in International Business* 12 (spring 1980): 59–94.

Hufbauer, Gary Clyde and Howard F. Rosen. *Trade Policy for Troubled Industries.* Washington: Institute for International Economics, 1986.

Hunsberger, Warren. *Japan and the United States in World Trade.* New York: Harper & Row, 1964.

Ikenberry, G. John, David A. Lake, and Michael Mastanduno, eds. *The State and American Foreign Economic Policy.* Special issue of *International Organization* 42 (winter 1988).

Inoguchi, Takashi and Daniel I. Okimoto, eds. *The Political Economy of Japan: The Changing International Context.* Stanford: Stanford University Press, 1988.

Jackson, John H. "The Birth of the GATT-MTN System: A Constitutional Appraisal." *Law and Policy in International Business* 12 (spring 1980): 21–58.

————. "The Changing International Law Framework for Exports: The General Agreement on Tariffs and Trade." *Georgia Journal of International and Comparative Law* 14 (1984): 505–520.

————. "The Crumbling Institutions of the Liberal Trade System." *Journal of World Trade Law* 12 (March-April 1978): 93.

————. "Dispute Settlement Techniques between Nations Concerning Economic Relations—With Special Emphasis on GATT." In *Resolving Transnational Disputes through International Arbitration*, edited by Thomas E. Carbonneu, 39–72. Charlottesville: University Press of Virginia, 1984.

Jackson, John H. "Perspectives on the Jurisprudence of International Trade: Costs and Benefits of Legal Procedures in the United States." *Michigan Law Review* 82 (April-May 1984): 1570–1587.

Jackson, John H. *World Trade and the Law of GATT: An Analysis of the General Agreements on Tariffs and Trade.* Indianapolis: Bobbs-Merrill, 1969.

Jackson, John H. *The World Trading System: Law and Policy of International Economic Relations.* Cambridge: MIT Press, 1989.

Jackson, John H., Jean-Victor Louis, and Mitsuo Matsushita. *Implementing the Tokyo Round: National Constitutions and International Economic Rules.* Ann Arbor: University of Michigan Press, 1984.

Jackson, John H. and William J. Davey. *Legal Problems of International Economic Relations.* St. Paul, Minn.: West Publishing, 1986.

Jacobson, Harold K. "Deriving Data from Delegates to International Assemblies: A Research Note." *International Organization* 21 (1967): 592–613.

————. *Networks of Interdependence: International Organizations and the Global Political System.* New York: Alfred A. Knopf, 1984.

Jacobson, Harold K. and Michel Oksenberg. *China's Participation in the IMF, the World Bank, and GATT: Toward a Global Economic Order.* Ann Arbor: University of Michigan Press, 1993.

Johnson, Chalmers A. *MITI and the Japanese Miracle.* Stanford: Stanford University Press, 1982.

————. "Political Institutions and Economic Performance: The Government-Business Relationship in Japan, South Korea, and Taiwan." In *Political Economy of The New Asian Industrialism*, edited by Frederic C. Deyo. Ithaca: Cornell University Press, 1987.

Kahn, Alfred K. *The Economics of Regulation: Principles and Institutions.* Cambridge: MIT Press, 1988.

Keohane, Robert O. *After Hegemony: Cooperation and Discord in the World Political Economy.* Princeton: Princeton University Press, 1984.

———. "Reciprocity in International Relations." *International Organization* 40 (winter 1986): 1–28.

Keohane, Robert O. and Joseph S. Nye. *Power and Interdependence: World Politics in Transition.* Boston: Little, Brown, 1977.

Koh, B. C. *Japan's Administrative Elite.* Berkeley: University of California Press, 1989.

Kohona, Palitha Tikiri Bandara. *The Regulation of International Economic Relations through Law.* Boston: Martinus Nijhoff, 1985.

Krasner, Stephen D. *Defending the National Interest: Raw Materials Investment and US Foreign Policy.* Princeton: Princeton University Press, 1978.

———., ed. *International Regimes.* Ithaca: Cornell University Press, 1983.

———. *Structural Conflict: The Third World against Global Liberalism.* Berkeley: University of California Press. 1985.

Kratochwil, Friedrich V. *Rules, Norms, and Decisions: On the Conditions of Practical and Legal Reasoning in International Relations and Domestic Affairs.* New York: Cambridge University Press, 1989.

Krauss, Ellis S. and Simon Reich. "Ideology, Interests, and the American Executive: Towards a Theory of Foreign Competition and Manufacturing Trade Policy." *International Organization* 46 (autumn 1992): 857–899.

Krugman, R. Paul. *Strategic Trade Policy and the New International Economics.* Cambridge: MIT Press, 1986.

———. *Trade with Japan: Has the Door Opened Wider?* Chicago: University of Chicago Press, 1992.

Kuznets, Paul W. *Economic Growth and Structure in the Republic of Korea.* New Haven: Yale University Press, 1977.

Lake, David A. *Power, Protection, and Free Trade: International Sources of Commercial Strategy, 1887–1939.* Ithaca: Cornell University Press, 1988.

Lardy, Nicholas. *Foreign Trade and Economic Reform in China, 1978–1990.* New York: Cambridge University Press, 1992.

Laudan, Larry. *Progress and Its Problems: Towards a Theory of Scientific Growth.* Berkeley: University of California Press, 1977.

Lenhardt, W. Christopher and Michael P. Ryan. "Rules, Power, and Outcomes in GATT Dispute Settlement." Paper presented at the American Political Science Association annual meeting, Washington, D.C., 2–5 September 1993.

Lenway, Stefanie Ann. *The Politics of US International Trade: Protection, Expansion, and Escape.* Marshfield, Mass.: Pitman Publishing, 1985.

Leo, Robert J. "An Update of the Japanese Auto Export Restraints." *Brooklyn Journal of International Law* 8 (winter 1982): 159–175.

Li, K. T. *The Evolution of Policy behind Taiwan's Development Success.* New Haven: Yale University Press, 1988.

Lim, Linda. "Engines of Regional Integration in Asia." In *AFTA after NAFTA*, 145–159. Washington: Korea Economic Institute of America, 1993.

Lincoln, Edward J. *Japan's Unequal Trade.* Washington: Brookings Institution, 1990

Lindblom, Charles E. *Politics and Markets: The World's Political Economic Systems.* New York: Basic Books, 1977.

Lindell, Ulf and Stefan Persson. "The Paradox of Weak State Power: A Research and Literature Overview." *Cooperation and Conflict* 21 (1986): 79–97.

Ling, Andrew M. "The Effects of Derecognition of Taiwan on US Corporate Interests." *Loyola of Los Angeles International and Comparative Law Journal* 6 (winter 1983): 163–184.

Lodge, George C. and Ezra Vogel, eds. *Ideology and National Competitiveness: An Analysis of Nine Countries.* Boston: Harvard Business School, 1985.

Long, Olivier. *Law and Its Limitations in the GATT Multilateral Trade System.* Boston: Martinus Nijhoff, 1985.

Loo, Tom and Edward Tower. *Agricultural Protectionism and the Developing Countries.* Canberra: Centre for International Economics, 1988.

Lowi, Theodore J. *The End of Liberalism: The Second Republic of the United States.* New York: W. W. Norton, 1979.

Mardon, Russell. "The State and the Effective Control of Foreign Capital: The Case of South Korea." *World Politics* 43 (October 1990): 111–138.

Marquiles, Irving P. *The Commerce Department Speaks on Import Administration and Export Administration.* New York: Practicing Law Institute, 1984.

Mastanduno, Michael. "Do Relative Gains Matter? America's Response to Japanese Industrial Policy." *International Security* 16 (summer 1991): 73–113.

———. "Setting Market Access Priorities: The Use of Super 301 in US Trade with Japan." *World Economy* 15 (November 1992): 765–788.

Matsushita, Mitsuo and Lawrence Repeta. "Restricting the Supply of Japanese Automobiles: Sovereign Collusion?" *Case Western Reserve Journal of International Law* 14 (winter 1982).

Matsushita, Mitsuo and Thomas J. Schoenbaum. *Japanese International Trade and Investment Law.* Tokyo: University of Tokyo Press, 1989.

McGovern, E. "Dispute Settlement in the GATT: Adjudication or Negotiation?" In *The European Community and GATT,* edited by Hilf, Jacobs, and Petersman, 73–84. Deventer, Netherlands: Kluwer, 1977.

McKeown, Timothy. "Firms and Tariff Regime Change: Explaining the Demand for Protection." *World Politics* 36 (1984): 215–233.

———. "The Limitations of 'Structural' Theories of Commercial Policy." *International Organization* 40 (winter 1986): 43–64.

Meyer, Friedrich Victor. *International Trade Policy.* New York: St. Martin's Press, 1978.

Milner, Helen V. *Resisting Protectionism: Global Industries and the Politics of International Trade.* Princeton: Princeton University Press, 1988.

Milner, Helen V. and David B. Yoffie. "Between Free Trade and Protectionism: Strategic Trade Policy and a Theory of Corporate Trade Demands." *International Organization* 43 (spring 1989): 239–273.

Mohr, Lawrence B. "The Reliability of the Case Study As a Source of Information." In *Advances in Information Processing in Organizations,* edited by Robert Coulam and Richard Smith, 65–93. Greenwich, Conn.: JAI Press, 1985.

Neu, Charles. *The Troubled Encounter: The United States and Japan.* Malabar, Fla.: Robert E. Krieger, 1975.

Nye, Joseph S. *Peace in Parts: Integration and Conflict in Regional Organization.* Boston: Little, Brown, 1971.

Odell, John S. "Latin American Trade Negotiations with the US." *International Organization* 34 (1980): 207–228.

―――. "The Outcomes of International Trade Conflicts: The US and South Korea, 1960–1981." *International Studies Quarterly* 29 (September 1985): 263–286.

―――. *US International Monetary Policy: Markets, Power, and Ideas As Sources of Change.* Princeton: Princeton University Press, 1982.

Okimoto, Daniel I. *Between MITI and the Market: Japanese Industrial Policy for High Technology.* Stanford: Stanford University Press, 1989.

Palmeter, N. David and Thomas L. Kossl. "Restructuring Executive Branch Trade Responsibilities: A Half-Step Forward." *Law and Policy in International Business* 12 (1980): 611–642.

Panzarella, Jay L. "Is the Specificity Test Generally Applicable?" *Law and Policy in International Business.* 18 (1986): 417–454.

Pastor, Robert A. *Congress and the Politics of US Foreign Economic Policy, 1929–1976.* Berkeley: University of California Press, 1980.

Patrick, Hugh, ed. *Japan's High Technology Industries: Lessons and Limitations of Industrial Policy.* Seattle: University of Washington Press, 1986.

―――, ed. *Pacific Basin Industries in Distress: Structural Adjustment and Trade Policy in the Nine Industrialized Economies.* New York: Columbia University Press, 1991.

Pauly, Louis W. *Opening Financial Markets: Banking Politics on the Pacific Rim.* Ithaca: Cornell University Press, 1988.

Pearson, Margaret M. *Joint Ventures in the People's Republic of China.* Princeton: Princeton University Press, 1991.

Pescatore, Pierre, William F. Davey, and Andreas F. Lowenfeld. *Handbook of GATT Dispute Settlement.* Ardsley-on-Hudson, N.Y.: Transnational Juris Publications, 1992.

Plank, Rosine. "An Unofficial Description of How a GATT Panel Works and Does Not." *Journal of International Arbitration* (December 1987): 53–102.

Porges, Amelia. "Explaining Radical Economic Policy Change in Japan: The Case of the US-Japan Beef and Citrus Trade Deal." Paper presented at the University of Michigan, Ann Arbor, MI, 12 March 1990.

―――. "GATT Dispute Settlement Panel: Japan-Trade in Semiconductors." *American Journal of International Law* 83 (April 1989): 388–394.

Porter, Michael E. *The Competitive Advantage of Nations.* New York: Free Press, 1990.

Porter, Roger B. and Raymond Vernon. *Foreign Economic Policymaking in the United States: An Approach for the 1990s.* Cambridge: Center for Business and Government, John F. Kennedy School of Government, Harvard University.

Prestowitz, Clyde V. *Trading Places: How We Allowed Japan to Take the Lead.* New York: Basic Books, 1988.

Putnam, Robert D. "Diplomacy and Domestic Politics: The Logic of Two-Level Games." *International Organization* 42 (summer1988): 427–460.

Rabushka, Alvin. *The New China: Comparative Economic Development in Mainland China, Taiwan, and Hong Kong.* Boulder, Colo.: Westview Press, 1988.

Ray, Edwin J. "Changing Patterns of Protectionism: The Fall in Tariffs and the Rise in Nontariff Barriers." *Northwestern Journal of International Law and Business* 8 (1987): 285–327.

Rhodes, Carolyn. "Reciprocity in Trade: The Utility of a Bargaining Strategy." *International Organization* 43 (spring 1989): 273–300.

Richardson, J. David. "The Political Economy of Strategic Trade Policy." *International Organization* 44 (winter 1990): 107–135.

Riskin, Carl. *China's Political Economy: The Quest for Development since 1949*. New York: Oxford University Press, 1987.

Rosenthal, Paul C. "Industrial Policy and Competitiveness: The Emergence of the Escape Clause." *Law and Policy in International Business* 18 (1986): 749–794.

Rostow, W. W. *The United States and the Regional Organization of Asia and the Pacific, 1965–1985*. Austin: University of Texas Press, 1986.

Samuels, Richard J. *The Business of the Japanese State: Energy Markets in Comparative Perspective*. Ithaca: Cornell University Press, 1987.

Sato, Ryuzo and Julianne Nelson, eds. *Beyond Trade Friction: Japan-US Economic Relations*. New York: Cambridge University Press, 1989.

Sato, Ryuzo and John A. Rizzo, eds. *Unkept Promises, Unclear Consequences: US Economic Policy and the Japanese Response*. New York: Cambridge University Press, 1988.

Sato, Ryuzo and Paul Wachtel. *Trade Friction and Economic Policy: Problems and Prospects for Japan and the United States*. Cambridge: Cambridge University Press, 1987.

Saxonhouse, Gary. "Tampering with Comparative Advantage in Japan?" Ann Arbor: Institute of Public Policy Studies, 1986.

————. "What Does Japanese Trade Structure Tell Us about Japanese Trade Policy?" *Journal of Economic Perspectives* 7 (summer 1993): 21–44.

Schattschneider, E. E. *Politics, Pressures, and the Tariff*. New York: Prentice-Hall, 1935.

Schelling, Thomas C. and Morton H. Halperin. *Strategy and Arms Control*. Washington: Pergamon-Brassey, 1985.

Schlosstein, Steven. *Trade War*. New York: Congdon & Weed, 1984.

Schott, Jeffrey J. *Completing the Uruguay Round*. Washington: Institute for International Economics, 1990.

Sheehey, Christopher. "Japan's New Foreign Lawyer Law." *Law and Policy in International Business* 19 (1987): 361–384.

Shirk, Susan. *The Political Logic of Economic Reform in China*. Berkeley: University of California Press, 1993.

Simon, David L. "Legal Developments in US-ROC Trade since Derecognition." *International Trade Law Journal* 7 (summer 1982–1983): 203–230.

Sletmo, Gunnar K. and Gavin Boyd. *Pacific Industrial Politics*. Boulder, Colo.: Westview Press, 1994.

Sklar, Martin. *The Corporate Reconstruction of American Capitalism, 1890–1916*. New York: Cambridge University Press, 1988.

Slater, Valerie. "The US Importer's Perspective on US Antitrade Actions Against Korea and Taiwan." *Michigan Journal of International Law* 11 (winter 1990): 403–409.

Snyder, Jack. "Richness, Rigor, and Relevance in the Study of Soviet Foreign Policy." *International Security* 9 (1984–5):89–108.

Stegemann, Klaus. "Policy Rivalry among Industrial States: What Can We Learn from Models of Strategic Trade Policy?" *International Organization* (winter 1989): 73–100.

Stein, Arthur A. *Why Nations Cooperate: Circumstance and Choice in International Relations.* Ithaca: Cornell University Press, 1990.

Stern, Robert M., ed. *US Trade Policies in a Changing World Economy.* Cambridge: MIT Press, 1987.

Strange, Susan. "Protection and World Politics." *International Organization* 39 (1985): 233–259.

Sussman, Michael J. "Countervailing Duties and the Specificity Test: An Alternative Approach to the Definition of Bounty or Grant." *Law and Policy in International Business* 18 (1986): 475–515.

Sykes, Alan O. "Constructive Unilateral Threats in International Commercial Relations: The Limited Case for Section 301." *Law and Policy in International Business* 23 (spring 1992): 263–330.

Thomson, James C., Peter W. Stanley, and John Curtis Perry. *Sentimental Imperialists: The American Experience in Asia.* New York: Harper & Row, 1981.

Tien, Hung-mao. *The Great Transition: Political and Social Change in the Republic of China.* Stanford: Hoover Institution Press, 1989.

Twentieth Century Fund Task Force on the Future of American Trade Policy. *The Free Trade Debate.* New York: Priority Press, 1989.

US Department of Commerce. *Study of Foreign Government Targeting Practices and Remedies Available under the Countervailing Duty and Antidumping Laws.* Washington: DoC, 1985.

US House of Representatives Committee on Ways and Means. *Overview and Compilation of US Trade Statutes.* Washington: Government Printing Office, 1989.

US International Trade Commission. *Review of the Effectiveness of Trade Dispute Settlement under the GATT and the Tokyo Round Agreements.* Washington: ITC, 1985.

US Senate Committee on Finance Subcommittee on International Trade. "United States-Japan Structural Impediments Initiative." Hearing, 20 July 1989–5 March 1990.

US Trade Representative. *Japanese Barriers to US Trade and Recent Japanese Government Trade Initiatives.* Washington: USTR, 1982.

———. *National Trade Estimates Report on Foreign Trade Barriers.* Washington: Government Printing Office, 1989–94.

Van Der Meer, Cornelius L. J. and Saburo Yamada. *Japanese Agriculture: A Comparative Economic Analysis.* London and New York: Routledge, 1990.

van Wolferin, Karel. *The Enigma of Japanese Power.* New York: Knopf, 1989.

Vogel, Ezra F. *Japan As Number One: Lessons for America.* New York: Harper & Row, 1979.

———. *One Step Ahead in China: Guangdong under Reform.* Cambridge: Harvard University Press, 1989.

Wade, Robert. *Governing the Market: Economic Theory and the Role of Government in East Asian Industrialization.* Princeton: Princeton University Press, 1990.

Wagner, R. Harrison. "Economic Interdependence, Bargaining Power, and Political Influence." *International Organization* 42 (summer 1988): 461–484.

Wheeler, J. W. "Comparative Development Strategies of South Korea and Taiwan As Reflected in Their Respective International Trade Policies." *Michigan Journal of International Law* 11 (winter 1990): 472–508.

Wheeler, J. W. and Perry L. Wood. *Trade Policy Formation in Selected Developing Countries.* Indianapolis: Hudson Institute, 1986.

Whitt, Richard S. "The Politics of Procedure: An Examination of the GATT Dispute Settlement Panel and the Article XXI Defense in the Context of the US Embargo of Nicaragua." *Law and Policy in International Business* 19 (1987): 603–630.

Wightman, David. *Toward Economic Cooperation in Asia: The United Nations Economic Commission for Asia and the Far East.* New Haven: Yale University Press, 1963.

Wilson, James Q. *Bureaucracy: What Government Agencies Do and Why They Do It.* New York: Basic Books, 1989.

Wilson, James W., ed. *The Politics of Regulation.* New York: Basic Books, 1990.

Wolfers, Arnold. *Discord and Collaboration: Essays on International Politics.* Baltimore: Johns Hopkins University Press, 1962.

Wu, Yuan-li. *Becoming an Industrialized Nation: The Republic of China's Development on Taiwan.* New York: Praeger, 1985.

Yager, Joseph A. *Transforming Agriculture in Taiwan: The Experience of the Joint Commission on Rural Reconstruction.* Ithaca: Cornell University Press, 1988.

Yarbrough, Beth V. and Robert M. Yarbrough. *Cooperation and Governance in International Trade: The Strategic Organizational Approach.* Princeton: Princeton University Press, 1992.

Yoffie, David B. *Power and Protectionism: Strategies of the Newly Industrializing Countries.* New York: Columbia University Press, 1983.

Young, Oran R. *Compliance and Public Authority: A Theory with International Applications.* Baltimore: Johns Hopkins University Press, 1979.

Zartman, I. William. *The Politics of Trade Negotiation between Africa and the EEC: The Weak Confront the Strong.* Princeton: Princeton University Press, 1971.

Zartman, I. William and Maureen R. Berman. *The Practical Negotiator.* New Haven: Yale University Press, 1982.

Zysman, John and Laura Tyson, eds. *American Industry in International Competition: Government Policies and Corporate Strategies.* Ithaca: Cornell University Press, 1983.

Index

227